Praise for *A Different Kind of War*

"This collection of essays by J. Malcolm Garcia is a must-read for those who want to better understand the plight of common people victimized by the hardships of life outside and inside the belly of the beast. Being a visiting journalist in these "foreign" places, especially in Mexico and Central America, often comes with risks for the idealistic reporter: violence and death. These omnipresent threats don't stop Garcia from shining light on the daily struggles of these honorable and resilient people."

—Álvaro Huerta, Ph.D., author of *Reframing the Latino Immigration Debate: Towards a Humanistic Paradigm* and *Defending Latina/o Immigrant Communities: The Xenophobic Era of Trump and Beyond.*

"These engaging essays reveal J. Malcolm Garcia's keen eye which is always in play, his observances cinematic; the absence of children on a main thoroughfare, cats asleep in a stairwell, a woman selling cigarettes, and the feet of police officers moving past a basement window. All the potent minutia of daily life in a country under duress. This collection illustrates that while one writer cannot save the world and all its woes, he can write about those individuals risking their own well-being to help others, and in turn make a difference in all our lives by chronicling their stories of compassion, mercy and fortitude as Garcia so lyrically does in *A Different Kind of War*."

—Tina Schumann, editor, *Two-Countries: U.S. Daughters and Sons of Immigrant Parents*, and author of *Requiem. A Patrimony of Fugues.*

"I was riveted by these tales of mean streets and lost souls, just as I was inspired by the portraits of those brave people who face down despair every day, and persevere. It is these glimmers of life and faith that make J. Malcolm Garcia's beautifully written dispatches from Central America sing."

—Daniel Alarcón, author of *At Night We Walk in Circles, Lost City Radio* and *The King Is Always Above the People*

"J. Malcolm Garcia's *A Different Kind of War: Uneasy Encounters in Mexico and Central America* is anything, but an easy read. Why? Because he writes about people and places no one really cares about: orphans with swollen melon heads; abused children whose parents earn a dollar a day sifting metal and glass out of putrid garbage dumps; prostitutes selling themselves in fetid rooms for five dollars a pop to feed their children one hundred miles away; and so much more. Garcia is a selfless, often poetic, writer who records the heroics of nuns, priests and school teachers who feel a calling to work with the downtrodden. In many ways, *A Different Kind of War* is an update of Luis Alberto Urrea's powerful1993 book *Across the Wire: Life and Hard Times on the Mexican Border*, but what one discovers is that life has become even more precarious for the poor in Guatemala and Mexico. Read this book if you dare."

—David Unger, author of *Life in the Damn Tropics, The Price of Escape* and *The Mastermind*, among other Guatemala-based novels.

"J. Malcolm Garcia's courageous, unflinching collection of stories is a compelling portrait of the realities in Central America and Mexico from which most of the asylum seekers arriving at our border are fleeing. The lives of everyday people and activists are told with sensitivity, curiosity, and compassion, and the teller is present just enough to maintain perspective on the told. Garcia's narration is rife with all the urgency and painful details they merit. This book effectively connects the people to their struggles, to the complexity of their realities, and in so doing, pushes powerfully against the tide of dehumanization and othering."

— Katherine Silver, author of *Echo Under Story*, is an award-winning literary translator of Julio Cortázar, César Aira, Juan Carlos Onetti among other writers and does volunteer interpreting for asylum seekers.

Other books by J. Malcolm Garcia

The Khaarijee: A Chronicle of Friendship and War in Kabul;

What Wars Leave Behind: The Faceless and Forgotten;

Without A Country:
The Untold Story of America's Deported Veterans;

Riding through Katrina with the Red Baron's Ghost:
A Memoir of Friendship, Family and a Life Writing;

Fruit of All My Grief: Lives In the Shadows of the American Dream.

A Different Kind of War:
Uneasy Encounters in Mexico and Central America

J. Malcolm Garcia

Fomite

Burlington, VT

ISBN-13: 978-1-953236-18-0
Library of Congress Control Number: 2021931725
Fomite
58 Peru Street
Burlington, VT 05401

3/26/2021

Dedicated to Olga Contreras

"Being unwanted, unloved, uncared for, forgotten by everybody, I think that is a much greater hunger, a much greater poverty than the person who has nothing to eat."

— Mother Teresa

Contents

Introduction

From 2015 to 2019 I reported from Mexico, Central America, and the American Southwest, where I met many priests and nuns and activist laypeople advocating for migrants and those who remained behind. Whether it's the violence of gangs or corporations exploiting opportunities in undeveloped lands, a cadre of local religious leaders and people of faith stand up for families who don't have wealth and status. These are the stories of their work and of the people they've chosen to help.

Providing

No election posters here. Only a boy sitting alone in a doorway across from Parque Jocotenago and the shade its trees offer. Above him a sign: Hogar Marina Guirola Leal, the Home of Marina Guirola Leal.

Farther north, on Avenida Reforma, in the last days of the rainy season, you can see mildewed walls holding the remnants of campaign banners like worn wallpaper for television personality and comedian Jimmy Morales, the victor, and Sandra Torres, the loser, in the October 25, 2015, Guatemalan presidential election. See the half-hearted attempts by city workers to steam them off. See the shorn, sun-faded faces of the smiling candidates amid other, much more diminished posters depicting the missing from the civil war that raged from 1960 to 1996. Nunca olvidar. Never forget. Geckos dart across their lost faces.

But there are no posters here in Zona 2, the old part of Guatemala City on the northernmost side that dates back to the nineteenth century. It used to be wealthier, decades ago. Today it has settled into a kind of genteel middle class, descending rapidly into working class, and the politicians no longer expect any votes from here. Vacant homes left to rot fill with rain, to ultimately be torn down for parking garages. Some boys sell Chiclets to drivers stalled in traffic and other boys sit in doorways, heads down, drooling, nodding out from a drug high. They remind me of the homeless people I once worked with in San Francisco as a social worker before I became a reporter. The saliva gathering in the lower lip of their slack mouths. The sweat pebbling their skin. The half-passed-out slant of their bodies. The life around them continuing without notice. I too would have walked by if it were not for my ten o'clock appointment at Hogar Marina Guirola Leal with Sister Dolores Ochoa. How often did I see men and women like them in San Francisco? C'mon, Alabama, get up, I'd say to one homeless man I knew well. It's raining. Come inside. We have coffee.

Across the street in the park, a maid walks two collies, scooping their shit with a plastic bag she peels off her hand like a glove. Other women set plastic milk containers and paint buckets in vacant parking spaces. They charge sixty-five cents an hour to anyone who wants to park. One woman complains that another woman sold a space to me that belongs to her, and a fight ensues, and birds distressed by the commotion or perhaps giving into another impulse decreed by instinct lift off from trees and blacken the sky for an instant, fracturing bars of sunlight, and the woman walking the dogs stares up at them, pausing beside a man who, oblivious to her, heats beans and rice that he hopes to sell to whoever passes, a stack of white foam plates beside him livid with ants.

I lean over the boy and ring the doorbell to Hogar Marina Guirola Leal. The building is named for the woman who donated it to the Somascan nuns in 2000. The nuns use it as an orphanage for developmentally disabled children. The door swings open and a diminutive nun in a cream-colored habit greets me.

"Sister Dolores?"

"Yes."

She looks down at the boy and hurries away, returning almost immediately with a plate of scrambled eggs. He takes the plate with an unsteady hand, like someone just waking up, places it by his feet, and looks at it with suspicion as if he wonders what it might do to him.

"A drug addict," Sister Dolores says. "Glue sniffer. Still, he has to eat."

I follow her inside. We walk down a bright hall and I notice a slight limp in her right leg—a kind of sailor's gait she has acquired by incorporating what I imagine to be something painful into her otherwise determined stride—her head turning to the left and the right, nodding to volunteers, her voice almost a chirp as she greets another nun. She pauses beside a cracked statue of the Virgin Mary, paint peeling off the bowed head, falling in flakes onto the table supporting it.

"How can I help you?" Sister Dolores asks, looking at me through glasses a little too large for her narrow face.

Her open, friendly demeanor flusters me. I expect her to smile. She is unlike nuns I remember from my Sunday school days as a child raised in the Catholic church. Granted, that was a long time ago, but I still have distinct memories of nuns in long, black habits that touched the floor, the lace-up black shoes and the dominating bandeau, and the veil and coif that covered much of their foreheads. In church on Sundays, they sat in the two front pews, blending into one another like paper dolls, stoic and domineering.

Sitting now across from Sister Dolores in a neighborhood of drug addicts, I recall one particular Sunday morning in church when I was a boy. At the end of the Mass, Monsignor Burke mentioned that Sister So-and-So (I don't recall her name) had been transferred to a parish on the South Side of Chicago, a mostly Black area and considered a "bad neighborhood" by the congregants of the north Chicago suburban church my family attended.

After Mass, people spoke about Sister So-and-So's bad luck, and even as a child, influenced, I suppose, by comments I had overheard about how people should serve the poor, I wondered why her transfer was a bad thing. I asked my parents and received "yes, but" answers. Yes, it was good to help the poor, but no one in their right mind would want to go where Sister So-and-So had been transferred. They accepted the notion of the church serving the poor but could not hide their revulsion—or was it intimidation?—when someone they liked was going to a neighborhood they only knew through newspaper crime reports. I didn't understand any of this, but my child's mind noticed anyway.

Years later when I became a social worker—more out of curiosity about these forbidden neighborhoods, the sense of risk they conveyed, than any concern I had for the poor—my father scolded me for my choice of a career. It is fine to work with the poor as a volunteer, he told me, but it is no way to earn a living.

"What is it you would like to ask me?" Sister Dolores says, still smiling.

I am in Guatemala to write a story about the presidential election and what it means for the country—one of the poorest and most corrupt in the Western Hemisphere—to have chosen Morales, a man with no political experience, and who on his TV show portrayed a peasant who accidentally became president. He won by riding a wave of disgust with politics as usual after an investigation into a tax and bribery scandal convulsed Guatemala's political establishment.

The scheme had put millions of tax dollars into the hands of unscrupulous government officials, including the outgoing president and his vice president, both of whom were jailed. The story, I thought, was fairly straightforward. But the former social worker in me wondered what the election of Morales meant for Guatemala's poor. Scouring the internet, I learned that orders of nuns in the country provide care for some of its neediest citizens, especially children, in lieu of the government, mired as it has been in political turmoil. How do they manage?

I also became aware that Morales's election was supported by old-school political players including the membership of his National Convergence Front-Nation party. The party was founded in 2004 by retired generals determined to protect the interests of the military following the 1996 peace accords that ended a thirty-six-year civil war. Party members have been accused of being involved in the deaths of an estimated one hundred forty thousand to two hundred thousand people, encompassing civilian and indigenous communities, who were killed or disappeared.

Given Morales's lack of political experience and the institutions behind his election, I ask Sister Dolores if she has any faith in the president-elect. Did she think that his government, unlike its predecessors, would show an interest in the poor? She does not answer directly.

"One conviction I have," she says finally, "is God will provide."

Behind her, I see a young woman with one of the volunteers, a physical therapist. They hug and appear to be playfully roughhousing. The young woman's swollen face and enlarged head loom over the volunteer and she laughs in a loud, high bark.

Sister Dolores glances over her shoulder to see whom I am looking at. The young woman's name, she tells me, is Cindy. She has been in the orphanage since she was an infant. The swelling in her face comes from a cancerous tumor in her mouth that has spread to her eyes, ears, and feet. It can't be cured. Cindy likes to boss people around. Sometimes she gets in a bad mood and screams, *I don't love you.*

"You'd never know she was sick," Sister Dolores says.

"What will happen to her?"

"She will remain here until God decides to take her, and then there will be an extra space and no doubt another child to fill it."

The girl's distorted face disturbs me. I turn away and refocus on my questions.

"What help, if any, does the government offer you?"

"The government talks about work and housing, but in our

case—our special needs children who can't function on their own—you don't hear the government say anything," Sister Dolores says. "That's what brings me down."

She keeps a calendar with daily entries of what she needs to keep the orphanage operating from day to day, week to week, month to month. Meals: more rice and beans. Linens: more sheets and blankets. What else? The roof leaks. What else? The floor in the kitchen needs to be replaced. Who can do that? What else? Five staff members need to be paid. Who will donate their salaries? What else? Everything else.

"God provides," she says again, but the stress of her limited budget remains a daily worry that I hear in her voice.

I finish taking notes and close my notebook. Sunlight plays over everything as the morning approaches noon and the rose-tinted sky carries with it the coolness of spring.

"May I come back to see you if I have more questions?"

"Of course."

I have no more questions, really, no reason to return. I have what I need, a couple of quotes. I'll speak with a few more people, write the story, and be done with it. But the simplicity of Sister Dolores's faith and her comfort in it, even as she worries about how the orphanage will get by, impresses me. She carries herself with relaxed good humor. She laughs when she describes the antics of the children. She emphasizes their character, not their disabilities. She describes the difficulties of her work as if her problems were no more serious than an overcast day. She can't bring out the sun, but she can make the best of what the day has to offer. She makes me feel welcome, even though she knows the time she spends with me will not help her bring in more rice and beans, collect more linen, or mend her roof and floor. There is something about her I find warm and embracing.

I stopped being a practicing Catholic years ago. When I reached fourteen, my parents no longer required me to attend church. I can't remember the last time I stepped inside one. I moved on, left behind the routines of childhood for the confusing future of adolescence and young adulthood and all the posturing and fey cynicism that went along with it. But these days, I miss church as much as I miss other bygone routines, the security that comes with order. With doing the same things at the same time over and over: school, summer vacations, holidays, birthdays, work. The doing mattered. Church was about attendance every Sunday, not faith. We were not a family that discussed God or read the Bible. Our politics were conservative. We did not ask one another what we thought about this or that. There was no need to examine our religious beliefs. *What are you doing today?* was the daily question that was the substance of our existence, not what it meant to be Catholic.

Julio Prato sits in the living room of a mutual friend wearing a bullet-resistant vest beneath his gray suit jacket. He is thirty-six but has the boyish look of a teenager, someone eager to please. A district attorney, he serves as a member of the U.N. commission investigating team that broke the corruption scandal known as La Linea or The Line. His bodyguard waits outside the apartment.

In 2007, Prato was asked to join the ten-member commission. The commission was founded to look at importers, and it wire-tapped the phone line of a Chinese merchant. Within the first week, the commissioners heard the voice of a customs agent discuss a criminal organization that was taking care of shipping containers. The customs agent spoke to the merchants on a telephone line set up for that purpose, charged a fee—OK, you pay twenty thousand dollars—and if they agreed, let them through.

In April 2015, a phone call indicated President Perez Molina, "El Uno," and the vice president, Roxana Baldetti, "La Doc," were involved. The customs agent spoke about both. *El Uno told us to charge this. El Uno wants sixty-one percent. La Doc gets the rest.*

The commission released its initial finding the same month, causing a public outcry that led to massive street protests. The investigators concluded that Molina had received as much as three million dollars in bribes from importers in exchange for illegal discounts on their customs duty.

The size of the protests surprised Prato. He never expected the arrest of Molina and his vice-president. People especially hated the vice president; she had been implicated in other corruption cases. However, this time was different—the commission had documentation of the corruption. Proof. No one had presented a case against the president before.

"We took polygraphs every year to prove the honesty of the investigating team," Prato says. "I have a bodyguard. The people here resolve problems violently when you upset them."

I tell him about my visit with Sister Dolores. At one time as a district attorney, Prato represented abused and abandoned children. He tells me that the needs of abandoned children do not figure into the commission's work.

"They can't vote," he says. "They offer no corruption opportunities. The police appear, drop a child off at a church, and wash their hands of it. Your nun won't get any help."

It is dark when I leave my friend's apartment. I pass Prato's bodyguard in the hall. He approaches me, stops, and watches me get in the elevator. Outside, the streets of Zona 10, a commercial district, stir with traffic and pedestrians rushing into the Hard Rock Cafe.

Walking toward my hotel less than a block away from the Dubai Shopping Center, I mull over something Prato said: *Your nun won't get any help.* Every year in San Francisco, we faced state and city budget cuts. We paraded our most successful clients—the ones who had found jobs, minimum-wage day labor usually—and had them testify before the city's board of supervisors. Dozens of nonprofits did the same thing. Hundreds of success stories waiting in an expanding line to talk about why the other guy's funding should be cut. It lasted all day. A pointless exercise. The results were always the same: all of our budgets were cut. But like Sister Dolores, we survived. I can't say God provided as much as laying off staff did.

Not far from the Home of Marina Guirola Leal, Asociación Cultural de Misioneras de las Hermanas Somascas, the Cultural Association of Missionaries of Somascan Sisters, stands squeezed between other square structures of the same height on a cobbled street so narrow that cars park halfway on the sidewalk so that other cars may pass.

I lift a black knocker and rap on the door once, twice. A metal plate slides back and a nun peers out at me. I think of a speakeasy and almost laugh. Shutting the plate with a bang, she swings open the door and I follow her into a large room that feels bare despite the two couches and an empty fireplace. A chandelier hangs from a high ceiling.

I sit down, the damp air collecting around me, when another nun enters the room. She tells me her name, Sister Celestina Somoza. At forty-nine, she has been a Somascan sister for almost thirty years. She smiles shyly and cups her hands together, fingering rosary beads. Almost self-consciously, she asks for my credentials. Guatemala's civil war ended almost twenty years earlier but even nuns remain suspicious of people they don't know. During the fighting, talking to the media carried deadly consequences if you criticized the wrong people.

At one time, Sister Celestina explains, returning my press badge, the congregation served orphaned and abandoned children as Sister Dolores does now. It used to shelter only babies. As they grew older they were transferred to other orders. Special needs children, for instance, went to Sister Dolores. Now the order provides after-school care for children of poor families, mostly single mothers. Only seven boys are enrolled in the program.

The boys tend to remind Sister Celestina of her own hardships as a child in El Salvador. Her father was an alcoholic and her mother placed her four daughters in a boarding school for girls administered by the Somascan Sisters. The nuns impressed her by the way they conducted themselves. The habits they wore. Their education. Her mother, meanwhile, left El Salvador to work in the U.S.

Sister Celestina's oldest sister became a nun before her. But then she left the order to take care of their grandfather, father, and now their mother. Sister Celestina admits to feeling relieved that these matters did not fall to her.

"Life is much harder with an addict," Sister Celestina says of her father. "He is deceased now. May he rest in peace."

She joined the order, which has missionaries in El Salvador, Honduras, and Guatemala, in 1985 without any idea of how to care for babies and children. There were many infants to care for at that time, she recalls, and they made her nervous because they were so little, so loud. Gradually she learned to distinguish cries of hunger from cries of pain and tantrums, and she grew to love working with them. She misses those days. New laws governing orphaned children have interfered with the order's work.

In 2008, Guatemala was the leading country for adoptions by U.S. families. But in 2009, Guatemalan authorities chastened by an adoption scandal tightened the country's adoption process. Corrupt lawyers had ignited the crisis by buying and even stealing babies to sell to families seeking to adopt, filling a void that existed because no government agency had the authority to match willing birth mothers with prospective adoptive parents. But the new, strict, state-run adoption process has left orphaned children in limbo.

Now before an adoption can be arranged with a family outside Guatemala, the National Council of Adoptions must seek a Guatemalan family first, despite the fact that Guatemala, given its poverty, has very low adoption rates. The regulations have blocked agencies in other ways. Sister Celestina tells me the order would like to open a day care center. However, the new laws would require the order to install a stainless-steel prep table in the kitchen and have different cutting boards and knives for meat, fish, and chicken. The prep table alone, she said, puts the day care center out of reach.

"The government wants to know where our money comes from and how we spend it," Sister Celestina says, "but when it comes to helping out, it gives us nothing but new laws that make our work more difficult."

She mentions one young woman, now twenty-two, who has lived at the orphanage since she was abandoned as an infant. She needed a bone marrow transplant to treat a congenital illness, but the orphanage did not have the means to pay. With nowhere to go and no one interested in adopting her, she asked to remain here and the nuns agreed.

Her mind is fine, Sister Celestina says. Her name is Jennifer.

"May I meet her?" I ask.

Sister Celestina agrees, but first she wants to tell me about another orphan, Gloria, who has remained with the nuns. She was twelve when her father left her. Now thirty-nine, she wants to leave, but the nuns worry someone might take advantage of her. Sometimes she goes out in the morning, Sister Celestina says, but the thing is, she always comes back. She doesn't know why Gloria's father abandoned her. It may have been a case of abuse. Gloria talks very little and won't say.

I follow Sister Celestina down a dark, narrow hall that leads out into an enclosed playground with a red ball in one corner. It seems to me a terrible waste of space not to have children here. Sister Celestina agrees. At one time, she says, they could take up to one hundred abandoned infants referred by judges and hold them overnight. But with the new laws. . . Sister Celestina's voice trails off. We cross the playground and enter another hall to an open door. Jennifer's room. Sister Celestina knocks, and we enter.

Jennifer lies on a bed in blue pajamas, her legs curled beneath her, hands turned inward and propped against her chest. She has large, alert eyes, and her toothless mouth opens in a smile as she watches us step in. A TV sits on a shelf. Beside it, a wheelchair. The slate-colored walls are poorly illuminated by a single ceiling light in the windowless room. After I introduce myself, I ask Jennifer about her childhood. She frowns and says that she remembers when she was very little but has no specific memory to share. Growing up in the orphanage was good and nice. A lot of volunteers came and got to know her and they took good care of her. She likes to watch TV. She enjoys going outside. She likes to talk with the children after they return from school. She likes everything. She doesn't know what would have happened to her if the orphanage had not been here. The thought disturbs her, and she does not want to talk anymore and asks me to go.

Sister Celestina and I leave her room and follow the curve of the hall until we are back where we started, in the big room with the empty fireplace. I apologize for making Jennifer uncomfortable. Sister Celestina looks at me, my apology irrelevant, her mind elsewhere.

"Even if I could change things and bring in more children, I don't have the authority," she says, as if I've made some sort of accusation. "I can't make those decisions."

I return to Hogar Marina Guirola Leal the next morning. The parking-space ladies encourage cars to stop while boys rush out from behind trees and wipe down windshields despite drivers' objections. The aroma of boiling beans and rice rises from the pots and pans of the men cooking nearby, and the maid is out once more walking the well-groomed collies.

Inside the orphanage, seven children sit in a half-circle in the courtyard in wheelchairs, a piñata dangling from a string before them. The courtyard walls depict sailors in boats balanced on the tips of blue waves, *Hogar Marina*, written in fat letters above the water. I have arrived for what Sister Dolores calls coloring time. A girl shows a boy the black squares she has shaded with green and orange crayon. She jerks back and forth in her wheelchair to get his attention and he takes the paper slowly and looks at it, contemplating the colors. She watches him, eyes alert but no other indication of what she might be thinking. The paper falls slowly from his hand and she watches it land on the ground. Sister Dolores limps over and picks it up and gives it back to the girl, who takes the paper and clutches it to her chest. Sister Dolores glances at each of the children and the young adults around her:

Gabie, eighteen.

Juan Pablo, twenty-eight.

Walter, twenty-two.

Juan Jose, eight.

MarMaria, twelve.

Filioman, sixteen.

Geraldo, sixteen.

Juan Pablo was abandoned at San Juan de Dios Hospital. The orphanage took him in when he was just three. Some families leave children with their hospital bracelets still on, like Juan Pablo, their names written with a felt-tipped pen. Other families abandon them with no information. Sister Dolores names those children.

Juan Pablo wants only to put his head on my shoulder. He pulls at my clothes. Should I resist, he grabs my shirt and reaches for my hair and pulls harder. He has hydrocephalus, a disorder that fills the skull with fluid. Doctors have tried to drain the fluid into his stomach but his head remains enlarged.

Geraldo sits next to Juan Pablo; he likes rock music. I watch him bounce to the beat of the Beatles' "Helter Skelter" in his wheelchair, the raucous music loud and distorted. Courts referred Geraldo to the orphanage when he was an infant. Sister Dolores knows nothing about his mother and father.

"Do they ask about their parents?" I inquire.

Sister Dolores shakes her head. They never knew them, never see them again. They have new parents now. They call a volunteer male nurse "papa," and the nuns "mama." The mother of one child, Maria, does visit once a year. She comes from far away to look at her daughter. She does not speak a word to her, only watches her for ten, fifteen minutes and then she leaves. Maria had been enrolled in special education classes at a public school. But the school did not provide physical therapy and she was forced to drop out. Now through the help of a volunteer, she has learned to walk. Unlike many of the other children, she reads and talks. Sister Dolores tells me that Maria is quite bright and needs to be in school, if only the orphanage could find someone to sponsor her. Sometimes people respond with donations, but not often.

Sister Dolores laughs when I tell her how children at first intimidated Sister Celestina. It takes some getting used to, she admits. She has served at Hogar Marina Guirola Leal since 2010. Before this assignment, she worked with elementary school children in Mexico for twelve years and then high school students in Honduras for fourteen years. At first the work at the orphanage left her feeling sad and helpless. Because most of the children can't talk, she didn't understand when they tried to communicate with her. Through trial and error she made progress. She began dancing with them to make them laugh. She pretended to talk to them on a telephone, sticking her thumb in her right ear and talking into her left hand. She learned to follow their signals. Like Juan Pablo. When he tugged at her clothes, she gave in and let him pull her toward him. That is how she learned that he wanted to rest his head on her shoulder.

She wonders sometimes what would have happened to Juan Pablo and the other children if the orphanage did not exist. They would have died, she says, answering her own question. Here they receive special attention in all sorts of different ways, the kind of care a poor family could never provide. The best their families could do was abandon them.

On occasion she will hear from former students she taught in Mexico and Honduras. A few visit. They thank her. They recall she was very strict. She would not let them get away with anything. Now some are doctors, lawyers. They tell her that their accomplishments are a result of her discipline. Sister Dolores is always surprised to see her former students. When she left Mexico and Honduras, she did not say goodbye to any of them. She just couldn't. They would cry, be sad. Of course, so would she. It would only have been normal. She had to move on to new children without the distractions that memories would bring. The nuns would call and tell her how her previous students were doing. Still, there was this emptiness she felt.

Sister Dolores steps away to ask a volunteer a question and her limp catches my attention once more. When she returns, I ask her about it. Her walk has been affected by an operation she had in the summer, she says matter of factly as if I had asked about the weather or her plans for this afternoon. Doctors found cancer and performed a full hysterectomy. They told her there was a fifty percent chance the cancer might return. She has received thirty radiation treatments and she sees her doctor every six weeks. If she continues doing well, her medical appointments will be reduced to once every three months and then, God willing, once every six months until she won't need to see her doctor again.

"I'm sorry," I say.

I wish I had not inquired. She gives no indication of illness. I once had a biopsy to check for prostate cancer. I tell her how scared

I felt until the doctor called with the results. Negative. I regret she did not have the same good luck.

Sister Dolores holds my hand but makes no comment. She tries to be the same person she was before the operation, she says, pausing between words. She doesn't dwell on being sick. The way she sees it, if this is her time, if her life is over, OK.

Her voice catches. She recalls all the weight she lost. How skinny and pale she looked. She took two months of sick leave. The children noticed her absence. She didn't want them to see her weak. They asked for her and were told she was sick. At night they put their hands together and prayed for her. When she returned to work, they clapped. "You know they are happy when they clap. It's their way of signaling emotion."

She sounds almost clinical. I understood what their clapping meant without her telling me. I suspect she is trying to keep the memory and how it must have moved her at a distance, so the tears that I see in her eyes and that she held back when she left her students in Honduras and Mexico do not overwhelm her now.

Seven years after I stopped working with homeless people, I stood at a bus stop in Haight-Ashbury and noticed a man staring at me. "Malcolm?" he finally said. "Yes," I replied. And then I recognized him. Archie Tate, a homeless man who could be a mean drunk. I don't know how many times I had checked him into detox programs. We hugged, Archie's body was rank, flies flitting about his hair. I paid his bus fare, and the two of us sat together.

I had tried to help Archie and others like him for fourteen years. Their slow self-destruction began to destroy me too. They left me exhausted, depressed. I did not feel a higher calling for my efforts on their behalf. I had no big-picture context in which to place my efforts. My work became a deadening, day-to-day grind in which I watched the Archie Tates of the world slowly killing themselves with booze and other drugs. Eventually, I quit social work. I had always enjoyed writing and decided to pursue journalism.

That afternoon on the bus, however, took me back and for a moment I felt as if I'd never left social work. I asked Archie if I could help him get into detox. As we talked, voices inside his head started to distract him. He began mumbling to himself, got agitated and at the next stop bolted out of his seat. I watched him running down the street, a piece of my life dashing off without so much as a backward glance.

Mauricio Chaulon Valez, a professor of history and anthropology in the school of political science at the Universidad Rafael Landivar, a Jesuit university in Guatemala City, stands at a white board in his office, drawing circles and lines extending into more circles to help me understand the connections to powerful people that led to Jimmy Morales's election.

"You have to understand, Jimmy is trying to present a fresh face but it's not so. He's backed by business and the military, all of whom are tied to traditional structures of power. Jimmy has no political background. He can be controlled."

Mauricio points to a circle representing protesters.

"The traditional groups of power took advantage of the protest groups' need for a fresh face and gave them Jimmy, someone these groups can control," he says. "Jimmy Morales is like a normal citizen, a common man. During the campaign he adopted visual symbols like rolling up his sleeves. He invoked God and biblical references. He took very conservative stances on abortion and feminism that resonated with some elements of the public."

Mauricio loops a few circles into one big circle, jots down, "Orbit of Power." More lines. Beneath one line, he writes, "traditional military groups." Beneath another: "economically dominant groups."

What happened, he explains, is that corruption became so normal that as long as it didn't seem to touch the pockets of the middle class, nobody cared: it's OK if you steal as long as it doesn't affect me. When they saw it affected them, they threw the president and vice-president out; OK, they said, that's enough. They were so unused to change like this that they did not consider a more radical position.

Mauricio puts down his marker and sits.

"So now, Jimmy Morales is president," he says. "But the ideological pattern remains the same: This president is not working; let's exchange him for a new one. We exchanged one face for another face, but it's still the same face. That is the culture of the middle class. The state's job is to promote productivity and individualism, not social justice. That won't change. Nothing will change."

Fatima Children's Home, named after Our Lady of Fatima, stands at the top of a hill in a residential area that overlooks downtown Guatemala City, far from Sister Dolores's orphanage and the impoverished women selling parking spaces.

The director, Barbara Cofino, meets me at the door holding fliers promoting her work. Before she opened the orphanage, she had been a human rights attorney. She can't explain exactly why she switched careers; trying to find meaning in her life, perhaps? She shrugs. As an attorney, she saw how poor kids were violated by drug-addicted parents, pimps, and abusive police and it made her sad and angry. She has four children of her own. Grown now, all attorneys, except the youngest, still in school. They volunteer at the orphanage. The work has heightened their humanity, their compassion. They act as older siblings to the kids. A bond has grown between them. Imagine, she says, if other well-off children made similar connections with these children.

Barbara accepts children as young as two months old, even younger sometimes. More girls than boys occupy the orphanage. The macho culture of Guatemala: men don't value daughters as much as sons and dispose of them easily. The girls want to be teachers or nurses. The boys, pilots.

On occasion, an uncle or a grandmother brings a child in, but not often; when they do, Barbara never hears from them again. Any problem children can have, they have. Sick, malnourished, bruised, with parasites on their scalps. Most don't get adopted and remain at the home until they reach eighteen, when they must leave and fend for themselves. Barbara won't accept developmentally disabled children. Those she leaves to the Somascan sisters.

A preteen child, Barbara believes, will adapt more easily to a new family than a teenager. The older they are, the harder it is for them to heal emotionally. They mourn too much inside and get depressed. Younger children, however, are like seeds in fertile soil; you can cultivate them, work with them, and watch them grow. She sees all sorts of cases. A five-year-old boy and his infant sister, for instance. Their mother was killed in a holdup. The ten-month-old girl took a bullet to her stomach. Her brother was shot in the ankle. Two years later, they were adopted.

Another case: Joshua, a fifteen-year-old boy, came to the home when he was five after his father gave him up. The boy's mother had died of cancer and the father said he had no one to care for Joshua. He told a judge that he hoped the boy would be adopted by loving parents. A family had expressed interest but in the end decided against taking him.

Joshua, Barbara says, will most likely remain at the home until he ages out. He likes making model houses and wants to be an architect. He has become an older brother to the younger children. Barbara feels she has no choice but to let him stay. If she discharged him, he would fall victim to gangs or be bullied by other children on the street. What will happen to him when he turns eighteen, she does not know. Here at the house he has lived a sheltered life. She avoids talking to him about his parents. A psychologist advised her not to delve into his past. Of course, if he doesn't talk about it, there will always be that pain. Sometimes Barbara does not know what to do.

Another case: At one this morning, the police brought her a forty-day-old baby. They called her X. Barbara named her

Katherine. One o'clock in the morning. Imagine. She received no advance call.

Another case: A five-year-old boy who stayed with her in 2011. The police brought him. His mother had been killed in a shooting. He had seen the paramedics take her on a stretcher and thought she was in a hospital. He hid cookies and candy in his bed for Barbara to give to his mother. She couldn't bring herself to say, Your mother is dead. She left that task to a psychologist. A family adopted the boy in 2016.

If Barbara has no room; she tells the police, tells the courts, *I'm sorry*. What else can she do? She has limits like anyone else. People ask her, why do you do this? My children are grown, she says. This work fulfills me. She gets by on donations and selling old clothes to a man who markets them as rags. She plants vegetables. The children like radishes.

Barbara won't comment on the election of Jimmy Morales. She doesn't think it would be safe. People might consider her an agitator and stop donating to the home. Instead, she says the government is not worried about hospitals and education, much less abandoned children. It is like that in all of Latin America.

When I see Sister Dolores the next day, I ask her a question that occurred to me in the middle of the night: Did her cancer diagnosis make her feel closer to Cindy, the girl with the tumors, than the other children?

Actually, Sister Dolores says, she feels closest to Douglass, a nineteen-year-old who she worries spends too much time alone.

She tries not to get attached to any one child, but Douglass singled her out for his love, and despite her efforts not to play favorites, his devotion won her over.

Douglass suffers from fetal alcohol syndrome. He was abandoned at a hospital when he was one month old. He moves stiffly with his head leaning as far back as he can stretch his neck, his chest jutting outward. Somehow, he walks a straight line without bumping into anything. When he sees Sister Dolores, he rushes to her and asks for fruit juice and cookies. He needs to eat all the time. Perhaps his hunger is caused by anxiety. Sister Dolores does not know.

In the dormitory, Sister Dolores shakes him by the shoulder to wake him and Douglass stirs, eventually sitting up, his head instantly stretching backward between his shoulders. He leans his head back and his eyes roll as if he is trying to see the floor.

"Douglass, don't you want to eat?" Sister Dolores asks him. "It's time."

He kicks his legs out from beneath some sheets and she helps him put on his shoes.

"Come this way."

Douglass walks away from her between rows of beds. Just as it appears he might step into a wall, he veers left and walks into the courtyard and Sister Dolores follows him.

Two children have died since Sister Dolores began working at the home. One of them, Gustaveo Adolfo Pina, had cerebral palsy and could not talk. He liked to paint, but because of his disability he was unable to control his hands, so the nuns strapped a paint brush to his forehead and he composed landscapes with thick splotches of varying shades of yellow, blue, green, and red. He looked through magazines for inspiration, but he never copied. He had a special wheelchair that he could control with his head, and he'd go all over the orphanage. When Sister Dolores scolded him, he would drive it against her to show his displeasure.

Gustaveo was abandoned when he was two months old, the first disabled child the orphanage took in. The day before he died, he wrote on a sheet of paper with a paint brush, "Someday I'll marry." He liked girls. One female volunteer gave him a cell phone filled with music. He turned it on with his nose and moved to the beat in his wheelchair.

At night, he slept with hands beneath his chest so they would not shake and hit the walls. He died of heart failure on December 6, 2013, in the middle of the night. No noise. A nun came to wake him for breakfast, and his body was already cold.

Then there was a girl, Carolina. Calm. Lovely smile. She couldn't understand much, but if Sister Dolores showed her affection, she'd smile. She had a cold and stopped eating. She didn't last more than two days. Dead, also of heart failure. God gives these children the grace not to suffer too much once their hearts stop.

When Gustaveo and Carolina died, Sister Dolores told the other children that they were sick and a doctor would check on them. After the doctor left, she explained that they had gone to join Jesus and were waiting for the rest of the children to meet them when it was their time, and although they were gone they remained among them and could still see them. The bodies were taken to the chapel and the children participated in a Mass. Some of the boys and girls cried and for a few days refused to eat.

"That's how we dealt with it," Sister Dolores says.

I nod my head, recalling how my staff and I would hold memorial services for homeless people who had died. We would sit in a circle and talk about so-and-so. I'd often realize at these moments that I never knew the deceased's real name, just their street name: Too Tall, Gypsy, Alabama, Red. Names that defined them in a way that Don or John or Carol never would. Those given names belonged to a world they were no longer a part of. We spoke about them as we knew them, and when the service was over we continued working and getting on with our lives, lightened and relieved we weren't the ones who had died.

I concluded long ago that everlasting life, if there is such a thing, comes from those values and behaviors we pass on to other people, who in turn convey them to others and so on. I remember Too Tall, Gypsy, Alabama, Red—men and women who had no homes, had no solid achievements I know of, but whose names and faces I remember, and I consider why I do, what it is about them that won't die.

Lawyer Gustavo Maldonado was one of thousands who protested the Molina government after investigators held a news conference revealing the La Linea scandal. Gustavo was working at home at the time. Five days after the news conference, he joined fifty people outside the presidential palace chanting, "Send the thieves to jail." The following week, twenty-five thousand people protested. Just masses of people coming through the streets. He was so moved he wept.

The police showed up but did not carry guns. Gustavo could not avoid the contradiction. Three months earlier, the military had moved in full force against indigenous farmers protesting against mine owners, killing some of the farmers. Here outside the presidential palace, unarmed police just watched as protesters, mostly middle-class, objected to how their taxes were being squandered by corrupt officials.

He is not surprised by the election of Jimmy Morales. Morales provides people with a superficial vision. They see this guy who has never been in politics. He is one of us, they think. Morales banalizes politics, Gustavo tells me. He opens a laptop and reads Facebook posts praising Morales:

God heard our pleas.

We have somebody clean and good that has become president.

He's like Ronald Reagan.

Nonsense, Gustavo says. Morales has three problems: He's tied to the military, he has no public administration experience, and he's willing to sell himself to attain power. Gustavo and his friends are calling for protests the day Morales is sworn in as president. They want him to know he is being watched, and they want him to know their demands: Reform election laws, civil service laws, and mining laws.

They do not have a specific demand about poor children, Gustavo concedes. He and his friends are against poverty, against an oligarchical system. They want to transform the class structure of Guatemala and thereby transform poverty. But a specific demand about alleviating the plight of poor children, no, they do not have one.

As a young social worker, I would stand with my colleagues every spring outside San Francisco City Hall and protest budget reductions in social services. We walked in a circle with placards that read NO MORE CUTS. We distributed fliers with photographs of homeless people who had died. We spoke into microphones, and some of us did tortured imitations of the Rev. Martin Luther King Jr.'s "I Have a Dream" speech ("I have a dream that there will be no more homeless people in San Francisco.") Then after an hour or so, we would leave and go to a bar where we liked to hang out after work with those homeless people that we had sort of adopted, the ones who volunteered at our agencies and whom we thought of as just like us because they appeared no different from us. They had teeth, clean clothes, were mentally together, and did not drink themselves drunk. They joined us as we congratulated ourselves for our protest. We had shown *them*. We pontificated about human rights and made all the proper lefty declarations, jotting notes on bar napkins for future actions. Then our homeless friends returned to the streets or a shelter, the line between our lives and theirs accepted without question—amazing, now that I think of it, that none of us saw the separate-but-equal hues coloring our relationships—and we went home to our apartments, social justice clocking out until the next workday, our lives no different, really, than those people who slashed our budgets.

On my last day in Guatemala City, I drop by Hogar Marina Guirola Leal to say goodbye to Sister Dolores. I have a folded envelope with one hundred dollars in my pocket. A donation. I have thoughts of doing volunteer social work when I return to the States. But when I leave here, I suspect my mood will change. Something will be severed. I have bills to pay, a car that needs repair, work, and other life intrusions I can't ignore and that will allow me to rationalize how I won't have time to do anything else.

I find Sister Dolores in the courtyard watching volunteers push the children in their wheelchairs out into the sun. To one side, on a mat, I notice an eight-year-old girl on her hands and knees trying to maneuver through hoops. University students studying physical therapy hope to teach her to crawl.

Sister Dolores thanks the volunteers and then sees me. Smiling, she holds my hands and kisses my cheek. I notice she is not limping. She exudes a quiet confidence. Perhaps she is healing. Perhaps it is a confidence that comes from leading a life devoted to the welfare of others.

I give her the envelope and apologize that I can't give her more. She dismisses my apology with a don't-be-silly look. People give to the order but not many, she says. Some of them drop by with a donation but don't want to see the children. Most people don't even do that. I ask her what she thinks her life would have been like had she not become a nun. She would have married, she tells me, and had children. Whoever that man might have been was spared, she says and laughs. The choice to join the order was less a calling than an intellectual decision—like you becoming a journalist, she says.

When she was fourteen or fifteen, Sister Dolores would see nuns walking through her village. Nicely dressed. Clean. Men were deferential to them. Sister Dolores worked with her father in the fields picking corn. Her parents approved of her becoming a nun, but her father said he would miss her working beside him. She didn't want to pick corn for the rest of her life. She wanted to be like the sisters: to wear clean clothes and have an education and feel fulfilled and be respected as a woman even by men; in short, to be useful to others in more ways than just bearing children.

I follow her into the boys dorm where she checks on Douglass, who has been melancholy the past few days. She worries about him. Is he in pain? she wonders. It must hurt holding his head the way he does. Maybe she'll encourage him to come outside, or perhaps she should leave him alone today.

"Douglass," she calls.

He doesn't respond. She has no idea what will happen to him. She knows she will care for him until he dies. Who wants these children? No one. When God summons Douglass there will be an empty space filled almost immediately by another abandoned child. And another nun, too, will come after her. The orphanage will continue. God will provide.

The Dump

I sit in an office of Francisco Coll School with teacher Sister Gloria Xol. A breeze blows a paper off the table, and I pick it up and give it to her and she reads it aloud: If the school doesn't pay one hundred dollars within thirty days, the electricity will be shut off.

"Money makes our lives difficult," Sister Gloria comments impassively.

She gives a resigned smile and shakes her head and puts the bill aside. Through the open office door, I see boys and girls chasing one another in a courtyard; their voices bouncing off concrete walls. In the distance, the office buildings of downtown Guatemala City, no more than ten minutes away, are visible through a brown haze.

Sister Gloria teaches fifty third-grade boys and girls and finds them a very hard group to handle. The small, confined classrooms exacerbate their bad behavior. The slightest thing—a look, a word—that's all it takes to start a fight. Take this one boy who beat a classmate the other day. He lives with his alcoholic stepfather and mother. The mother told Sister Gloria that she hits him with a cable when she gets angry with him. She wanted to send him to a boarding school but couldn't afford it. How do you handle a boy like this? the mother asked. With violence.

Sister Gloria told the boy what his mother had said and he began crying and told her how much the cable hurt. Sister Gloria told him that the way he felt when his mother hit him was the same way other students feel when he strikes them. She thought she might get through to him but he didn't change. He remains aggressive and continues to be beaten at home. The boy's grandmother worries that his mother will lose control and kill him. Sister Gloria would like to get into the hearts of the boy and his mother and remove the pain they cause each other, but she does not know how.

"Your grandson is a child of God and deserves a chance," she told the grandmother.

I learned about Francisco Coll School when I visited Guatemala in 2015 to cover the presidential election. My translator, Olga Contreras, introduced me to a friend who volunteered at the school and I asked to see it.

Named after a Spanish priest and saint, it opened as a grammar school in 1995. Next door, International Samaritan administers a middle school. Most of the students in both facilities live in a barrio beside the Guatemala City garbage dump, the largest landfill in Central America. The dump holds more than a third of the country's trash and provides work for scavengers who recycle as much as a million pounds of garbage a day. In the process, they expose themselves to toxic fumes, hazardous materials, and landslides of waste that can bury people alive.

Olga's friend and I followed a school administrator through a network of alleys choked with bottle-filled sacks, cans, and other recyclables collected from the dump. Mattresses dried against shacks cobbled together from corrugated metal and discarded boards. The remains of collapsed hovels were used to ignite cooking fires. Sagging lines of laundry offered a bit of color.

We stopped at the shack of a single mother and her three daughters. The mother was working in the landfill but the girls were home. The two youngest attended Francisco Coll. The infant daughter of the oldest sister fussed in her arms. Piles of damp clothes covered the floor and their mildewed funk told me they were ruined. The younger girls explained that they were sorting the shirts and pants for the school to sell at a bazaar. Their sister did not look at me as we talked. She held the baby away from her body awkwardly, as if she'd rather have someone else take her, and she did not look at her either.

"We're trying to help this family," the administrator said after we left. "They are a tragic case. The father is in jail. The girls are his children. He committed incest. The baby you saw is his child."

The next morning, I left for the States. When I got home, I sent an email to my editor and she agreed I should write about the school. The following spring, I return to Guatemala.

Sister Gloria Xol introduces me to the principal of Francisco Coll, Sister Gloria Marlena Guadron Castillo. Sister Gloria Marlena has a pleasant smile that doesn't conceal the worry lines around her eyes. She tells me she has been at the school just four months. The lives of the children in el basurero, the dump, as locals call the barrio, shock her. Her childhood in a small village outside Santa Tegla, El Salvador, was so much different. Families had very little, of course. People earned less than a dollar a day, but violence was rare. As a young girl she didn't like her teachers because they yelled at the students and provided textbooks that looked one hundred years old. She thought she could do better and dreamed of building her own school for poor children.

"You know kids and how they think adults are incompetent," she tells me.

Her ambitions changed when three nuns with the order of Dominican Sisters of the Annunciation of the Blessed Virgin came to her village. The sisters called a meeting where they discussed living a life devoted to God, and afterward, they went house to house and asked families to send their children to Sunday school. Sister Gloria Marlena was among the children who attended.

At sixteen, she joined a weekend spiritual retreat and read a biography of the saints. Their simplicity and concern for others moved her, and when she finished the biography she decided to devote her life to God. As a young nun, she served in remote parishes in El Salvador and Guatemala for eleven years before her superiors transferred her to Francisco Coll.

For the past few weeks, she has focused much of her attention on three orphaned students, two brothers and a sister. When they were small, their father was shot in front of the boys. Recently, their mother was murdered. The older boy, a sixth-grader, has vowed revenge on his parents' killers. What does she say to such children? Sister Gloria Marlena wonders. Vengeance is not yours to give? You should pray? Do they even understand what prayer and faith mean at their age? Is prayer as real to them as a gun? Before she came here, she had never asked herself these questions.

After school, Sister Gloria Marlena escorts me to a building about a block away where lay teacher Juan Pablo Rivas tutors students in math and Spanish grammar. He volunteers on Monday, Wednesday, and Friday, from two in the afternoon to five and sees about forty students. The work, he tells me, drains him. Some of the children have poor hand-eye coordination. They don't understand the simplest things and they rarely sit still. Their moods fluctuate like a breeze, one moment gentle, the next blustery. This afternoon he tells them to write an essay about the meaning of honesty. He hopes they will reflect on their own behavior and that of their parents.

My life, one student writes. *Sometimes I'm really happy and sometimes I'm really sad. With my Mom I'm really happy. But on the other hand my father is no longer here but I am really happy with God and my family too.*

Another student begins her essay: *My name is Jennifer and I would like to tell you about my life. My life is happy, nice, but sometimes it is sad and at those times I don't want to be without my father. He was shot. I would like to be a dentist or a doctor or a vet. I adore my family but want my father. I want to be somebody in life. That is why I need to study so I can look for a nice job and help other people and so I'm able to take care of everybody else.*

A third student offers a wish list: *I would like to do more things in my life such as going to the country. I'd like to go alone to the video games and I'd like to be able to have boots. I would like to tell my parents thank you because they are the ones struggling and suffering to support the family. I have an older brother who helps us out. I have a teacher who loves us very much and I have never had such a nice teacher before.*

The essays sadden Juan Pablo. Such a tragic world these children live in. He recalls a six-year-old boy he tutored who had gotten involved with gangs. He picked fights so Juan Pablo told him to leave, and he hasn't seen him since. Then there was a twelve-year-old girl. Juan Pablo helped her as much as he could but she had problems at home. Sometimes she lived with her father, a gang member, and sometimes she lived with her mother and grandmother, alcoholics both. The girl got very violent. She tried to act older than she was but she was just a kid, a troubled kid. She got into so many fights. Juan Pablo doesn't see her anymore, either.

Other students give him hope. Like nine-year-old Francisco. Francisco is doing well. He comes from a very poor family but his mother and older sister support him. He stays off the street and completes his schoolwork.

"Would you like to meet him?" Juan Pablo asks me.

He shouts, "Francisco," and a boy stands. His stained, orange T-shirt hangs off his slim body like a rag suspended from a hook; his blue jeans spill over his sneakers, and Juan Pablo leads us from the classroom to the hall and finds three chairs. Francisco sits beside him, head down. I imagine he wonders why he has been called out of class. I introduce myself and apologize for making him nervous. "OK," he says, and shrugs, posturing a nonchalance he does not feel. However, as he answers my questions, Francisco relaxes, and I soon realize he enjoys talking about himself.

He tells me he lives on a big, quiet street without much traffic. It twists and turns and gets slippery when it rains. Yesterday it poured and Francisco's house flooded and got very wet inside. When it does not rain, Francisco roller-skates, but the bumpy pavement makes him fall too much. On smooth roads, he really gets going. Francisco enjoys school because he's good at math. He has not yet memorized his multiplication tables but when he does, he thinks he'll like math even more.

This week in his catechism class, Sister Gloria Marlena read a Bible story about a robber who got caught. The class talked about how no one should take things from other people. If they need something, they should pray for it. A friend of Francisco's told her he asks God to stop his mother from beating him.

After school, Francisco helps his mother at his grandmother's tortilla shop. His grandmother has not been feeling well so his mother fills in for her and Francisco stands beside her, mixing tortilla batter and daydreaming about becoming a firefighter and saving people.

When Juan Pablo dismisses the class, I walk with Francisco to his home. We stop at a shack patched together with aluminum siding, wood, and blue plastic tarps. He knocks on an ill-fitting door but no one answers. His mother, he says, must still be at the tortilla shop. We cross the alley and he raps on the door of a neighbor who watches him when his mother works.

A young woman holding a baby answers and Francisco introduces me to Carmela. Her two younger sisters peer around her. I recognize them all. These are the girls I met on my first trip; the family with the baby born of incest. A toddler and a baby sleep on a mattress on the dirt floor and Carmela notices me looking at them. Her boyfriend is the father of that one, she says pointing to the infant. She doesn't mention the father of the toddler. Her two teenage sisters, Cindy and Jaqueline, say they saw me at Francisco Coll where they are students. Carmela dropped out years ago.

"There are no opportunities here," Carmela says of el basurero, "so why should I go to school?"

Just the other night, two men pointed pistols at her and took her money and cell phone. Jaqueline has also been mugged, ten times in two years. Sometimes when she walked to school, other times on the bus. She cries talking about it.

Three men stopped Cindy and her mother one afternoon. The men had guns and demanded money but Cindy and her mother had only a little change. The men took it and let them go. Toward the end of each school day, Cindy has trouble concentrating. She thinks of the walk home alone.

"My sister was mugged," Francisco says in a me-too kind of way, as if he feels a need to compete for our attention. In 2014, she was walking to a store to buy underwear and a guy stabbed her in the belly. She survived but she stayed in a hospital for many weeks. That same year, Francisco continues, a shooting took place in front of his house and he looked through a crack in the wall and saw a man running, bleeding from his right arm.

"But you were never mugged," Carmela says.

"No," Francisco agrees, looking a little downcast. Then he pipes right back up. He doesn't worry about being mugged because Sister Gloria Marlena told him he should only fear God.

The next morning, I return to Francisco Coll and sit in on a social studies class taught by Sister Carlotta Merida. Sister Carlotta grew up in San Marcos, Guatemala, and worked in Cameroon, Ivory Coast, and Rwanda for twenty-three years before she returned to Guatemala in 2015 to care for her ailing mother. She had never seen such poverty as she did in Africa. People could not grow food in the parched soil, and their children starved. The boys and girls here, she tells me, at least can get something to eat even if it comes from the landfill.

"What do you want to do when you grow up?" she asked a boy here one afternoon.

"I want to be a professional killer and thief," he told her.

She knew he didn't understand what he was saying but she did not scold him. Many of her students' parents are thieves, prostitutes, and gang members. Children love their fathers and mothers no matter how flawed. Instead, she asked the boy more questions: What else would you like to be? A policeman? He agreed being a policeman would be fun.

Sister Carlotta wants her students to understand the meaning of respect, love, and truth. Don't steal. They know that one. That's easy. Many of them know what it's like to be robbed. She gives them a goal once a week and asks them to explain what they must do to achieve it. This week she assigned two objectives: avoid saying bad words and show respect to your teachers. One student told her he had behaved well in his math class a day after he was sent to the principal for fighting.

"That's an accomplishment," Sister Carlotta told him, "write it down."

The boy who wanted to be a professional killer has changed too. He sits still in class and has stopped hitting other kids and doesn't get up and leave without permission. Who knows what his future holds.

Layperson Jessica Gomez teaches a fourth-grade composition class across the hall from Sister Carlotta. She instructs the class to list the main characters in the day's reading. "Then we'll work on our writing and our vocabulary," she says.

Jessica graduated from Francisco Coll in 2010. Her mother, Altagracia Arevalo, is the school janitor. Jessica has seven siblings. She never knew her alcoholic father; he died when she was young. Her mother grew up in Jutiapa, Guatemala, near the border with El Salvador, and moved to el basurero in search of work before Jessica was born.

When Jessica completed high school, she decided to become a teacher and chose to work at Francisco Coll because she had attended the school and understood the students. Besides, a teacher's salary is so small, where else could she live but the barrio? People around here know her and she has never been mugged. Criminals respect her for being a teacher because some of their siblings and children are her students.

"What's the main character?" Jessica asks, shaking a rattle to get one boy's attention.

"Where do these characters live? A farm, a town?"

The boy grabs the hair of another boy and wrestles him to the floor and Jessica breaks them up. The first boy walks around making faces.

"It's not nice for you to be out of your seat," Jessica tells him. "Where's your book? If you don't work, I'll send a note to your mother."

"She'll beat me," the boy says.

"Then sit down."

Jessica glances around the classroom. She doesn't see Francisco, one of her better students. Sometimes, he doesn't show up. At the beginning of the year, Jessica confronted Francisco's mother about his absences. She told Jessica that Francisco was exhausted from helping her in the tortilla shop and she had let him sleep in. Jessica replied that she was also tired but she still did her job. Francisco had two jobs: to help his mother and attend school. Francisco's mother agreed and sent him to school the next day.

Another student, Stephanie, reminds Jessica of herself. Stephanie's mother works in the landfill, leaving Stephanie to care for her three younger brothers and a sister after school. Stephanie feeds them and puts them to bed, just as Jessica had cared for her younger siblings when her mother toiled in the landfill.

"I'll give you five more minutes to finish the assignment," Jessica tells the class.

The two boys who had been wrestling tap their chests, their

fingers spread into Vs, a gang sign. They stop when Jessica shakes her rattle. After school, she sees them wandering the streets with older boys.

Another student, Aracely, also can be difficult. She does not pay attention, talks back. Aracely has five younger sisters and her father is an alcoholic. She and her siblings don't have enough to eat, and Jessica takes food to Aracely's mother and encourages her to send her daughters to school.

"That is how her life will be different from yours," Jessica tells her.

In her office next to Jessica's classroom, Sister Gloria Marlena considers a sketch drawn by an eight-year-old girl of a stick figure holding a gun with a gang insignia. Jesus stands on the other side of the page, a yellow crucifix above his head, and he holds a rope that the stick figure holds too.

"Let Jesus pull you across," Sister Gloria Marlena had told the student. "Don't be afraid."

The student had been absent from school for days until Sister Gloria Marlena visited her mother. "She's a bright girl," Sister Gloria Marlena said. Her mother agreed, but she had never attended school and doesn't understand its importance.

At noon, the recess bell rings and the students bolt out of their classrooms and into the courtyard. Sister Carlotta, who serves snacks from a wagon, and I watch Cynthia, the daughter of the man convicted of incest, take a box of M&Ms and sit on a stone bench, and I join her.

"Have you always lived here?" I ask.

She shakes her head. Their first house stood near the landfill but not as close as the house they have now. It flooded all the time and the dirt floor would turn to soup. They put a mattress down to absorb the water and she, her mother, and her sisters slept together on a blanket in a part of the house that wasn't wet. In the morning, they ate cold rice and beans. The mattress, soaked with mud, stunk and they put it outside to dry.

They have a better house now with good doors. The first house didn't have doors at all, only a piece of wood to cover the entrance and it fell off all the time. When she has a house of her own, Cynthia wants it to be like this house but bigger with very large doors.

"I met you last year, do you remember?" I ask her.

"A little," she answers. "You did not stay long. Sometimes foreign people with NGOs come by and look at us and don't stay long either."

Cynthia likes to read books her mother finds in the landfill. Some of them look new while others are dirty and torn. She enjoys stories about fairies and nature and animals, and she likes to draw the characters. Tigers are her favorite animal because their fur has lovely coloring. Cynthia would like to be an artist.

Even more than reading and drawing, she enjoys spending time with her mother. Her mother has dark skin and is short. She can be very easygoing but sometimes she gets quite angry if Cynthia and her sisters don't make dinner and clean the dishes afterward. Cynthia once had a beautiful dream she shared with her mother: Her entire family was reunited and happy. They lived in a delightful house. She remembers this dream fondly because it made her mother smile.

She looks forward to seeing her father when he's released from jail. When he lived with them in their first house, he let her play with friends outside. Then he went to jail and her mother brought her and her sisters to el basurero and Cynthia never saw her friends again. She does not know why her father is in jail anymore than she knows who fathered Carmela's first baby. Her mother and Carmela scold her, "Stop asking questions." No one in the family tells Cynthia anything.

An hour passes and recess ends. Some of the boys and girls drift into the classroom of Sister Gloria Xol. This afternoon, she teaches math.

Sister Gloria: Attention! Sit in your seats. Put your food away right now and copy the assignment on the board.

$$15 - (8 \times 2) =$$

$$2 \times 15 + 2 \times 8 \times 2 =$$

Sister Gloria: Who doesn't understand? I will explain. Multiply eight times two and subtract the total from fifteen. If you have fifteen minus sixteen what do you have?

Boy: Negative one.

Sister Gloria: Good. (to another boy) Did you copy everything?

Boy: I don't have a pencil or pen to write with.

She gives him a pencil.

Sister Gloria: Be sure to give it back. Pay attention, this will be on the exam.

A boy throws a pen.

Sister Gloria: What are you doing? Why aren't you paying attention?

Girl: I don't have a pencil.

Sister Gloria: What are we going to do if we keep forgetting our things?

A boy sings a rap tune: I never asked to be born, and death's no question/The sun's still shining off the same old lessons/Then why does life feel like an educated guess?

Sister Gloria: Pay attention!

I leave Sister Gloria's class and follow Altagracia Arevalo, the mother of Jessica Gomez, through the barrio in search of truant children.

"I feel bad for the boys and girls whose parents work all the time and are not around to support them," Altagracia says. "They have to work, I understand. I have to work; we all do. I'd rather not, but that is not possible. My two sons, both mechanics, have been laid off. Another son lost his job at a chocolate factory. I am still supporting my family."

Altagracia labored in the landfill for twelve years. Twelve years, she repeats, shaking a finger at me. She earned just a dollar a day collecting and selling glass bottles and cans. Some things she kept for her children, like clothes and shoes. Once or twice she found a hat to block the sun. She competed with children—little ones, not just teenagers—who could stoop over longer than she could, rummaging through the garbage without their backs aching. One boy licked something off his fingers and died. Altagracia almost died too. Years and years ago, when she was three months pregnant and very hungry, she ate from a can of rancid meat. Doctors had to pump her stomach.

Altagracia stops to confront a boy pushing a wheelbarrow holding another, smaller boy, sound asleep.

"Why are you not in school?" Altagracia asks.

"I have to watch my brother," the older boy says.

Altagracia asks the boy where he lives and he takes her to a shack beside a gutter flush with gray water and a swollen, dead puppy. Altagracia pokes her head through an open door and sees a woman washing plates in a bucket. Chickens settle on a bed beneath a bare lightbulb and more chickens cluck on a sack of clothes beside a woodpile.

"You need to get your son to school," Altagracia tells the woman.

"I know, but I needed his help. Last night's rain flooded the house."

"School is important."

"I know. I want my children to learn something in life. To read and write so they can find work. I am allowing them to study. I just needed their help today. I worked seven hours in the landfill yesterday. Today, I'm not feeling well."

"Did you eat something you collected?" Altagracia says.

"No."

"Good."

The woman says she only gathers bottles and cardboard, not food. She earns about six dollars a day. On Saturdays she stays longer and makes a little more. A mugger killed her husband in an attempted robbery in 2007. Since then, she has been with other men. It's good to have a man in the house for protection, she explains. Men, however, come with a price. She has eight children, ages twenty to a year and a half. She is pregnant now with her ninth child. The father, like those who came before him, left once she became pregnant.

"A woman is one thing for men," she says. "A baby, quite another."

"You get pregnant and they don't want you, is that it?"

"Yes," the woman says.

"You make excuses," Altagracia says.

"No," the woman says. "I talk about my life."

Back at school, Cynthia stops Altagracia. She shows her a pencil sketch she drew of a two-story house with a tall door. A large tree provides shade. One of its branches curves over the roof and turns into a mountain on a distant horizon. Cynthia remembers seeing a house like this when she was small. It's one of her first memories. She made several versions of the drawing before deciding to save this one.

"I like it very much," Altagracia tells her.

"This house would never flood," Cynthia says.

At two o'clock the children leave for the day, streaming out of the school past Ramon Gonzalez, a thin, muscular man throwing bottles into barrels. He wears sunglasses to protect his eyes from flying bits of broken glass. After he fills one barrel he starts in on another and then loads them into a pickup and drives to a recycling factory. He earns less than one dollar per barrel.

Ramon drove a garbage truck but quit after a few years. Collapsing mountains of landfill trash almost buried him alive more than once. The landfill is a living, breathing monster, he tells me. Every so often something sets it off and it needs to feed.

It rains in the evening and the next morning Francisco skips school to help his sister sweep water out of the house. His grandmother remains ill and his mother takes her to a hospital. She won't tell Francisco what's wrong; she cries when he asks her. He sweeps and sweeps but the water always rolls back and he gets a bucket and scoops it up and tosses it as far as he can but still it drifts back. When his mother returns home, she praises him for his hard work and sends him to school. He does not ask about his grandmother.

The tortilla shop stands at the end of an alley near a closed gate. Behind the gate, piles of junked cars provide homes for feral cats. Francisco's mother, Christine Ixcoi, flattens dough and tosses it between her hands before she drops it into one of two wood-burning ovens that give off an intense heat and she steps back, wiping her grimed face with an apron.

If her mother were well, Christine would be working in the landfill sorting through garbage for about eight hours a day. However, her mother is not well. At the hospital this morning a doctor said she had ovarian cancer. He urged Christine to try homeopathic medicine. She does not know where she will get the money.

Christine moved to el basurero with her mother in 2009 because it costs nothing to live beside a garbage dump. Otherwise, she would never live here. Young men do drugs on the street, and their families say nothing. They are poor, and too preoccupied with their poverty to discipline their children. Christine's first husband left her when she became pregnant with her daughter, now twenty. The father of Francisco also abandoned her.

Of her two children, Francisco is the most even-tempered. He enjoys helping around the house. An observant boy, he sees everything—the good and the bad. She hopes he has a life far different from hers and attends high school and graduates and finds work. She doesn't care what kind of job, as long as it's not in the landfill.

Seated in her office, Sister Gloria Marlena receives a disturbing phone call. The mother of a student tells her that her nephew and his friend were shot and killed by two robbers while they sold Chiclets on a bus. Sister Gloria Marlena can't believe it. Why? They wanted their money, the woman tells her in a flat, hopeless voice.

Why did the woman call? Sister Gloria Marlena wonders. What did she think she could do? Did she want help? Help how? Listen, offer support, pray?

Twelve-year-old Fernanda Mayen sits outside Sister Gloria Marlena's office. Fernanda left her composition class to use the bathroom without permission and her teacher, Sister Carlotta, sent her to Sister Gloria to be punished.

Fernanda lives in a part of el basurero that has the fewest families and where she and her friends feel safe to play. She has good friends but no best friends. People move too often for her to have a best friend. As much as she likes playing outside, Fernanda knows to be careful. Some people bully girls when they see them alone. They drink and get high and chase them and throw rocks and grab their dresses.

On sunny days, she spends as much time as she can away from her ugly house where everything is filthy. It stinks. Fernanda lives with an uncle and aunt. She does not remember when her father died. Her uncle told her he was mugged and shot. Her mother died near their home when Fernanda was in second grade. Not in this neighborhood, another one, sometime at night. She had been toiling in the landfill and she was killed on the way home. A friend found her body. Fernanda always stayed with her uncle when her mother worked. That night, he told Fernanda she would not be going home.

She thinks she has a picture of her mother but she doesn't know where she put it. Her mother had red hair and was a little fat with fair skin, her face darker than her arms and legs. She was really fun. Her mother talked a lot and liked to gossip with friends and never hit her. Life without her has been hard for Fernanda. Sometimes her uncle eats before she gets home from school and doesn't save anything for her. He gets angry all the time about the rain and how it floods his house. He threatens her, If you get anything wet and dirty, I will pull your pants down and beat you with my belt. If she goes to a store for school supplies, he shouts at her, You're always spending my money! Fernanda's uncle is a big man. He works with trucks and has strong arms good for beatings. He hits her brothers. They attend fourth and sixth grade. The older boy wants to buy a gun and murder whoever killed their mother. Fernanda's uncle tells him to shut up about that. She thinks her uncle likes being angry.

Fernanda enjoys school. The neat and tidy buildings appeal to her so much more than her home. Of her classes, she likes math the most. The math teacher sings little rhymes: *Two plus two is four / not one numeral more.* Fernanda wants to be a teacher so she knows all the things her teachers know. After school, she feels sad because she has to go home. Sometimes, her uncle lets her do her homework. Other times, he has her clean the house. He doesn't care if she attends school. Her aunt always asks about her grades. Fernanda likes her even though she yells a lot too.

One night, Fernanda dreamed about her mother. She was dressed in white and sat with Fernanda and then Fernanda had to use the bathroom. When Fernanda finished, her mother was gone and Fernanda woke up.

In the morning, I ask a garbage man near my hotel if he will take me into the landfill. He agrees, providing I tip him and don't mention his name. I meet him hours later, after he has finished his trash route.

As I pull myself into the cab, he starts the engine and we drive past Francisco Coll and el basurero to a pitted road that winds into the landfill. The dust we churn up reduces visibility. Avoiding some deep holes, we veer into an area filled with idling garbage trucks, where I watch men hauling sacks of recyclable material larger than their own bodies, running, feet dancing for balance, the weight of their loads propelling them toward a row of lean-to shelters where recyclers wait beside their scales to weigh the pickings.

The garbage man parks and we get out. He has been picking up trash for twelve years. His brother, also a garbage man, got him the job. No prior work experience required. He can't read or write and feels very lucky to be working. He starts at two in the morning and finishes at six at night four days a week. He'll do this for as long as he can, the rest of his life, maybe, who knows? He's only twenty-six but it's steady work.

We wait for a recycler to weigh the garbage man's sacks of cans and glass and bundles of cardboard. He earns about a dollar a pound. Trash unsuitable for recycling he'll dump elsewhere in the landfill and people from el basurero will sift through it and no doubt, he says, will find something to recycle that he missed. He collects garbage in mostly residential areas and sorts through it all and has found all kinds of things, including metal shelves, cabinets, car parts, gold chains and shoes. He keeps the shoes and wears them on the job. He found two guitars once that were in good shape. He can't play but he kept them.

The garbage man drops me at my hotel. After dinner, I am watching a televised soccer game when a photo of the landfill interrupts the sportscast. "A massive heap of garbage fell," an announcer says. "At least twenty-four garbage pickers are missing."

The photo vanishes and the soccer game resumes. I call Sister Gloria Marlena.

"It's very bad," she tells me.

Her voice shakes. She had been teaching catechism when the cell phones of some of the children began ringing. Then all their phones started ringing.

"Mother! Mother!" one boy yelled. "The landfill caved in and washed away the people!"

He ran out of class and the students and Sister Gloria Marlena chased after him. She doesn't know yet if any students were in the landfill. She can't imagine what families must be feeling. The only thing she could do was stand with them outside the landfill and wait for updates but none came. Eventually she walked home and prayed.

In the courtyard of Francisco Coll the next morning, somber-faced children stand in small groups and don't speak. Their weighty silence cuts off everything else, even the noise of the recycler Ramon Gonzalez, still throwing bottles into barrels despite everything that has happened. Sister Carlotta holds two candles and asks the boys and girls to remember and pray for the dead. She tells me that families remain lined up outside the landfill impatient for news of a husband or son, brother or wife, grandparent or sister.

The father of one student is missing. Three other students lost their grandfathers. A stepmother of another student also died, and a former student just fifteen was buried alive and his body hasn't been found. Everyone called him Chico. His parents also worked in the landfill. Chico's father was holding him by the arm but could not maintain his grip and Chico was sucked down. Chico's father yelled, "Chico! My Chico!" and then he was gone.

I accompany Sister Gloria Marlena as she walks through el basurero to check on families. At one house, a girl tells her that her grandfather was taken out of the landfill barely alive.

"My family is OK," another student tells her.

He points to a shack.

"The grandfather of that family, he's missing. There's no news. The family went to a hospital, but he was not there. They have looked for him all night. The police have stopped looking for him in the landfill."

"We'll drop by again to see if you've found him," Sister Gloria Marlena says.

Another boy tells her that his mother was supposed to be in the landfill but went into labor and did not work. She named the baby "Suerte"—Lucky.

When Sister Gloria Marlena and I return to the school, a volunteer, Angela Hernandez, stops us. She had been in the landfill when the garbage gave way.

"You're working and the next thing you know you sink down," Angela says.

She was scared and ran as fast as she could. The noise sounded like the roar of some big animal chasing her. Angela has worked in the landfill since she was seventeen. One time, she sank so deeply into the garbage that only her head stuck out and it took a half-dozen men to pull her out. She had no other job so she returned the next morning. Now at fifty-six, she puts in twelve hours a day sorting and picking and reselling what she can. It is the only work she knows—that and volunteering at the school cleaning toilets to earn money for food.

"I think forty people are missing," Angela says. "One day of rain and this happens. Imagine what it will be like during the rainy season."

In the school courtyard, I see Cynthia and ask about her mother.

"Alive," she says.

Her mother was leaving for the landfill when she heard people screaming and wailing. Then the noise of ambulance sirens drowned out their shrieks. Cynthia was home and heard a really loud bang. She worried her older sister Carmela might be in the landfill but Carmela was running errands. Cynthia didn't know that, and wouldn't go to bed until Carmela came home. Now everyone is home and she can sleep. Her mother gathered ten sacks of aluminum cans before all the upheaval. The cans will support the family until the landfill reopens.

The older brother of Fernanda Mayan saw people perish in the trash. He told Fernanda that the garbage dragged people down into the ground and he started running. He had never seen or heard anything like it. Noise like rolling thunder. He began shaking as he talked and could not stop crying.

Fernanda tries not to think about what happened. Her uncle says it is part of living in el basurero. She worries about her brother. What will he do now? How will he earn money for the family if he can't work in the landfill?

Sister Gloria Marlena eases her way through the students and stands alone in a corner of the courtyard. Every day she urges parents to support their children's education. What does that support mean when they can die in the landfill? How many more families will the landfill take? How many students?

She looks at me but does not expect an answer. In her prayers, she puts the children and their families in God's hands.

"How many will continue to fall through his fingers?"

"Do you question your faith?" I ask.

"No," she says. "I question my strength."

Francisco stops me as I leave the school. He says he was with Juan Pablo, the tutor, when the landfill caved in. His mother had been selling tortillas to street vendors. Her brother drives a garbage truck. Concerned, she called him and he told her he was OK. Francisco heard a story that a gold mine lies at the bottom of the landfill and whoever looks for it will not come out. His mother pushes Francisco to study so he can get a good job and not be tempted to work in the landfill. Earlier in the day, before the landfill collapsed, Jessica Gomez gave Francisco ninety points on a math quiz. Ninety points! He looks forward to the next test and hopes he'll get one hundred points. Today is a sad day in el basuero, but tomorrow may be better. He thinks it will be, but he doesn't know.

Land Rites

The humid heat of San Miguel Ixtahuacán leaves me sweat-soaked and out of breath from the steep climb to the house at the top of the hill. A woman opens the door.

"I have an appointment with Sister Maudilia Lopez," I say.

"Come in. I'm her assistant, Magdalena."

Magdalena leads me through a dim, cool hall that opens into a rustic dining room where a warped wood table occupies most of the space, surrounded by sagging shelves of spices and canned food and metal bowls, and I follow Magdalena through a back door to a garden. Sister Maudilia stands off to one side with a hose, watering roses, the water splashing her bare feet. She is short and compact and wears a long skirt and a loose blouse patterned with the geometric and floral designs typical of Maya culture, and her dark hair falls evenly between her shoulders. An indigenous nun, Maudilia does not wear the habit of the sisters I knew from my Catholic upbringing.

"It's hot and they are dying of thirst," she says of the roses.

Sister Maudilia shuffles from one rose to the next as water drips off the leaves and creates streams on the dry ground. Palm trees rise above us and insects hum in tufts of grass at our feet as she shifts the hose into her other hand and, without intending to, sprays a cat. It springs away to take cover beneath a fallen palm leaf and hisses. Sister Maudilia ignores it, continues watering. The water comes from rivers whose source lies in the mountains above San Miguel, where tributaries and land have been destroyed by a gold and silver mine.

Owned by Montana Exploradora de Guatemala, a subsidiary of the Canadian company Goldcorp, the Marlin Mine began operations in 2005 in the regions of San Miguel and Sipacapa, communities composed largely of indigenous Mayas who still speak their native languages. The Mam, of which Sister Maudilia is a member, is one of many Maya nations in Guatemala and makes up the majority population, numbering at more than six hundred thousand in Guatemala's western regions. The mine brought jobs and prosperity to some among the Mam, but not all. It generated more than $4 billion in revenue for Goldcorp and indelibly altered the countryside. It also divided the community, converting many among the agrarian Mam into devotees of consumer culture who came to view the land as a profit center, while others maintained their spiritual connection to their farms.

Sister Maudilia responded politely but without urgency when I contacted her from the States and explained I wanted to write about the mine. Now that I'm here, in May 2016, she speaks little, appears almost indifferent. She just waters the plants while I watch her. I don't feel ignored but rather accepted into her day as much as the plants she tends and the humid heat she can do nothing about.

She clearly feels no need for niceties, no need to ask, How was your drive? and other polite but rote questions that would hold no interest for either of us. She agreed to meet and put me up in her house, but compared with what concerns her—the mine—my presence is negligible.

When she finishes watering, Sister Maudilia winds the hose and I follow her inside. She rinses red beans in a bucket and cuts potatoes. The cat tries to follow her inside, but she shoos it away.

"Dinner," she says of the beans and potatoes.

I tell her I've heard she has received death threats but she denies that. Mine workers have bad-mouthed her for her opposition to the mine: They've yelled at her, called her on the phone, and said things like, "Why are you doing this? Don't meddle." But death threats, no. Not yet.

Before I left Guatemala City for San Miguel, I met with a Goldcorp spokesman and a company lawyer. Their office took up most of the ninth floor in a tall downtown building sheathed in glass. They took me into a large conference room with bare white walls. We sat on opposite sides of a long table. They wore matching black suits and ties and gold cufflinks. As they gave me their business cards, they said their names could not be used. They both hoped I'd visit some of Guatemala's beaches and historical sites. Enjoy your stay, the lawyer said. Yes, enjoy your stay, the spokesman urged. They talked in clipped sentences, each precise, rehearsed word anticipating a trap and fencing off all unapproved stray thoughts that might slip out of their mouths. Their forced small talk, I knew, would vanish once I finished the interview, and they walked me out with smiles that did not conceal their feeling that all media are suspect. They understood as I did that dozens of studies excerpted in news outlets had found little good to say about the Marlin Mine.

A report by the World Bank's Office of the Compliance Advisor/Ombudsman office in 2005 found a "genuine difference in understanding amongst the parties about the purpose of consultation with and disclosures to local people." The report asserts that documents submitted to the leaders of indigenous communities "did not at the time have sufficient information to allow for an informed view of the likely adverse impacts of the project," casting doubt on the appropriateness of the consultation.

"The government of Guatemala has not been able to provide effective guidance about this issue and meet the expectations of civil society with respect to consultation," the report said. Tensions increased when people who anticipated being hired by the mine were not. Many families sold their land to the mine and bought trucks thinking they would be needed for jobs that never came.

The Goldcorp spokesman said that at its peak the mine employed more than eight hundred people, most of whom lived nearby. He insisted that up to 95 percent of its workforce still comes from the local population, and no more than 5 percent from outside Guatemala.

"The real problem is that the employment is not sustainable," economist Edgar Pape, a retired economics professor at San Carlos University in Guatemala City, told me later. "People can't replicate that kind of income once the mine closes."

According to the Central American Institute for Fiscal Studies in Guatemala City, the entire mining sector in Guatemala paid an annual average of $50 million in taxes and royalties between 2009 and 2014. This, she said, was equivalent to a tax burden between about 4 and 6 percent. For every one hundred dollars in profits, the government received less than six dollars in taxes and royalties. But Goldcorp's spokesman said the company pays the state nearly 40 percent of the Marlin Mine's earnings in taxes and royalties, a level that has been verified by independent studies.

"Whether the amount is sufficient is a judgment call for the political leadership. It should be their position to add or not to add additional tax," he insisted.

In addition, Goldcorp is registered as a maquiladora, a program whose main purpose is to increase employment among low-skilled workers, train a workforce, and increase exports. However the program can also be used by foreign companies to access low-cost labor and favorable duty or tariff rates on imported equipment and machinery, so that the companies benefit from a lower income-tax rate. The spokesman rejected the characterization because, he said, it suggested a sweatshop.

"It is nothing more than a law that helps with exports," he said. "It has certain tax-related incentives that make it attractive."

He added that the company was in regular contact with the Ministry of Energy and Mines. He said the company would pay for the closing of the mine and apply international standards and "best practices."

Ministry officials declined to speak with me.

For years, environmentalists have accused the mine of releasing dangerous pollutants. In 2009, the Pastoral Commission for Peace and Ecology found arsenic and other chemicals in the Quivichil and Tzalá rivers downstream from the mine's wastewater reservoir. E-Tech International, a New Mexico nonprofit that provides environmental technical support to poor communities in developing countries, reported in 2010 that "the mine wastes have a moderate to high potential to generate acid and leach contaminants into the environment." The Goldcorp spokesman said the company applies "rigorous" compliance and international environmental standards to the mine, and that the Ministry of Energy and Mines and the Ministry of Environment and Natural Resources monitor it.

"We have had no judicial process or finding of any sort of irresponsible handling of industrial wastes," he said. "We have complied with all laws required beyond what local regulations would demand from us. We have had no rulings against us."

However, an anthropologist at the University of the Valley in Guatemala City, Regina Solis, whom I'd interviewed earlier, told me that the real damage was less tangible but equally important:

"When the mine started the construction process, they built roads, took water from community rivers, and this process caused the Maya community to feel displaced because their land was being altered," Solis said. "The Western vision of the land is very different from the Maya vision."

Standing in Sister Maudilia's kitchen, I offer to set the table and she points to the cabinet where she keeps the plates. Sister

Maudilia never anticipated that she would become an anti-mining activist. She had only wanted to leave Comitancillo, the small village about thirty-five miles outside of San Miguel where she was born. Not even a village, really. Just a group of houses. As a child she dreamed of liberating her mother from her abusive father—and herself too. She did not attend school then, but worked in a pottery factory making food trays. She never wanted to be a doctor or a lawyer. She did not even know those careers existed—or anything else other than farming and factory work. When she was twelve, a priest came to Comitancillo and offered religious education to young girls so they could become nuns. Fifteen girls participated, including Sister Maudilia. She saw the classes as a way out of Comitancillo and began dreaming of joining the church. She did not fully understand what it would require of her but she wanted a better life. With the priest's help, she entered a convent at fifteen and took her vows in 2003 when she was thirty-one with Hermanas Guadalupanas, an order that allowed her to incorporate Maya ancestral beliefs into Christian spiritual life.

At the convent she learned about women who studied to become doctors and lawyers, but by then she had her heart set on becoming a nun. She did enroll in school, however, and earned a degree in theology. Now she is studying for a graduate degree in social anthropology in Quetzaltenango, Guatemala's second-largest city, a four-hour bus ride from San Miguel.

Sister Maudilia moved here in 1996, becoming the only nun in the small parish. In those days, San Miguel was a very quiet town, but to Maudilia it was so much bigger than Comitancillo, thirty-five miles away, that it was almost like a city.

About the same time that she moved, a company offered San Miguel's farmers seeds and financial loans to grow broccoli. Once the broccoli was ready, the company bought it from the growers and shipped it to other countries but the farmers did not like this arrangement. A belief persisted that the company was not looking out for their best interests. Company supervisors would tell them to harvest the broccoli and pack it in crates, and on a certain date they would inspect the loads. If they found one bad piece, they would reject the entire crate and decline to pay for it. Eventually, the farmers refused to grow broccoli and the company left after two years.

In 2003, people started gossiping about another big company coming to town. Rumors suggested it was a cement company. That made sense because San Marcos had big rocks in its rivers and people told Sister Maudilia that rocks were needed to make cement. Then one afternoon a silver Toyota pickup circled the square. Over a loudspeaker, a man inside the truck invited people to a meeting. He said there would be food and drink. At the meeting, he would inform everyone of a new company that would soon establish itself in town. He said nothing about the meaning of the colors of the mountains that were home to the people here: Red, the energy of Mother Earth; white, the spiritual life of their ancestors; yellow, the crops that people eat; blue for the sky and water; and how his plans would affect all of this.

For weeks in the month of June the pickup drove around town, building excitement in the community. Sister Maudilia and others asked themselves, Should we attend? What is this really about? They wondered what they should wear for something that seemed to portend something significant was about to happen. The streets filled with families walking to the meeting at city hall, the expressions on their faces alternating between solemn and giddy as they crowded together. Men in dark suits stood before them and slowly revealed their plans. Not for a cement factory, but a gold and silver mine. Everything was set. Jobs would be offered and the local economy would prosper. The meeting was not a consultation, but an announcement of intentions. The company had bought and leased land long before the meeting and told the property owners not to mention the transactions to anyone. Plot by plot, the company took over farms. When opponents of the mine found out, it was too late. The land had already been sold.

Among those who attended the first meeting was Bishop Alvaro Ramazzini.

The slender streets of Huehuetenango, a Mayan settlement before the Spanish conquest where many people of Maya descent remain, bustled with heavy foot and car traffic the afternoon I arrived to speak to Bishop Ramazzini on my way to San Miguel, about an hour away. Dust, black with diesel soot, layered a scrim of grit on the uneven storefronts grouped like pieces of an ill-fitting puzzle. The one-way streets allowed for little maneuvering, and traffic jams turned into screaming matches as drivers refused to budge for one another. I used these moments of inertia to ask for directions to Immaculate Conception Parish, where the bishop lived. When I got moving again, I drove in circles, detoured from the given directions by one-way streets that did not allow me to turn where I'd been instructed. Eventually, I found the church, when by chance I noticed a steeple rising behind a closed metal gate.

The gate opened to a parking lot and a garage, behind which stood the church; a mechanic from the garage led me to it. Inside, I followed a hall to a door that led into a large room with open windows. Shadows extended over the tile floor, and breezes removed the afternoon heat and lifted curtains over a sofa and two chairs in a corner. The spacious room seemed vast compared with the constriction of the streets outside and I felt as if I had to walk a long way just to reach one of the chairs to sit.

Bishop Ramazzini walked in a short time later, a stout man wearing a white gown. His sandals flapped against the tiles and he paused to wipe his glasses. He had been a priest in San Miguel for twenty-three years before he was named bishop in 2012. He presided over thirty-two parishes in western Guatemala that include San Miguel and Sipacapa.

Sitting near me, he steepled his fingers beneath his chin and closed his eyes for a moment as he contemplated my questions about the Marlin Mine. He remembered the first days of the mine well, the mystery of it. The people of San Miguel didn't know anything about it when its representatives first came to town in the late 1990s. There had been rumors before then, sightings of outsiders, but nothing concrete. Bishop Ramazzini helped organize community meetings with mine representatives to learn their plans. There would be jobs for many people, the representatives said, and there were. More than a thousand at first, Bishop Ramazzini said, but to function, the mine needed to blast tunnels, level trees, and build roads. The community became divided between those who opposed the mine, seeing it as destructive, and those employed by it. You had men working in the mine, and their in-laws disapproving of it. Bishop Ramazzini told mine representatives several times that the mine would produce social conflict and benefit only a few, but they were concerned with the extraction of gold and nothing else.

The jobs carried a price. Streams filled with poisons, including arsenic. Entire mountains were leveled. Houses developed cracks from the blasting. After the initial buildup, the company laid people off.

As a young priest, Bishop Ramazzini realized he did not know Guatemala. He had spent his childhood in Guatemala City, not the countryside. His first three years in San Miguel taught him what it was like to be poor. He saw malnourished children in homes with dirt floors and no bathrooms. Women working twelve- to fifteen-hour days in farm fields, earning less than one dollar a day. They had no money to send their children to school. He met landowners who hired these women but who disliked them because they were descended from Mayas rather than Spaniards.

Bishop Ramazzini finds little has changed. The needs of the people are the same now as they were then. Only the population is bigger.

Sitting across from Sister Maudilia in her kitchen, my plate of potatoes and beans steaming, I tell her what Bishop Ramazzini said. Like him, she tells me, she saw the mine as a threat. She watched engineers and surveyors converge on San Miguel with their big cars and phones and promises of wealth. People who believed those promises applied for jobs. Some were turned away and became envious of those who were hired, many of them farmers who had sold their land to Goldcorp. The layoffs began after the startup phase, and the unemployed left town to find work elsewhere. Families who for generations had lived and worked in San Miguel, gone.

In 2008, a group of friends told Sister Maudilia to join them in a protest against the Marlin Mine. They sat in a line and prevented bulldozers from leaving the mine to dig up more land. It was a temporary success, but eventually the mine found ways to move around the women. The action left Sister Maudilia inspired, but at another protest, demonstrators burned mining equipment, infuriating her. The action only benefited the mine, she told them. Now the mine people could say, "They attacked us. We can use force."

The last significant protest occurred in 2011. A demonstrator was doused in gasoline and set alight by hooded men who identified themselves as mine supporters. The protester survived but suffered severe burns and left San Miguel. Perhaps the horror of this act contributed to the decrease in demonstrations in the years that followed, Sister Maudilia muses. Perhaps because the mine had been in San Miguel for nearly ten years, people had reached a point of apathy. It had become part of their life, like a new neighbor who after a number of years is no longer new—appreciated by some but not by others. The mine, Sister Maudilia has concluded, is an assassin. It kills community and family bonds. It kills the spirit.

Sister Maudilia shows me to a bedroom by the front door and when she leaves I stretch out and stare at the ceiling through the dark. I am struck by her phrase, "mine people." Like another life form, I think, before falling to sleep.

In the morning, I wake up and look out the window at layers of mist. After I dress, I wander downtown. Vendors move through the fog erecting white tents. Tables beneath the tents display fruit, meat, clothes, shoes, and tools, and men hurry past me to unload tent poles from rusted pickups, shouting, *Aqui! Aqui!* to coworkers, pointing to where the poles should go. The day brightens, easing into the hours ahead with a rising humidity that accompanies the crows of roosters. Families converge downtown before the tents have been fully raised, fingering the items on display. I introduce myself and listen to conversations about the weather, politics, and the mine:

> Ernestino Garcia, a fruit vendor: I have seen the benefit of the mine myself because some of my family works there. The mine is fine. I've not seen any damage.

> Maura Diaz, a butcher: We've lived here all our life. We've heard of people being badly affected by the mine but we have no complaints because we don't

know anyone who works there. We are businesspeople. Whatever brings in money is good.

Esperanza de Leon, a mother of two: I live three miles from the mine. My house has been cracked by tremors for more than ten years. Four and five in the morning and five at night I hear explosions. Some engineer came by last year and said the damages were not the fault of the mine. He had an engineer leave a machine in my house for fifteen days to measure the explosions and to see if the explosions caused any damage. An engineer named Nelson. I thought he was an American. He hooked up the machine to a wall socket. It was about the size of a small TV. The machine didn't make a sound. It had some lights. It didn't measure anything. It stayed quiet. The lights didn't blink. The man came back two weeks later. He looked at it and said the machine shows nothing; you don't have a problem. The thing is, I don't believe the machine. I can see new cracks and they are growing. I am frightened something might happen when my children are sleeping. I have been told the tremors are due to the explosions. I feel the earth move.

Oralia Velasquez, the owner of Tienda Alexis, a convenience store: Before the mine, San Miguel was a lost and forgotten town. Every business has picked up now. I have a brother-in-law working in the mine. My husband tried but couldn't. He applied for a security job but they did not hire him. I hope the mine stays and I pray to God that the mine hires my husband so we have a chance at a better life. Thanks to the mine, we have new roads and a new bridge. Only a few have not seen its benefit. In many small towns we have cobble streets. They don't want to change to paved roads. They are simple people.

Ruben Bautista Domingo, an unemployed truck driver: I live less than a mile from the mine. Around July 2015 I noticed two big cracks in my ceiling that ran down the wall to the floor. Just two cracks, nothing else. I have been hearing explosions, feeling tremors. It always happens at five p.m. and has been going on for months. Nothing like this has happened before. I am fearful because I don't know to what extent my house has been damaged. Is it unsafe? I don't know. Nobody from the mine has spoken to us.

I walk out of the bazaar to the outskirts of town, where the white building of a hospital funded by Goldcorp sprawls before me, bathed in sunlight. A few families linger in the empty parking lot. In 2012, Goldcorp provided a little over two million dollars toward the building and supplying of the facility, which the company called a short-term clinic, one of more than one hundred community projects—including computer labs, schools, teacher training, recreation halls, sports fields, roads, water and sewage systems—that Goldcorp had funded. The Ministry of Health and Social Assistance took over the facility in 2014, but did not set aside enough money to operate it at full capacity.

"When children are sick they have to go to another clinic," forty-year-old Pedro Cinto, a father of four, tells me. He brought his children for flu shots but the hospital has no syringes.

"They dispense advice here but not medicine," he says.

I walk inside and onto a gleaming white tile floor. A boys wipes the walls with a sponge. Near him a nurse in a blue uniform explains birth control to a couple. She offers them a pamphlet with information. The hospital does not have birth control pills, condoms, or anything else, she explains. The man asks if his wife can have an operation to prevent future pregnancies.

"Yes," the nurse says, "but not here."

I follow the couple outside. The man tells me his wife does not want any more children because they have three already. He would like more, but his wife says no. What can he do? He thinks the hospital is fine for birth control information. It is elegant but offers very little. Just some secretaries and a policeman guarding the front door and this nurse who gave them the pamphlet. The name of the hospital is the Center for Permanent Attention, the man tells me, but he calls it "the center for permanent referral." He laughs. For colds, diarrhea, and other problems, he takes his children to another hospital more than two hours away. He supposes he and his wife will drive there for birth control.

From the hospital, I return to Sister Maudilia's house and find Magdelina, sweeping the kitchen floor. I offer her some mangos I bought in the bazaar. She puts them on the table. Sister Maudilia is out running errands, she says.

As we share a mango, I tell Magdalena some of the comments I heard about the mine. It surprises her that some people spoke critically. The mine has spies all over San Miguel. Infiltrators, Magdalena calls them. If they hear someone complaining, they will tell on that person. So with strangers, the people say they like the mine. The people here are very cautious. They took a chance talking to me.

I find her comments a little over the top, even paranoid, but I keep my thoughts to myself. However, she suspects my doubt.

"At one time, I had been a stranger like you," she says.

Magdalena moved to San Miguel from Guatemala City in 2008 as part of an indigenous women's group the church had organized to attract more indigenous people to the Catholic faith. In those days, Magdalena would buy peaches and avocados bigger than her hands. These days, peaches and avocados are half that size and have no flavor because the water is polluted, she says. White foam floats on the streams. When it rains, the white stuff washes into town. One time, cattle drank water as the white stuff sat like clouds on top and the cattle died. Before the mine came, the mountains had been a holy place for Mayas. They held religious ceremonies among the peaks, praying for good crops and health. Now the land has been poisoned and the mountains no longer hear their prayers.

We finish our mangos and as I wipe the table, Magdalena offers to take me into the mountains to see the mine. Driving out of town, we follow a twisting road of broken pavement, passing small houses that lean into the mountain as if seeking a foothold, and dogs watch the car from beneath bowed porches where children sit by outdoor sinks and piles of pots and pans. A few trees grow at a slant and cast a thin shadow across the road, and fallen boulders stand unevenly in the scrub. As we round a curve, I notice three women outside a small house. We stop and I approach them to ask about the mine. Two of the women refuse to speak to me, but one, Maria Belaskez, agrees. She takes me to a tree away from her friends.

"They work in the mine," she says, waving a hand as if brushing at flies. She does not care what they think. Let them turn their backs on her and hide in the house. She will talk to whomever she chooses. Her concerns center on her grown sons and not on what people think of her talking to an American about the mine. Her sons have teaching degrees, but San Miguel has few jobs for teachers so they applied for jobs at the mine, as she and her husband have, but no one has offered them work. The family owns a small field where they grow corn. After the harvest, they travel by foot to the coast to work the coffee fields, but corn and coffee pay very little. Less than five dollars for every one hundred pounds. On a good day, Maria can pick one hundred pounds of corn and coffee in two hours but she needs to earn more than that.

"How is it in Guatemala City?" she asks Magdalena. "Any jobs?"

Before Magdalena answers, Maria turns to me.

"How about the United States? Do you know if there would be jobs for my children?"

"How would you get there?"

"If I can walk to the coast for coffee, I can walk to the United States," she insists.

Magdalena and I drive farther into the mountains until we reach a plateau overlooking a valley. We stop and walk to the edge. In the hazy heat, I see dump trucks and front loaders on plowed ground dried by the sun to a white powder. Sunlight blinks off tin-roofed shacks, and eighteen-wheelers stand idling amid hills of rubble beside a conveyor, the noise of grinding gears rising up to us.

Two men, one much older than the other, sit outside a nearby house. The younger one offers Magdalena a chair and introduces himself. Cecilio Gonzalez. The older man, Luis Mejia, is his grandfather.

"We were looking at the mine," I say.

"Ah, yes, the mine," Cecilio says.

Luis remains quiet.

Cecilio tells us he has a cousin works who works in the mine. Another cousin plants trees for the ministry of the environment. That cousin opposes the mine. Preserving nature, making a profit, how do you choose? Cecilio wonders.

"Have you been to the hospital?" he asks.

"Yes," I say.

"The mine paid for it but it has no equipment."

"I saw."

Luis turns to the road, his profile a landscape of shaded wrinkles and lines. When he speaks his gaze remains focused elsewhere. He says he thinks about the long-term effect of the mine. What will be left behind? No one knows. Whatever the problems, the people will have to deal with them. The mine changed everything. Mountains have been destroyed. What has happened to the soil? Has it been poisoned? Luis drinks the water and has not become ill, however he knows others who have. He assumes tunnels have hollowed the ground beneath the mountains and that one day everything will cave in. The water will get more polluted or dry up. The mine people insist there will be no damage when they leave, but they have already damaged the land. What if they ruin it more?

Miners in orange suits and white helmets trudge along the road as Magdalena and I continue driving, and she raises a hand in greeting, but the men ignore her. A mud-brick house at the top of a hill looms before us; a woman stands in the door. Wind tugs at her pink blouse, and her black hair blows about her face. She waves to us and we stop. "You have a flat tire," she shouts. I get out and look. She's right. The front left tire is almost out of air. I hadn't noticed on the bumpy ride. She gives me a hand pump and I fill the tire. When I finish, she offers us water and tea and we sit on her porch overlooking the road and she goes back into her house and returns with a tray of crackers. Her name is Gregoria Cristina Perez. I tell her why I am in San Miguel.

Gregoria smiles.

"I have much to tell about the mine."

To begin with, she says, it was unbelievable how fast the mine company bought up land. The first people to sell their property received much less than those who waited and negotiated. Gregoria's parents owned two parcels near the mine and Gregoria owned one herself. The mine people told them they worked for a big Canadian company called Goldcorp that dug for gold and silver and that the company needed her land. You need to sell it to us, they told her. Her parents went to the mayor of San Miguel and asked him, What is this project? Who is this company that wants to buy our land? The mayor told them not to worry. Nothing will happen. The company specializes in orchids not minerals.

That didn't make sense to Gregoria's parents. The mine people said nothing about orchids. Gregoria's parents demanded answers and the mayor, unused to being pressured by constituents, broke down and told them the truth. You should thank God for this blessing, he said. Make the most of this opportunity and sell. With the money, you can buy trucks, animals and more land. Her parents sold their land. When will we have an opportunity like this again? they asked themselves. The company had not approached Gregoria and she had no intention of selling her land if it did. Then in 2004, the mine people asked to install wooden utility poles for electrical lines on her property. Your neighbors had allowed poles on their land, they said. Nothing was damaged. The poles will blend with the trees. Neighbors, however, told Gregoria that the mining company had cut down trees and dug up their land. Those areas were no longer good for planting and grazing.

No, Gregoria told the mine representatives, you cannot put poles on my land.

When she came home from the market the next week, Gregoria saw men installing a half-dozen posts and she told them to leave. The supervisor stopped the work and said he would speak to his office. He asked for her phone number. Later that day Gregoria received a call from a mine representative.

Look, he told her. Don't be a problem. He wanted her to sign a contract authorizing the use of her land but she refused and complained to the mayor. The mining company has a waiver, the mayor told her. They can come on your land whether you allow them or not.

Gregoria returned home and, with her son's help, cut down the posts. The company filed a complaint and the police came to arrest her but her neighbors surrounded her house to prevent their entry and they left. The mine did not pursue the matter after that. Gregoria, however, has little to celebrate. The mine has polluted the land and water and her property is worthless now. Nothing is any good. What did she achieve? There is no happy ending.

Sister Maudilia sits in the kitchen stringing Mayan prayer beads when Magdalena and I return. She tells me that our conversation from the previous night left her in a reflective mood. She thinks about the mine and the trouble that followed it, how for years there seemed to be a protest every other day. The protests could be very exciting. The energy fed on itself and mushroomed into shouts and Mayan chants, but sometimes the protests could get out of hand and protesters had to be very careful, especially when the mine sent people in to disrupt and provoke. They needed to know how to respond and to stand firm without getting hurt. The mine supporters don't see the poison in the soil. Please respect the land, Sister Maudilia tells them, but they ignore her.

This evening, I decide to go out for dinner. On one darkened street, I see a hotel and assume it will have a restaurant. The gray block building does not look particularly inviting, however, and appears even less so when I enter the dim lobby.

"Who stays here?" I ask a bored looking desk clerk.

"Mostly police and the military to protect the mine," he says and yawns. He points me to the restaurant through a pair of glass doors and I sit at a table. A waitress watches me, but does not move until I call her over. About the same time, two women in platform shoes, short skirts, and tight T-shirts that expose their stomachs walk in and take a table near mine. They check their cell phones.

"Did you pay the taxi?" one of them asks.

"I put it on my bill here. I have an account."

She puts her phone on the table.

"Listen."

I hear the sound of a man moaning and a woman's voice calling him baby, baby, baby. The moaning gets louder and the two women laugh until the moaning stops.

"Who was that?"

"The policeman from last night."

"In your room here?"

"His car."

They laugh again. The waitress approaches them.

"The same as always," the woman with the phone says. "Put it on my account."

As I place my order after them, a twenty-four-year-old man named Jaime Perez Lopez gets ready for bed on the final night of his life. He starts work in the mine at four in the morning and his family will later tell me he always went to bed at seven. He likes his job and is a good employee. He works twelve to twenty-four hours a day, depending on what has to be done. He graduated from high school with a degree in public accounting but had been unable to find a job until the mine opened. After work, he helps his family around the house. A healthy, nice young man, his aunt will say of him.

His bus ride to the mine will take him past Juan's Fabric Repair Shop, Velasquez Tailor, Tigo Mobile Phones, and Cafeteria Maya, among other shops and restaurants, and the local parish, home to Father Eric Gruloos. Father Eric has lived in San Miguel for thirty-one years. There were only fifteen priests in town when he first came here; now there are thirty-eight. Time. Father Eric can't fathom how fast it moves. He is a tall, lean man. He wears glasses and has a full head of gray hair that he runs a hand through as he considers the passage of years. As a young man, he had thought about a nursing career. He didn't have a clear idea, really, of what he ought to do, but he wanted to help people. In the end, he decided to become a priest for the free education and the inspiration of being among a group of men who had a calling to help others. He does not think about his youth much now, the whys and whats that determined his life. These days, he feels motivated solely by the love of God. Men and women who are like he was as a young person, people who don't have a clue of the spirit, can fall into a trap, into the hands of bad people, manipulative forces. They don't understand the power that people like that have over a mind that holds nothing dear other than surviving day to day. The presence of the mine makes this very clear.

When times were simpler, rumors about the mine spread like birdsong rising from the trees every morning. A mine is coming, people said. Many didn't believe it, including Father Eric. Why would anyone build a mine here? he wondered. Of course, the rumors were true. The mine did come. San Miguel had always been poor. Then just like that, some people in the community were hired and made money. With this money came bars and prostitution. Men flush with cash left their families for mistresses. Here people who had lived together through Guatemala's civil war engaged in a second civil war, a struggle of neighbors with money from working at the mine against neighbors without. Once the mine began operating, when the shafts had been dug, buildings erected, trees cut down, many of the neighbors with this new money lost their jobs. They were cast aside and became poor once more; they had nothing and left. The land and the water have also suffered. People complain that scales and sores cover their bodies after they bathe in the rivers. Farmers fear the water they use to irrigate their land. The mining s company has land where it grows vegetables and cattle to show that the water is safe, but the people believe otherwise. One day a teacher took a photo of a child with skin problems. Mine supporters accused him of manipulating the photo and he fled San Miguel amid threats against his family. Too many people, Father Eric has concluded, don't want to know the truth.

Father Eric has also been accused of riling up opposition but he insists he has done no such thing. He attends protests as an observer only. He poses questions, asks people to think for themselves. If a river became polluted after the mine began operations, a river that had never known pollution, what does that mean?

As a young priest, Father Eric worked in Peru for a year. The water in a river near where he lived always looked clear, but at one time runoff from a mine had poured into it, and although the mine had been shut down for at least one hundred years, farmers would not use even one ounce of the river's water for irrigation. No one fished it and no animals drank from it. The book of Genesis reminds Father Eric that man manages the land but does not own it. The land is on loan for the length of one's lifetime. The earth is for everyone. Or had been.

The next morning, hours after Jaime drove by the church, Father Eric wakes up and turns on the radio. A tunnel in the Marlin mine has collapsed. One man killed. Father Eric wonders if there might be more fatalities. What will the mine people say about this? And their supporters? It doesn't matter. They will use this tragedy to their advantage. Trust no longer exists.

Sister Maudilia tells me about the mine when I come into the kitchen for breakfast. A friend called and told her the father of the dead man was already negotiating with the company for a financial settlement. The mine has all this money to buy people, even grieving parents. The family will get money and the problem will go away. According to her friend, the dead man's last name is Perez. A relative works in the mayor's office. I skip breakfast and hurry over there. The yellow, rectangular city hall stands not far from downtown. The closed doors of several offices face the street. A single open door exposes a foyer with folding chairs set in four rows before a desk where a woman sits, reminding me of a teacher in a classroom. I ask her about the mine accident and the Perez family, expecting to be turned away, but to my surprise she leads me into an office and introduces me to Facundo Diaz, a city council member.

"The father of the man who died in the mine used to work here as head of the municipal police," Diaz tells me. "He got laid off. This was some time ago. My understanding is that he was called to the mine to discuss the death of his son, Jaime. The people who work in the mine have been told to leave the area. They don't want anyone near the accident. The mine people are scared. Their security people fear a violent reaction to Jaime's death. Many people oppose the mine. My nephew works in the mine. I am talking to you in the hope improvements will be made and he will be safe."

Diaz gives me directions to the Perez family home, which stands behind the house of Jaime's uncle, a casket maker. I find his uncle's storefront, Vente de Caje Mortuary, at the end of a dirt alley. A teenage girl stands on a stairway leading to an apartment above the shop. Off to one side metal barrels, a sink, coils of wire, and piles of broken cinder blocks fill an empty courtyard. The girl looks at me with the expression of someone who just woke up and can't make sense of the morning. I ask her about Jaime.

"I am his sister, Fabida," she says.

Her parents learned what happened at six this morning when Fabida's father got a call from a supervisor. Jaime had been alone in a mine tunnel when it collapsed. Fabida's parents had already left for the mine when she woke up. Her aunt Albertine told her about Jaime.

At the mention of her name, Albertine emerges at the head of the stairs and shows me a photo of her nephew. His dark hair is combed to one side and he wears a blue shirt. His unblemished face stares at the camera without a smile. Albertine does not know the kind of work Jaime did in the mine but he was always full of energy; if she had not known him she never would have believed he worked such long hours because he always behaved as if he had done nothing all day and would help around the house. Once a week, he turned his salary over to his father, who drove a truck but earned very little.

"Jaime had no vices," Albertine says.

In the short time that I've been with Albertine and Fabida, small groups of people have been converging on the mortuary to pay their respects, including the family's pastor, Nixon Domingo with the Peniel Evangelical Church. He has just returned from the mine, he says; Jaime's parents are still there. The mine people told them that they were removing dirt from a shaft and they hoped to recover his body by nightfall. Of course it is all very sad, Pastor Nixon continues. Everything in life has a positive and negative side, including the mine. As long as the mine people abide by the law, he has no problem with them. He has his opinions, of course. The mine has created greed and jealousy, and even now with this family, people are saying how rich they will be when the mine pays them off. This kind of thinking is not good for anyone. For the good of everyone, people must learn to get along and keep their opinions to themselves.

I leave the mortuary for the mine, hoping I'll find Jaime's family. The guards make it clear, however, that I cannot enter. I ask a woman standing nearby what she knows about the accident. Her son stands beside her pulling on her hand as he balances on rocks, throwing pebbles into a stream.

"I don't know anything," the woman tells me.

The boy pipes up and tells me they are related to the dead man. His mother tells him to shut up. They are cousins of the dead man's father, she explains after some hesitation reluctant to say more. She is here to pick up her husband who works at the mine and does not want to jeopardize his position by speaking with me. He works in the public relations department and has been with the mine for ten years. No company or government has given more jobs to so many people as this mine has, she says. The people who oppose it get money from communist groups in the U.S. and Europe.

"How do you know that?"

She refuses to say more. Looking at her son she places a finger to his lips.

A woman wearing a wide, floppy hat herds a dozen goats along a hillside path near where I am parked. She saw me speaking to the woman and waves me over. Facing her, I see she has only one eye. Her name is Deodora Hernandez and I follow her and the goats across a narrow bridge above a stream she calls "the cyanide waters"—poisoned, she claims, by the mine. She does not know anything about the death of Jaime Perez, but heard that a tunnel had collapsed and that some people got out but not all of them. She feels bad for them but has problems of her own.

"I have been through a lot," Deodora tells me.

Her problems began when she and her husband, Carlos, refused to sell their farm to the mine in 2010. Deodora had chained herself to her fence to prevent work crews from entering her property. You are not going to take my land, she declared. The mine people told Deodora that the municipality could force her to give up her farm. The government will pressure you, they said. The company is huge and powerful and you are not. All of her neighbors had agreed to sell. However, to excavate the area, the mine people needed Deodora's property too, and they would not buy her neighbor's land unless she agreed to sell, but she refused. She was born in San Miguel and did not want to live anywhere else. Her neighbors turned on her and stole farm equipment and goats.

"You think you are better than us," they said.

Deodora attended a community council meeting to explain why she and Carlos declined to give up their home. You have been our neighbors our whole life, she said. Why do you enter our land and tear up our crops? You treat us like an enemy. You are not people of the mine. You are people of these mountains and streams as I am.

A councilman became so enraged by her refusal to sell that he struck the side of her head with the back of a machete blade. No one attempted to stop him. She picked herself up off the floor and stumbled outside, bleeding. The councilman did not follow. Deodora and Carlos reported it to the police, but they said she exaggerated. The councilman did not want to kill you, the police chief told her. I'm sure he only pushed you and you fell.

The next evening, two men in hoodies who said they were selling coffee stopped at her house and asked to come inside. Deodora and Carlos did not recognize them and turned them away, but the men complained that it was late and asked if they could spend the night in their barn. No, Deodora said, and shut the door. About an hour later, she stepped outside to bring in laundry suspended from a clothesline. She did not hear the gunshot that took out her right eye, but she remembers falling and covering her face. Carlos carried her to their pickup, then he rushed to the San Miguel hospital but it was closed. He then drove to San Marcos, about two hours away. Deodora lost consciousness by the time he reached the hospital there. At first, the doctors refused to treat her. Your wife is going to die, they told Carlos, and you are a poor man; let's not waste time on her. But Carlos insisted. Deodora remained in the hospital for a week before he took her home. Since then she has cried a lifetime's worth of tears. She has Carlos and their farm, but the mine has her eye.

This evening, I reach Gerardo Perez, the father of Jaime, by phone. He tells me he is very upset with the mine. He and his wife had asked to see the body of their son but the mine people took the body to a morgue in San Marcos without letting them see him. It was such an ordeal. All they had wanted was to see their son's body, so they drove to San Marcos. Gerardo did not recognize Jaime. He had been crushed, but not dismembered. The coroner had removed a dental bridge to make the identification. Gerardo's lawyer advised him to accept whatever the mine people offered him. They are very powerful, the lawyer said, and can buy the authorities and leave you with nothing. Gerardo agreed to the company's offer of twenty-seven thousand dollars in damages and liabilities.

"I better receive this money or I could be left without anything," Gerardo says. "What do you think? Should I have asked for more?"

"I can't answer that," I say.

"I think I should have asked for more," Gerardo says. "Of course you understand that it is a lot of money, but all the money in the world is not going to give me back my son."

In the morning, I accompany Sister Maudilia on a two-hour drive to a school in the mountains where she teaches traditional Mayan beliefs to unemployed teenagers. She wants young people to understand why she opposes the mine and how everyone needs to reclaim their roots and not just follow European beliefs that have nothing to do with Mayan culture.

The road takes us through an empty village and we stop so Sister Maudilia can use her cell phone to call the school for directions. I get out of the car and peer through the windows of vacant buildings that appear to have been recently constructed. No desks or chairs or curtains, nothing to suggest that at one time people ever filled these rooms. Trucks lumber past spewing dust and rocks and when the air clears, the vague echo of their engines drifts back to me. Sister Maudilia gets off the phone and calls my name and I get back in the car; about an hour later we reach the school, on a hill surrounded by scrub brush and a few trees. Two dozen teenagers in blue uniforms mill about our car and Sister Maudilia hugs them and squeezes their hands before she leads them inside to a classroom and asks them to sit in a circle.

"We come here with cars and phones and our desire for money and more things," she says. "We listen to foreign music but don't know what it means. Outsiders use our clothes for fashion but they don't know what the Maya designs on our clothes mean. We need to tell them. We need to learn to dance to the sun again, to the sky and the rhythms of nature."

Sister Maudilia understands the students come from poor families and knows they tend to feel shame for being Maya, embarrassed by their language that is no longer the national language, ashamed of their poverty. They want to be Westerners and that desire turns their humiliation into ignorance. If they are not aware of who they are, then anyone can convince them of anything. If they appreciate their heritage, a people rich in culture and tradition, neither the mine people nor anyone else will can make them feel inferior. They will stand up for the land and their history and themselves. They will understand that their past does not have to be past. Neither does their pride.

The Line

*S*ister Magdalena Pasquel stands on a street corner in downtown Guatemala City. Her black hair falls to her wide shoulders. Floral and animal-shaped designs decorate her blue blouse and catch the sun as she crosses the street and walks toward a bank of row houses. The afternoon humidity fogs her glasses, and every so often she makes a face to prevent them from sliding. Grime and diesel exhaust stain the pink, red, and green buildings she passes. These colors once may have indicated a bright, active neighborhood, but unrelenting sunlight and neglect have washed out the pigment and the sullen expressions of vendors without any wares to hawk have become diluted; they sit on the sidewalks silently, limply, perspiration dripping off their wrinkled faces, while bored prostitutes shift and slouch against the open doors of their rooms, weary of stares and waiting for their next trick. Hopelessness pervades the neighborhood. Sister Magdalena notices a skinny girl, the leader of a group of young prostitutes huddled around her, and approaches.

Sister Magdalena: Hello, how are you?

Skinny Girl: Hi.

Skinny Girl hurries away.

The other girls speak at once: Why are you visiting us? What do you want? Are you going to preach? Why don't you preach?

Sister Magdalena: It's in the small gestures we preach our beliefs.

Many years ago, Sister Magdalena sat on a bus with her mother. When the bus stopped near midtown Guatemala City, they stepped off and walked to a bazaar. On the way, Sister Magdalena looked down a street and saw women in doorways and men clustered around them. A railroad track ran through the center of the street, and men crossed the tracks to speak with the women. Sister Magdalena's mother saw where her daughter's eyes were focused and hurried her along.

Sister Magdalena smiles now recalling this moment—the ignorance and curiosity of a child and the discomfort of a mother shielding her daughter from the unpleasantness of life. What would her mother say now that she was working with those very women on that same street? La Linea, as it's known, the line, or the strip, a two-block area where prostitutes rent small rooms and offer their bodies for sex. An online sex guide to Central America's entry for La Linea reads: "La Linea is in Zona 1 of Guatemala City and runs along the railroad track north of 10a Calle between 13/14 Avenida and 15 Avenida. It's considered Guatemala City's Red-light district. For a landmark, it is just across the street at the east end of the Edeficio Central de la PNC (the national civil police central building) on 10a Calle. Prices are very cheap: Q25-100. Best hours on brothels in this area are from nine a.m. to five p.m. Be careful in this area, especially when it's dark."

Followers of the site offer their brutal assessment below the post. Guest Red Light Area Guatemala: *My friend told me the hookers in La Linea want something like fifty Guatemalan quetzals for sex. This is about six US dollars. Still very cheap I think.*

Goodguy1: *I went there like in 2004 and it was so dirty that I could never fuck a whore there. It was so nasty, burning garbage, weird guys walking around, no real windows at all hooker rooms. Price was only like five USD but NO! It was still great experience to see the worst Red Light District in my life. I'm tired of the whores in Tijuana.*

Guest john monger: *I like dirty.*

Sister Magdalena wonders, Who are these men? No different from the men milling around the row houses now. What happened to them that brings them here? Perhaps they are angry at women for inexplicable reasons. Perhaps they seek thrills, power. Perhaps they see women only as appliances for their pleasure. She can pray for them but not speak for them. Are they like the man who recently demanded more time with a La Linea prostitute, and when she refused, tried to stab her with a pair of scissors? Or like another client who stole her cell phone and used it to threaten and harass her and other women?

Sister Magdalena watches Guatemalan soldiers that she assumes are on leave walk past her and peer at the girls. Dogs run on the train tracks alongside them, snapping at one another over garbage, and dark clouds hold in the clamminess of the sweltering afternoon. Young men on motorcycles drive in circles on the street, even on the sidewalk. Some of them are trying to see the women having sex, others want to know who they have solicited. They ride throughout the day without stopping. Sister Magdalena doesn't understand. Why don't they leave? What can they accomplish driving endlessly back and forth, back and forth? What thoughts course through their minds? Everything about La Linea makes her feel lost, unbalanced.

A black, metal door open to the street reveals a dim, nine-by-twelve room in a pink La Linea row house. There is a cot with one white sheet and a roll of toilet paper and a box of crackers at the foot of the bed. Bare concrete floor, green walls. A light bulb hangs from the ceiling. Above a small table holding perfume bottles, a cracked mirror. The young woman leaning back from the door wears a black miniskirt and a tank top. Strands of her dark hair cling to her sweating shoulders. Her name is Andreas. She has a tough look, a look of no expectation, of a life lived with no soft edges. She is thirty years old, married, and has two children, ages nine and fifteen. Her unemployed husband stays at home with her mother. She has been a prostitute for eighteen months. When she started, she worked occasionally, but when her husband lost his construction job, she put herself out on La Linea six days a week. On Sunday, she stays home with her family.

Sister Magdalena: Hello, how are you? I haven't seen you for a while. I hope you are OK.

Andreas: I've been working another place one block away.

Sister Magdalena, offering Andreas a card: I'm giving you this.

Andreas, reading aloud: *Make your best effort and be brave.*

A man walks past and checks her out.

Sister Magdalena: Study the phrase, apply it to your life.

Andreas: I try to be brave. When I am with my husband he's rough. He wants to reclaim me from the men I have been with.

A man whistles.

Sister Magdalena: What other work can you do?

Andreas: I don't know.

Sister Magdalena: Think of something. Have a dream and pursue it. We can discuss it when I see you again. Where is Margarita? I haven't seen her for a while. How is she?

Andreas: She had a problem and is no longer working because she got into a fight with some of the other girls. She was in the purple house across the street and had had a poor month, no clients, so she had witchcraft done to bring in clients and the other girls didn't like that and told her to leave. That's when they fought. I had a dream about her and looked for her to tell her the dream so it would come true because it was a nice dream in which she had stopped working but I did not find her.

Sister Magdalena: Life here is difficult and you've been lucky nothing happened to you. You don't know what her story is. It is nice of you to have nice dreams about her.

Andreas: Yes.

Sister Magdalena: I am not asking you to change, only you can do that. But I am here for anything you may need. If you see your friend, tell her we don't want anything bad to happen to her.

Andreas: Yes.

Sister Magdalena: I don't see you as a soul going to hell. I just care about you and your well-being.

Sister Magdalena had not expected to see Andreas. Normally, she hustles for clients farther down the street. Andreas had her guard up. Perhaps she had had a bad client. Perhaps business was slow. Sister Magdalena knows not to pry. She chose instead to ask Andreas about her children to show she was interested in her family so Andreas would see she had value no matter her work. Sister Magdalena may not see Andreas again for weeks. Disappearances happen. The girls argue with one another and leave or they get sick and stay with family, and when they return their room has been taken over by another girl. Almost all of them have children. The children stay with grandparents or live nearby, watched by a neighbor. Sister Magdalena is reminded of a forty-five-year-old prostitute, Angelica. One afternoon, Angelica stood outside a row house in a gray dress, white blouse, and a gray vest, and if Sister Magdalena had not known she was a prostitute, she would have assumed she worked as a secretary. She cautioned Angelica not to stay out in the sun too long but Angelica told her not to worry, she used face cream. Angelica was sad that day because she hadn't earned much money. She hoped to attract one more customer. If not, she would go home to her children. They lived with her mother at the top of a hill. When they see her walking toward the house, they run and hug her.

At her age, Angelica told Sister Magdalena, she did not think she could find other work. She had applied to be a cook in a fast-food restaurant but the restaurant owner had asked for her high school diploma and letters of reference. She had neither and wasn't hired, and even if she found a job, what then? She would always face the risk that a former client would see her. Even now she worries that someone will recognize her and say something in front of her children.

Sister Magdalena listened but said nothing. Sometimes she can't think of anything to say. She has crossed paths with many prostitutes and their families. The women glance at her and hurriedly turn away and she keeps walking, staring straight ahead as if she had not noticed them, respectful of their privacy, a silent prayer for them on her lips.

A colleague, Sister Maria Enriqueta Valdes, introduced Sister Magdalena to La Linea in 2014. Sister Maria had worked with prostitutes in Mexico and El Salvador for twenty-nine years before she transferred to Guatemala in 2012. During that time, she had learned to earn their trust by not acting like a social worker. She didn't attempt to convert them, either. Instead, she asked what they needed and offered them inspirational sayings. She knew when to talk and when to walk away. Sister Magdalena followed her example.

That first day on La Linea, she smelled the stink of trash in the streets and the putrid, muddy pools of water the mange-ridden dogs drank from and the air felt as thick as bad breath. When she met with prostitutes, the odor of perfume and the smell of disinfectant the women washed with after sex overwhelmed her and made her nauseous and she tried to keep a straight face as her stomach churned. She felt bad for the women living as they did. Some of them, she saw, were indigenous Mayas like herself. Sister Magdalena grew up in the province of Santa Cruz Chinautla. Her family identified as Mam, one of many Maya nations that make up rural Guatemala. The people of Santa Cruz Chinautla molded clay pots and farmed. It was a town almost insignificant in size. A river ran through it, and the black water carried waste from Guatemala City. Still, Sister Magdalena recalls a happy, cheerful childhood, the dirty river just part of life's struggle.

She was thirteen when nuns from the order of Saint Francis came to Santa Cruz Chinautla and approached her and other girls. The nuns paraphrased the apostle Paul: Show me your faith and I will show you my work. Sister Magdalena had never thought about becoming a nun, but she was intrigued by the sister's belief in a spiritual world beyond the mortal one she knew. The nuns told her that as a novice she would receive an education and the opportunity to leave Santa Cruz Chinautla.

However when she decided to devote herself to a religious life, Sister Magdalena did not choose the order of Saint Francis. Instead she took her vows with the Oblate Sisters of the Most Holy Redeemer. The order's mission, to work with women involved in prostitution, attracted her. She knew how poor women struggled to support their families in Santa Cruz Chinautla. Oftentimes they left, and rumors abounded about what they were doing to make money. If they returned, villagers shunned them. Sister Magdalena felt sorry for them and as a small girl began her practice of saying "Hello. How are you?" to let them know she was not ashamed of them.

Of the women Sister Magdalena meets on La Linea, the indigenous prostitutes leave the deepest, saddest impression. Some can speak only a Mayan language. One girl, Maria, no longer wears Mam clothing. Sister Magdalena pulls her aside to remind her that traditional dress means everything. The patterns, the colors,

celebrate the power of earth and water, sun and sky. Clothes identify one's Maya nation. For Maria to replace her clothes with hot
pants and skimpy blouses and platform shoes means she has abandoned her roots, her identity.

Sister Magdalena: You've changed. I didn't recognize you. Your
look, especially the way you dress.

Maria: Yes, it is a huge change.

Sister Magdalena: I didn't recognize you.

Maria: Men like me this way better. I get more clients. The
first day I dressed this way, I felt naked. Now I'm used to it. I pray
to God to help me get through this.

Sometimes Sister Magdalena sees women from La Linea working
Sexta Avenida, a commercial district and pedestrian walkway in
midtown. They are older women, fifty- something. On La Linea,
they work at the end of the train tracks with other women their age.
Younger prostitutes solicit at the head of the tracks. As a result, the
older women complain to Sister Magdalena, they see fewer clients.

On the avenue, however, the women do not face age discrim-
ination. They move about wherever they like. Most often they sit
on benches near bus shelters and wait for men to approach them.
Sister Magdalena has suggested they consider other work but the
women say to do that would mean taking time off the street and
sinking deeper into debt. Every day they need money. Their grandchildren don't ask them what they do. They just want to eat.

One woman, Monsita, a fifty-year-old prostitute, stands
between an eyeglass store and a pharmacy. She leans on her left

leg and thrusts her hip out as a few men glance her way. After they pass, she sighs, her face expressionless, and shifts to her right leg.

Monsita: I have four children to baptize.

Sister Magdalena: Come by and we will discuss when and where.

Monsita: They are not my kids but my grandchildren. My daughter abandoned them and I don't know if the infant has a birth certificate.

Sister Magdalena: OK.

Monsita: A guy beat me. He pushed me down some stairs. For six weeks I couldn't work. I still can't move my arm. I got an x-ray. The doctor said I need physical therapy.

Sister Magdalena: Go back and get therapy or find a doctor to tell you what to do. I'm glad you're OK. I'm glad to see you.

Monsita: A woman said I should wrap my arm in leaves, hot water, and alcohol.

Sister Magdalena: See a doctor.

Sister Magdalena leaves the avenue and returns to La Linea. Some of the women she spoke to earlier watch her. Behind each woman is a complex, sad story. She cannot look at them through her own eyes; she must imagine taking off her shoes, and putting on theirs.

In this room, a soccer poster hangs on one wall. Beside it another poster shows how to use a condom. A third poster depicts a woman with her fist in the air: Sex Workers, You Have Rights! Bottles of hand cream and perfume clutter a folding table. A can of Red Bull too. Silver shoes with heels lie on their side beneath the table. The woman renting this room, twenty-seven-year-old Margarita, sits in a chair reading a newspaper.

Sister Magdalena: Hello, how are you?

Margarita: Good morning. I have no time. I have no day off. I have to make fifteen hundred quetzales[1] to pay for this room. Plus, money I give my family. I pray to God to help me get through this.

Sister Magdalena: Take care and have time for yourself.

Margarita: Yes. Someday I wish I could run from here to a faraway place. But I can't do that. I am trapped in this life.

Sister Magdalena: I can't help you economically, but I can help you find other ways to live when you are ready to learn them. You can trust me. Who else can you trust?

Margarita: Only God.

Sister Magdalena: Yes, of course. But he works through people, friends, and family. He will not come down and help you directly. He will have friends and family to help you directly. Start with me.

Margarita: I am trapped.

Sister Magdalena offers her an inspirational card similar to the one she gave Andreas and reads from it: *Be brave.*

Every so often, Sister Maria Enriqueta Valdes still accompanies Sister Magdalena to La Linea. More often than not, however, she works alone. She considers La Linea a sacred place. Few people see it that way, she knows, and other nuns are scared for her. They would not dare go into La Linea. A very old church and a major tourist attraction, Our Lady of the Rosary, stands not far from the row houses but the priests don't care about the prostitutes. They

---

1 about two hundred dollars

choose not to see them. Sister Maria invites prostitutes to celebrate Mother's Day and special holidays at the church. She meets them in the parish, but the priests restrict her to an area separate from the rest of the parishioners. She takes small comfort in that. At least they are allowed into the church.

Sister Maria knew several La Linea prostitutes who have been murdered. She learned about one of the cases on television. A news report showed a photo of the girl's room and an inspirational card with a quotation from the Book of Matthew that Sister Maria had given her: *The tax collectors and the prostitutes are going into the Kingdom of God ahead of you. For John the Baptist came to you showing you the right path to take, and you would not believe him; but the tax collectors and the prostitutes believed him.* The killer had strangled the girl and stuffed her under a bed. Another prostitute found her body there three days later. Sister Maria had only known her street name, Kimberly. She was short and in her twenties and very pretty; a single mother from El Salvador or Honduras, no one knew for sure. The other girls said she cried between customers.

A red and black dress thrown across a bed. The sheet rumpled. One chair. A calendar peeling off a wall patchy with yellow paint. A small swivel fan turning back and forth beside a green, leafy plant taking up one corner and gathering dust. An empty table with a thin cloth covering it. The woman in the door wears black leather hot pants, a T-shirt, and a leather vest.

Sister Magdalena: Hello, how are you? I am Sister Magdalena. I've never seen you here.

Woman: My name is Miriam.

Sister Magdalena: Is that your real name?

Miriam: Yes. I have two children, girls. Eleven and six. Both are in school. Fifth and first grade. I live near the border with El Salvador.

Sister Magdalena: Does your family know you're here?

Miriam: No, I told them I'm a waitress. I go home every two weeks to bring them money.

Sister Magdalena: You are brave and strong to keep going. How old are you?

Miriam: Twenty-eight. I have worked here a year and a half.

She looks at Sister Magdalena.

Miriam: Are you a nun?

Sister Magdalena: Yes.

Miriam: God is good to me. I don't deserve it. But he comes through.

Sister Magdalena: You may not think you deserve it but we all do. Make an effort.

Miriam: In what?

Sister Magdalena: Fighting for your life.

Miriam: I'm getting off the street soon. The younger girls earn more money but spend it. I save it. What they are doing is not the way to leave the street. This one girl saved to go to a concert. She spent a ridiculous amount of money for her and a boy. I told her: Listen to me. If you saved the money you spent on the concert you would not have to work for a long time. Don't spend it on things like that.

Sister Magdalena: You have more experience. Use this wisdom and give it to others. Tell them what your experiences are.

Miriam: I do. Some are not receptive. I have a lot of bad experiences to share with other girls.

Sister Magdalena: Let's keep in touch. I'm glad to see you doing well.

Why this life? Sister Magdalena asks herself. She could be doing other, more uplifting and inspiring work. Helping old people, for instance, or children. Why this? She can't say. She knows only that since that moment long ago, when she was a young girl watching the women on La Linea and her mother pulled her away, her life has led her back here. For reasons she will never fully understand, these women have given her purpose. She can't explain it any other way. If an explanation were even warranted. Faith is believing without reason.

A mop in the corner, the concrete floor damp. Toppled perfume bottles clutter a table. One bare, gray mattress, no pillow. The woman inside wears a black bra, blue jean shorts, and black, high-heeled shoes. Her name is Angelica. She looks out at the street and faces Sister Magdalena. Her expression, youthful but hard, changes to curiosity.

Sister Magdalena: Hello. How are you?

Ballerina and Bird Lady

B ird Lady is less than excited when I request an interview.
   "What will you ask me?"

"Questions about your life," I say.

She stares at me through her sunglasses, my warped reflection trapped in the thick, dark lenses. I don't see her eyes. The stifling July heat of downtown Guatemala City clings to us, pushing back against me and making simple note-taking a burden.

"What life?" Bird Lady says.

"Why are you here? How long you've been doing this."

She frowns but relents. She reminds me of someone about to see a doctor for some dreaded medical procedure.

"OK, I am ready for you," she says

Ballerina, on the other hand, working across the street from Bird Lady on Sexta Avenida, a shopping district, eagerly agrees to an interview. He embraces me, flexes his arms to show how years of working as a car mechanic have toned his body. He smiles, exposing gaps teeth once occupied. He wonders if I'll take his photo.

"Yes," I tell him.

He asks me to send copies.

"Of course," I say. "Email them as an attachment? Send them to Facebook?"

Ballerina looks panicked. He tells me he does not have email or a Facebook account. He starts dialing family and friends on his cellphone.

"This is Luis. Luis! I'm being interviewed by this journalist," he explains to someone he has called. "An American! He came all the way here to Guatemala to interview me! Me!"

I am amused he sees me as some sort of big-time reporter. Amused and pleased. I admit for a moment I enjoy my elevated status. However, I don't want to create false impressions and try to tell him I don't have the stature he imagines, but he dismisses me with a wave of a hand.

"Why? Because he heard of my dancing. Do you have Facebook or email? He wants to send me photos he took of me dancing. You don't have? OK, OK. Thank you."

As Ballerina dials another number, I cross the avenue to talk with Bird Lady again. The avenue stretches for blocks and permits no vehicles. Families fill the sidewalks on this Sunday afternoon, lingering in front of cafes. Vendors take advantage of the foot traffic. They hawk souvenirs and draw attention to the restaurants and stores they stand near and whose bold banners promote sales. Somber armed guards stand in front of the stores, reminders of the thirty-year civil war that ended in 1996 and turned Guatemala into a killing zone. These days the killing continues in many parts of the city where gangs extort businesses that cannot afford guards.

I have just finished a reporting assignment here and have some down time before I return to the States. This morning, I decided to walk the avenue and play tourist. I don't know when my story will run. Even when it is up, I won't know if anyone has read it or noticed my byline. The news site I write for has no icon to indicate how many "hits" a story receives.

I explain all this to Bird Lady so she does not have the exaggerated expectations of me that Ballerina has but she shows no interest in the vagaries of an internet news site. She sits on a plastic stool in front of St. Francis Church, selling palm-size packets of bird seed for parishioners to feed the pigeons swarming her feet.

"Feeding the birds brings you luck," she says, "because you are feeding God's smallest creatures."

She does not feed the birds, herself. Perhaps it would bring her luck if she did. She doesn't know. She decided long ago not to waste the seed on something that might not be true. She sells it, gets her money and expects nothing more. She leaves luck to others. Money in hand is true. Money in hand, she takes a bus home to Zona 7, a settlement outside of downtown where poor people squat on land no one wants and build shacks using discarded aluminum siding and plastic tarps, and the shacks turn into ovens on hot afternoons like today's and list when it rains, the mud floors turning to soup.

"Semilla!" Bird Lady calls out. Seed.

A man stops beside her holding the right hand of his daughter. He buys a bag of seeds. He and his daughter walk into the stone courtyard of the church and the man crouches down beside his daughter, pours seeds into her hand and watches as she tosses the seeds into the air. The pigeons jump and flap their wings, pecking at the pavement. The girl opens her mouth wide in amazement. Her father smiles and holds her close. I feel somehow invigorated, despite the heat, by the girl's reaction to the pigeons. The birds shift back to Bird Lady. She does not move, her eyes concealed behind the dark lenses of her sunglasses and her thoughts, too. I don't know if she delighted in the girl's joy, as I did, felt refreshed by it, or even noticed before the oppressive heat reasserted itself and I forgot all about the girl.

"Do you know who am I?" Ballerina shouts into his phone. "Remember me? Yes, that's right, Luis. Do you have email?"

He notices the wind blow his cardboard donations box off the sidewalk and drops his phone into his pocket and chases after it, arms outstretched before him, half crouched, and a few people laugh, including some guards at his awkward strides as he lunges for the box. He catches it and weights it down with a water bottle. He puts a cassette into a boombox and then preens in front of the window of La Curacao, an appliance store, where he dances on weekends to draw customers: Straw, pachuco-style hat tipped down over his forehead, tinted sunglasses set just right. His blue satin shirt clings to his chest and a knotted white and navy blue-striped tie hangs loosely from around his neck. Black ironed slacks fall evenly over his patent-leather shoes. He combs his dyed black hair forward over a bald spot.

The boombox kicks on, the gyrating, static-filled music stunning the crowd, mouths open. A few people pause and look as

Ballerina jumps up and down, one arm raised above his head. He turns, tapping one foot, a poor imitation of flamenco.

The music finishes and he stops to catch his breath. He tells me he is known as the best dancer. The best dancer of what? His neighborhood? Guatemala? He does not say.

"All over," he says when I push him for an answer, "all over. Everywhere."

His dance moves show his influences. The moon walk of Michael Jackson, the turns and spins of Fred Astaire, the athleticism of Gene Kelly. He likes the applause, likes being looked at and admired. He tells me that while he appears to have the body of a fifteen-year-old, he is sixty-two.

He stares out at the street, the groups of people walking past. He notices Bird Lady. She calls him Ballerina, the king of dance, he says. She doesn't know his name, Luis Peña, or his life any more than he knows her name, Julia Lainez, or her life. They know one another only by what they do, he says. She feeds birds. He dances. What else do they need to know?

"Semilla!"

Bird Lady sweats in the afternoon heat, her arms oiled in perspiration. Her white floppy hat limps down over her forehead, burdened by the sun. People walk past. She recognizes a few of them: the shopkeeper who holds her unsold seed overnight without charge, a priest who lets her work here in front of the church, a woman who brings her water, the man who dances.

"He says you call him Ballerina, the king of dance."

"I've never spoken to him," Bird Lady tells me.

A woman offers Bird Lady a ham sandwich on white bread. Bird Lady takes it and gives her some money. Bird Lady says she owes this woman one hundred twenty dollars she borrowed recently for medicine and food. The woman stops by every week for a payment. Bird Lady thinks it will take her a year to pay off her debt. The sandwich isn't free, either, she says.

"Yes, hello. This is Luis. Do you have Facebook?"

The music Ballerina plays insinuates itself among the noise of people lingering outside La Curacao. They listen, hesitating between a RadioShack and Parque Publica, a clothing store. Some people watch Ballerina, puzzled: Who is this man? Why is he dancing?

When he was twelve, maybe thirteen, Ballerina can't say exactly but around that time, he and his friends would sneak into parties held by older boys. They'd follow teenagers they saw on the street wearing suits. They'd overhear them say they were going to a party. They followed the boys to the party and then showed them their moves. Everyone saw how well Ballerina danced. They saw his passion. He liked the disco years. He was really something then. He visited Mexico with a friend one year and learned different dance styles: Mambo, merengue, salsa, duranguense. He started dancing for local music groups that played at weddings.

During the civil war, he never danced on the street as he does now. Too many shootings and kidnappings. He'd only dance at parties and weddings. People kept low profiles during the war, he says. At home, sometimes when he practiced, he tapped his feet to the rhythm of gunfire.

After he danced at a party, he would return home well past the ten o'clock curfew his father had set for him, and his father would hear him and whip him with a belt no matter how quietly he slipped into the house. Ballerina barely knew his mother. She left for another man when he was very small, taking his two older siblings with her. He has not seen his siblings since, does not know if they are alive or dead. His mother died long ago. He did not attend her funeral, but he gets sentimental now should someone mention her to him. Reminders of his father, deceased just two years, touch him, too. He has two children of his own and feels guilty about the worry he caused his father coming home late those nights when he was just learning to dance. He can't stand it when someone close to him dies. Maybe because his mother abandoned him but the suddenness of death, the abrupt absence that follows, the vacancy of ghosts gets to him, puts him in a depression for days.

His grandmother helped raise him. She owned a small shop in the central market. She would slap him so he learned how to read and write and complete homework. He never sat still. He always played around. She would strike him with a ruler on the tips of his fingers until he cried out in pain. He learned to read, he says, by blood. He still remembers his math, history and science lessons. When he completed his homework, he danced in his room until he no longer felt the pain in his fingers.

"Semilla!"

Bird Lady has worked in front of St. Francis for two years. She started this job with only three pounds of seed. She earned enough in two weeks to buy more than double that amount. In those days, a priest would chase her away. He bought bird seed himself from someone else and laced it with poison to kill the pigeons. He didn't like the smell of the bird shit.

Years ago, Bird Lady sold fruit and cake every day. Before that, she cleaned houses until gangs shook down her employers for how much she doesn't know. Her employers left for the United States, leaving her in "Guat" as the locals call Guatemala City. Bird Lady has worked since she was fourteen. She wanted to be a lawyer or a teacher but her parents did not have enough money to send her to school. She is fifty-six now. She would like to sell fruit again but a fruit vendor, she says, has a high overhead. A car struck her four years ago. She still limps from her injuries. It would be difficult for her to push a fruit cart.

Bird Lady knows by sight individual pigeons. She calls them her girls. She knows when one is injured. She does nothing for them. If they die, they die. What has anyone done for her? The seed is their bond. She sells it, they eat it. She does not ask any more of herself or them. A couple stops by once a week with their son. He can't be more than two. They buy fifty bags of seed and spend an afternoon feeding the birds. Those are good afternoons.

It saddens her to see so many people with money buying whatever they want while she sits here stuck doing this small job. She earns eight to ten dollars a day, a little more on weekends. She walks to the church every morning in time for seven o'clock Mass. Even at that early hour, people want to feed the pigeons. She sits in the damp, gray dawn and remembers the light receding from her mind when she woke up. She assumes the light signifies her dreams retreating to where dreams come from. The dreams move away too fast for her to remember them.

"Hello, I'm having an interview. Who I am? This is your father, for God's sake! You don't have Facebook? Do you have email? An important American journalist wants to send me pictures of me dancing."

Ballerina envisions himself dancing on a ship, skipping down a flight of stairs to a dining hall filled with well-dressed people. Or on a stage. Do ships have stages? he asks me.

"Yes," I tell him.

"Good."

Ballerina would like to perform abroad. For people in Europe to see his skills. All he needs is a bottle of water and a light lunch to keep going. He would dance all day if he could.

I tell him how Bird Lady sees her dreams fade away when she wakes up. Does he remember his dreams? I ask.

No, Ballerina says, because he does not dream. His dreams have already become a reality. He is a dancer. Three or four stores in addition to La Curacao ask him to dance to attract customers.

"I am a professional," he says.

No, the stores don't pay him, Ballerina admits, but it doesn't matter. He is dancing. He will do this even when he is eighty and needs a cane. He will tour different countries: USA, Canada, Venezuela, Japan and all of Europe.

"OK, so you say you can't receive the photographs? That's fine. I understand."

Ballerina pockets his phone. No one he knows has Facebook or email. I suspect his friends are not as impressed with me as he is. They may not even believe I exist, that Ballerina is making the whole thing up and I am nothing but a figment of his imagination, and for a moment I feel almost as if I am an apparition, here but not here. Big-time journalist, ha! Very funny, Luis! Ballerina shakes his head. He doesn't understand. He shrugs, looks at me. After a moment, he grins.

"Bring the photos when you return to Guatemala!" he declares, problem solved.

"I don't know when that will be," I tell him. "It depends on my next assignment."

He waves his hand. No matter. Japanese people have taken his picture and now me, an American journalist. Someone important will see the photos, he is certain. Someone will call him with an offer to work abroad.

"When I dance, I am center stage," he tells me, "and every-body is looking at me, admiring me. The cheers fuel me. I am high. When I dance, I am flying."

He tips his hat over his forehead, drops his arms to his side and waits for another song to start on the boombox. I hear a rising mix of accordion, electric guitar, conga, piano, trumpet and saxophone amid the static. I watch Ballerina move his feet in a four-beat pattern: three steps to one side followed by a pause. He repeats the steps with a simple back and forth movement, advancing across the sidewalk. He closes his eyes and smiles. Turning his face to the sky, he throws his arms wide open. People walk past him, around him. I put money in his empty donation box.

"Semilla!"

Bird Lady appears to be staring at Ballerina from across the street, but her sunglasses continue to hide her eyes, revealing only the distorted images of those passersby caught in their orbit, and it is impossible to say who she may be watching, if anyone. I close my notepad, pack my camera. I have no more questions. I walk off, merging into the flow of people. Pigeons pirouette above Sexta Avenida, dipping and rising. Ballerina is somewhere among them, I'm sure, soaring. He has left Bird Lady and me behind never to know that feeling.

Where Are the Children?

I walk zigzagging down the crooked cobbled streets of Tegucigalpa. No kids. Playing, shouting, shining shoes, walking with their parents.

None.

Here in Tegucigalpa, the capital of Honduras, one of the poorest countries in the Western Hemisphere, where the average income is about thirty dollars a month, no street kids? Not even beggars?

Doesn't make sense.

I notice a woman making tortillas and the cornmeal that covers her plaid apron. Another woman selling cigarettes sticks her hands out to me. When I shake my head, she raises her shirt exposing her breasts and then jerks her chin toward an empty stairwell. I walk on. Honduran soldiers armed with AK-47s brush past, bumping against my shoulders when I don't step aside and I trip, stumbling around a corner before I regain my balance. Above my head, a sign sticks out above the sidewalk: *Tobacco Road*. A smaller sign beneath it: *For Backpackers*.

Through a bright yellow gate, I see two feral cats curled up asleep on a patio. A picnic table stands to one side. The swishing sound of a washing machine rises out of the shadows. To the left of the gate, a door opens to a bar.

"Hello!" I shout.

After a moment, a short, pot-bellied man with white hair tied back in a small ponytail approaches, scowling. He wipes his hands on his green polo shirt, slaps them against his blue jeans.

"Saw your sign," I say. "You get that from the Erskine Caldwell novel?"

"No," he says, his face relaxing. "I never read the book. At one time Tegucigalpa was the halfway point on the route taken by merchants trading tobacco."

He tells me his name is Tom, an expat from Miami, and we shake hands. Tobacco Road, he explains, is a bar and hostel.

"I've assimilated into the country very nicely," he says. "The hostel made good business sense. The backpackers are very happy, grateful for a place to stay. And then they're gone and new people come in. I love the excitement of new people coming in here. I don't have time to get old. Here I'm Peter Pan."

He unlocks the gate and leads me into a room where half a dozen square wood tables fill the tile floor and tall chairs with straw seats line a bar. Bright colorful paintings of local villages cover the wood-paneled walls. Red tile roofs. Green hills. Dirt roads. Several other paintings of mostly naked women in skimpy lingerie take up more space. Above these paintings hangs a sign prohibiting the use and sale of drugs on the premises. Below it, a mocking play on words:

To Do Is To Be - Descartes   God Is Dead - Nietzsche
To Be Is To Do - Voltaire   Nietzsche Is Dead - God
Do Be Do Be Do.- Frank Sinatra

Tom looks out the barred windows and checks the sidewalk. A woman carries a basket of laundry on her head. A phone booth across the street stands empty. An emaciated dog trots past. Tom hands me a beer.

"Tomorrow, Hondurans celebrate their independence day. It's against the law to sell alcohol the day before a national holiday. If the police come in, I'll tell them you're a long-lost dear friend I haven't seen in years and give them a few dollars."

I rub the cold beer bottle against my sweaty forehead and sit at one of the tables. Twisting off the top, I wipe the mouth with the tail of my shirt and take a long, cold swig. I explain that I'm a freelance reporter here for just a few days to write a story about street kids. Tom suggests I visit La Casa Alianza, an aid organization nearby that assists homeless kids throughout Central America. Taking a napkin, he jots down directions.

"I hate to say this, but they are vicious," Tom says of homeless kids. "They should be taken off the street. They can't be rehabilitated. They are as young as thirteen. They're like pygmies. They surround you and take everything you have at knifepoint, even your shoes. You hate to say it. You can blame it on poverty, world trade, the IMF. But they are beyond help. If the police want to kill them, good. That's the reality."

Two cops walk by followed by several soldiers and we hurriedly hide our beers between our legs. They look in at us. Tom raises his chin in greeting.

"We need long straws," he whispers.

I finish my beer, and tell Tom I'll see him later. Looking at his directions, I walk to La Casa Alianza. Crushed lemons and bananas stain the road and flies hover above the ruined fruit. Following a maze of narrow streets, I find La Casa Alianza near a line of vendor stalls beside the banks of the Rio Cholutacar. Vultures circle above mounds of garbage heaped on the river's weedy banks.

The agency stands behind a high gate. I pound my fist against a metal plate and a guard approaches and peers at me. After a moment, he lets me in. The guard says something, but his voice is drowned out by the noise of countless children in torn T-shirts and jeans swarming a courtyard kicking soccer balls, scampering up flights of stairs, and yelling from a cafeteria through windows protected by wire mesh. The noise rises in a crescendo of echoing shouts and shrieks, ricocheting off the cinder-block walls, an endless ping-pong of commotion. Distracted, I stumble over a girl drawing a chalk picture of an angel on a concrete bench. She looks up at me, startled.

"Policía?"

"No."

"I did not sniff glue," she tells me. She stands and backs away. "I lived on the street for two years. My father hit me and I left home. But I did not sniff glue."

"No one said you sniffed glue," I say.

"I didn't."

"What is this glue sniffing?"

"The children who sniff glue, they are the ones who are prostitutes," she answers.

"I don't think you're a prostitute."

"I didn't do it," she says and runs away.

I try to follow her but a group of boys stops me. They thrust their hands in my face and crook their small fingers in odd shapes, signing to me in street gang lingo. They slap my hand, drag their fingers along my palm and clutch my fingertips, rolling their hands into mine until we make a joint fist. Then they let go, snap their fingers and tap my hand with their fists and someone grabs at my pockets and I feel my wallet being dragged from my pocket. I slap that hand and push past the boys but they follow me, clutching at my shirt until the guard steps between me and them.

"Go," the guard tells me. "You don't belong here."

I return to Tobacco Road and ask Tom for a beer.

"That was quick," he says.

"I didn't get very far."

"Guess not."

I tell him about the girl and the boys.

"I warned you," he says.

Sighing, Tom runs a finger through a wet ring on the bar.

"You know, I never expected to move here," he says looking up at me. "Originally I had left Miami for Spain. In Spain, I had been a chiropractor, but I didn't get along with my partner," he says. "So

I decided to do my own clinic. I went back to the States to settle my affairs and decided to go to Central America. I had to rent my house in Miami—Central America was closer if there were problems. And I had already been to Mexico. I was just curious about Central America. I already knew the language."

He rented an apartment in San José, Costa Rica, and spent four and one-half years there running a bookstore. The store did well, but Tom gradually grew to dislike San Jose. Too many gringos. He wanted more of a Latin culture. Travelers who stopped in his bookstore urged him to see Honduras. He decided to visit and was struck by the friendliness of the people, the way they greeted him on the street. Two weeks later, he loaded a truck and moved to Tegucigalpa.

"You have a different set of hoops to jump through here than in Spain and Costa Rica. You can jump through the correct hoop, or pay someone to jump through a crooked hoop. You could lose your business because you went through the wrong hoops, which legally may have been the right hoops."

The next morning, I leave my hotel and walk past La Casa Alianza to the bottom of La Calle Campo Motagua, a narrow street that ends at the Rio Cholutacar. Wet, stomach-curdling garbage steams beneath the sun.

Boys stagger about as if they've been spun in a circle and made dizzy and can't regain their balance. Faces sheathed in sweat, they pause long enough to smear glue from baby jars into plastic bags, and hold the bags over their mouths and noses and inhale. Their eyes roll and saliva drips out of the corners of their mouths. More boys lie passed out around them, partially filled jars of glue in their hands. The odor of glue hangs over everything.

One boy straddles an inflatable tiger. Above him, vultures circle, rising on the updrafts. More vultures hop on the ground, flapping their wings as they approach the stinking carcass of a dog. They stop, sink their heads between their hunched shoulders and stare slit-eyed at the passed-out children.

The boy on the tiger thrusts his hips back and forth while other boys near him wrap their mouths around their glue jars and inhale. A vulture tears flesh off the dead dog.

The glue keeps us from feeling our hunger," the boy on the tiger tells me, stumbling over his words, eyes nearly closed.

"Life is a deception," he adds.

A glue-smeared bag floats away from his outstretched hand and lands on the back of a vulture and the enraged bird flaps its wings and shrieks as the bag whips and snaps stuck to a mat of black feathers. The boy watches the vulture's frenzied dance with unseeing eyes. He rides the tiger harder, waiting for it to carry him out of this place.

I stop at Tobacco Road on the way back to my hotel. A worn-looking man sits in the corner of the bar. He shows me a heavily creased piece of notebook paper with a long list of numbers printed in shaky handwriting. It's confirmation, he says, of a six-hundred-thousand-dollar loan he's been granted by the Honduran government to ship shrimp to Australia.

"It's in the bag," he says in an Australian accent.

He approaches Tom and asks him for a beer. When he returns to the table, I sit at the bar.

"Who's he?" I ask.

"He's the man with the plan. He always has a scheme, and the scheme always falls through," Tom says. "Each one is a little more outrageous than the last. He always has an explanation when it falls apart: Somebody ripped him off. Goddamn bureaucracy. As if it was even true in the first place. But he survives. Somebody always picks him up. Like today. I don't know where he got money to come in here."

I watch the man with the plan scribble notes on notebook paper.

"You smell like glue," Tom says.

I tell him about the children by the river.

"A lot of these kids are hiding," he says. "The government takes them to shelters if they see them. Are we talking about children who have no homes? How many is that? Five hundred? Or are we talking about children who work on the street for their families? Then there are many more."

"And it doesn't matter? They just take them away?"

"Yeah. Like that."

He snaps his fingers.

Where're the shelters?"

"I don't know, don't care. As long as they keep away from me."

A sixteen-year-old boy sits beneath a palm tree in the courtyard of La Casa Alianza and says he doesn't want to talk to me. A scar reveals where a gang tattoo was removed from his left arm. Since an anti-gang law was passed in 2003 in response to a surge in violent crime, the police have detained hundreds of tattooed teenagers and young adults. Gangs have carved up major Honduran cities into their respective turfs.

"How long were you in the gang Diez y Ocho?"

The boy hesitates. Maria, a La Casa volunteer, holds the boy's hands.

"Maybe four months," the boy says. "Since I was ten."

Maria heard I had been at La Casa the day before, and came by my hotel the previous night. After she introduced herself, she said she wanted me to meet a real success story, a boy who had turned his life around. He ran away from a gang to avoid joining it, she said. Imagine.

She stood in my door and clutched her hands together and her eyes brimmed with tears. Her enthusiasm for this boy appeared to overwhelm her. I asked if she wanted to sit but she said she couldn't stay. I agreed to see her in the morning.

"My brother was in the gang so I joined," the boy continues. "You have to live with them for six months. They hit you, beat you up to make you tough. Then you have to kill a member of another gang. I wouldn't do that so I ran away to Guatemala."

"You see," Maria says, "he ran away to leave the gangs. When he got to Guatemala, he went to the La Casa office there."

"Before you went to the La Casa office in Guatemala did you join a gang?"

"Yes. Mara Salvatrucha," he says. Better known as MS, "the gang from El Salvador."

"Why?"

"I didn't know anyone. Then I met a member of MS. He recruited me."

"How long were you in MS?"

"Five years."

"Five years?"

He looks at me and I hold his gaze and he knows he slipped up. Maria watches us and I can see that she too understands. She lets go of his hand. The boy nods at me as if he is giving me permission to ask the obvious question. The look in his eyes says, Let's get this over with.

"To join a gang you said you have to kill?"

"Yes."

"Did you?"

"I killed a Diez y Ocho gang member for MS."

"Shoot him?"

"Yes. I was called El Gino. Genius. Because of the way I killed. The way I sneaked up on them. They never knew what hit them. I killed many."

"From behind?"

"Yes. Always surprise your enemy. Like Osama bin Laden. Kick ass."

"Where are they? Other boys like you?"

"In gangs."

"I mean street kids. Beggars. The ones not in gangs."

"Hiding. The police sweep them up. Or we kill them. If they won't join the gangs."

Maria, her face drained of color, walks away. The boy watches her go, thrusts his crotch back and forth and laughs.

I leave the boy, imagine the gestures he is making behind my back, and stop at Tobacco Road for lunch. The man with the plan traces a map on the table with a tobacco-stained finger, explaining how a ship will come up from the south, pick up the shrimp from a port somewhere on the east coast, and then embark for Australia. He shows me a handwritten contract with his signature on another piece of beat-up notebook paper. He sips a beer.

"Police were in this morning," Tom says.

"What did they want?" I ask.

"I don't know. My landlord is a former general. I think he was into drugs. Maybe they want him. Maybe they want me. I shot a cop here once. He was harassing one of my bartenders. It was a warning shot, but I hit him in the spleen. I did twenty-one days in jail."

"Bastards," the man with the plan says.

"There's corruption on all levels. The police, military, the government. That's the one thing that might make me leave Latin America. The corruption."

"May I use your phone?" the man with the plan asks.

Tom hands him his cell and he steps into the hall.

"What I really want to know is what the police are up to," Tom says, looking at me.

"The deal's in the bag," the man with the plan announces, handing the phone back to Tom.

"What do you think they want?" Tom asks me. "The police."

"Just have to wait for the president to sign off on the deal," the man with the plan says.

"Do you think they're setting me up?" Tom asks.

I walk to the Rio Cholutacar to find some kids who can tell me where these shelters are that Tom told me about. I look around. No glue sniffers. Were they rounded up?

Empty plastic bags stick to garbage and brush. In a shack on La Calle Campo Motagua above the Rio Cholutacar, a woman ladles glue from a bucket into baby food jars to sell for a quarter. Teenage prostitutes file out of the sagging front door of a hotel and buy glue from the woman. They dip their fingers in it and smear it on plastic bags or just hold the jars against their mouths and inhale. An obese old man sits in the peeling orange hall of the hotel and reads a newspaper, his washed-out eyes wandering over the girls from time to time. His jowly balloon-like presence is squeezed into a chair too small for his bulk. Men wander in and he points to rooms. He calls the prostitutes by name and they follow after the men.

I take a coin out of my pocket and show it to one prostitute who holds a jar of glue under her nose. She looks about fifteen and wears a white blouse and short red dress but has no shoes. Her teeth shine with saliva and tiny bubbles of spit collect in the corners of her mouth. Her bloodshot eyes try to focus as I close my right fist over the coin. I open my hand and the coin is gone. Then I open my left hand and show her the coin. She laughs, her eyes for a moment shiny and alert. She raises the jar to her nose and I stop her by offering her the coin. She reaches for it and I close my hand around hers and ask, "Where are the children?"

She doesn't answer. She wants to write her name in my notepad. I give it to her. Rosa Rafael. In tight, even handwriting. She wraps a flourishing loop rising from the "l" in Rafael around Rosa. She draws two lines under her name and holds the pad out to examine her work. She learned to write somewhere and now her name and the decorative way she writes it are all she has to call her own.

Rosa!" the old man shouts.

"Perdón," Rosa says, standing.

She enters the hotel, bends her head, and inhales from her jar. Pausing in the doorway, she turns toward me, eyes rolling, face already becoming slack.

"Hogares de Protección Kennedy."

"Dónde?"

"Avenida de Kennedy."

She walks down the hall and I follow her, but the old man stops me and demands money. When I refuse, he takes a pistol from his pocket. I back away and raise my hands. A policeman comes up behind me and asks, "What is the problem?"

A door closes, the hall empty of Rosa. The old man waves his gun, complains about me to the policeman, who does nothing to stop the trade in sex. He sticks out his hand and I give him five dollars. Shoving the bill in his pocket, he tells me to leave. Behind the warped walls, I hear the shuffling of feet. Men's voices. The low, slurred tones of the girls' stoned responses.

Sometime after six o'clock. Tom and I sip beer at the bar. I just missed one of his customers who had been mugged at knifepoint this morning.

"I told you," Tom says. "Vicious."

Not all of them. When I left the prostitutes, I stopped and talked to a boy named Carlos at La Casa Alianza. He had spent four weeks in jail, charged with being a member of MS because of the "M" tattooed in his right arm. He said the letter honored his dead older brother Miguel. When he was released from prison, a doctor scraped off the tattoo with a knife, leaving a raw, bloated welt.

Several times since his release, he said, police have stopped and questioned him, examining the scar on his arm.

"All they do now is hit me. Sometimes gangs see me in a group and assume we're another gang and try to kill some of us. Sometimes the police think the same and want to arrest us. Social workers want to take me away. I have removed my tattoo. That is all I can do."

When I tell Tom this, he shrugs.

"That's too bad," he says without much feeling. "Maybe he's bullshitting you."

I'd thought of that too, but I resent Tom's hardness, his unwillingness to bend a little. Not all of these kids are vicious, and those who are didn't get that way by accident.

A few people sit at the bar with us. Just before I got there, Tom had thrown out the man with the plan. He had met a German couple on the street in need of a place to stay. He walked them here and asked Tom for a finder's fee. Tom reminded him of all the beers he had fronted him and told him to get lost.

"He's an embarrassment. How does he get up and look at himself in the morning?" Tom says, raising his bottle halfway to his lips. He stops, stares at the door.

I turn around. Two police officers stand in the entryway. They point their rifles at us and tell us to stand against the wall. We get off our stools and raise our arms. The police inspect each of us for tattoos. One cop pushes my head back, scrutinizes my neck. Nothing. I've never had a tattoo, although I've considered it. But I was never drunk enough and I'd never have someone jabbing needles in my neck.

The police leave without a word. We remain standing, hands up, and watch them go. Tom and I look at each other and then at the other barflies standing against the wall, arms up holding their beers. Without a word, we all put the bottles to our mouths and drink.

I take a cab to my hotel, afraid to walk alone, afraid the police might stop me on the street. I look through my duffel bag for a map of Tegucigalpa. I hold it up to the window for better light and trace a route from the hotel to Hogares de Protección Kennedy.

I hear voices and look out my window. On the sidewalk below and across the street by a restaurant, soldiers and police linger under halos of bugs swarming in the brothy glow of dim streetlights. They shout back and forth to one another. Some of the soldiers look up in my direction. Despite the late hour and the inky darkness beyond the streetlights, they wear sunglasses. They seem to stare right at me but it is impossible to tell. Perhaps they are looking past me to the roof. What are they thinking? What do they want?

Hogares de Protección Kennedy stands off a stone and dirt road surrounded by a concrete wall topped with barbed wire. Behind the walls, gray cinder-block huts appear along a cracked sidewalk that winds through the silent grounds. Weeds grow in sandy vacant lots pocked with muddy puddles. A swing set and a slide stand empty and a hard, wet wind blows.

Children stare at me through barred windows. They make no sound. Some of the wire is torn, and groups of children stick their arms out of the windows and wave to me. A guard explains that the children are locked inside because a staff person isn't available to watch them. The static of a television crackles behind the small faces watching me.

The guard lets me peer in one window. In one corner a boy sits on a black, metal bunk bed without mattresses. He walks toward me and stands on his toes to talk. He was about to buy candy with money he earned polishing shoes when police snatched him off the street four weeks ago and brought him here.

"I don't know where my family is. I don't like it here. Take me with you."

The guard escorts me to the administration office, a bare room with just a desk, chair, and phone. Moments later, the director, Lesbia Lagos, a short woman with black hair and a stiff, mannequin smile, strides in without pause as if she expected me. We shake hands and I explain to her why I'm in Honduras. Hogares de Protección Kennedy is one of four centers for street children, Lagos tells me. These centers, she says, are the reason I see so few kids on the street. She assures me the children are well cared for and will soon be referred to aid organizations that will help them to enroll in schools and find jobs.

"Some of these children are helping their mothers and fathers earn money, I know this," Lagos says. "But to work only without an education, they will become like their mothers and fathers: nothing."

She pauses, interrupted by a secretary carrying a tray holding a bottle of Coca-Cola and two ice-filled glasses. The secretary pours Coke in the glasses and gives one to me and one to Lagos.

"We find them on the street," Lagos says of the children, "and we work with the police." She pauses, waits for the foam in her glass to settle. "Normally, we talk to them, try to convince them to come with us willingly. They resist sometimes."

She takes a long drink and sets her glass on the desk, her small hand wrapped around it almost in a fist.

"They don't have a choice. What is worse? Sniffing glue all day, recruited by gangs, or placed in a center?"

Without waiting for me to answer or ask a question, Lagos gets up and sticks out her hand. Our meeting is over. I leave the center and catch a cab to Tobacco Road and join Tom at the bar. This is my last night in Tegucigalpa, I tell him. I fly out in the morning. He hands me a beer.

"On me."

"I got what I came for."

He raises an eyebrow.

"I found where they take the kids."

"Bad?"

"Depends on your perspective."

"No doubt."

"It's pretty bleak."

"Of course it is."

I still see the thin, disembodied arms sticking through windows at Hogares de Protección Kennedy, rising in the air, clutching at my passing shadow and I cover my face, press the heels of my palms into my eyes and shake my head.

"You all right?" Tom asks.

"Depends on your perspective."

He smiles.

"Always does."

A young man with a light patchy brown beard and a backpack slung over one shoulder rings the buzzer.

"You have a room?"

"Traveling through?" Tom asks. He opens the gate.

"Yeah. Just came from El Salvador."

"Where are you from?"

"Germany."

"El Salvador's a little country. I'm not impressed with it. How long will you be here?"

"Day or two," the backpacker says.

"I've been here going on eight years," Tom says. "I've been spreading rumors that this is a very dangerous town—to keep gringos out."

The backpacker laughs. Tom takes him to a room and returns to the bar.

"Nice kid," he says. "I love the flow of energy of backpackers coming and going. It's uplifting, this wave of energy."

A small girl in a dirty pink dress wanders in, interrupting Tom's rapturous outpouring of bliss. She holds out two grime-covered boxes of Chiclets and tries to sell me one, but Tom shoos her away. As she leaves, a policeman struts past and the girl shrinks against the door. When he passes from sight, she darts outside.

"That's part of the excitement of living here," Tom says, watching the girl run. "You're always susceptible to something bad happening to you."

In The Shadow of Berta Cáceres

July 8, 2016, noon: First stop: San Pedro Sula, Honduras. Interview with Father Cesar Espinoza. He has received death threats for his anti-mining stance. A friend of Berta Cáceres. He will be in San Pedro Sula for a conference and is staying with a friend. You will drive directly from the airport to meet him.

You don't look like a man under threat.

How should such a man look?

I don't answer because I have no idea. I only have my imagination and movie images to guide me. Jumpy, nervous, I suppose.

You're calm, I say finally. Very calm.

What would you have me be?

Again, I don't answer. Father Cesar wipes sweat from his forehead with a cold bottle of water. He uncaps it and takes a sip and sighs.

Nightmares plague his sleep and he wakes up perspiring. He has not sought therapy. That is a luxury he cannot afford. For a while, he broke down in tears in the middle of Mass. He suffered from back aches and headaches. That may be a result of age, he thinks. He smiles. He is thirty-nine.

I'm afraid, really. I have post-traumatic stress. Do I go about my life shaking in my boots? No, but if I'm driving and a motorcycle comes too close I am scared.

A motorcycle?

I was kidnapped.

When?

July 4, 2014.

He motions at a bottle of water he had given me.

Please, he says.

I twist off the cap. We sit on the second floor deck of a rectory in downtown San Pedro Sula. It rained earlier and gray clouds still layer the sky and the warped boards of the wooden deck hold the damp. A clingy humidity enwraps us.

I am in Honduras to write about environmental activists opposed to mining, similar to the work Sister Maudilia was doing in Guatemala. From San Pedro Sula here in the north, I will travel south, visiting towns along the way affected by mining until I reach Choluteca near the border with El Salvador.

The divide separating pro- and anti-mining factions assumed lethal proportions two months before I left the States when gunmen shot and killed Honduran environmental activist Berta Cáceres. Just one year earlier, she had won the prestigious Goldman Environmental Prize for preventing a hydroelectric dam from being built in the western part of the country on the Gualcarque River. The river is sacred to indigenous people who depend on it for their livelihoods.

I had not been familiar with Berta's work before her death. At least four assassins entered the gated community where she lived on the outskirts of La Esperanza in southwest Honduras. A checkpoint at the entrance to the town—normally manned by police officers or soldiers—was left unattended on the night she was killed. News reports alleged that a former soldier with the U.S.-trained special forces units of the Honduran military had included Cáceres's name on a hit list months before her assassination. Her death was seen by many activists as a warning that environmental protests would be dealt with in one way and one way only. My fixer, Olga Contreras, with whom I'd worked in Guatemala, told me all of Central America mourned Berta. She was considered the Rev. Martin Luther King Jr. of Honduras. Olga arranged my travel schedule and sent me emails detailing my itinerary.

On the night I was kidnapped, I had been invited to a party at the U.S. Embassy, Father Cesar tells me. I went to talk about mining with ambassadors and people from international aid organizations. That's the only reason I went. I don't like parties. I was by myself, and on my way back home I picked up a human rights advocate and a friend, another priest. For two hours the kidnappers held us. Then they dropped us off at a sleazy motel, the kind used by prostitutes. They took our money and cell phones. They took our car and luggage. They kept those things but gave back our money and cell phones. OK, one of them said. You've been warned. You can get a restraining order. It won't help you. This is how we do things in Honduras.

Father Cesar takes another sip of water and rubs his face with a worn washcloth. He is a large, muscular man with a paunch and a helmet of black hair. I notice the pockmarks on his face and recall my tortured teenage fight against acne. How strange, I think, the memories that cross my mind in places so unrelated to my life. How neither Father Cesar nor I, as teenagers, could have imagined we would be facing one another, an anti-mining, activist priest confronting death threats and a reporter who grew up in a Chicago suburb and whose parents locked the doors at night out of habit, not fear.

When the kidnappers stopped us, I thought they were drunken people, Father Cesar continues. They were five men with assault weapons and they took over our car. Two of them sat in front. I was in back. Be quiet, don't say anything, the two men said. A car followed us. There was a police car in front of us but it did nothing. I was thinking of my life. Indeed, life does flash in front of you. I thought, Where are they going to take us to kill us? I thought about so many things. I thought, This is a terrible way to end my life. At first, I thought it was a normal robbery. I told them I'm a priest. I work with the church. Like trying to mediate. We were coming from Tegucigalpa to San Pedro Sula. They stopped us at Siguatepeque, a town in a tourist area. When they let us go, they left us in Esperanza near where Berta was killed. The location was not by chance. It was a message to us, I suspect.

Father Cesar stops talking. What do you think? the expression on his face asks me. I don't know. How do I find parallels between my life and an experience unlike anything I've known? I say nothing, jot down notes, and avoid his look by staring over his shoulders at laundry lines extending between houses; rusted metal siding separates each one. Shards of glass are strewn across the tops of walls to deter intruders, and traffic drones somewhere beyond the palm tree-lined road.

After the kidnappers let us go, once we felt safe, we called the police, Father Cesar continues. The police came and drove us to the town of Arizona. The kidnappers got away with it. They haven't been caught. To this day, I ask myself, Why wasn't I killed? If they could kill Berta what stopped them from killing me, a priest from a small parish? When activists were killed, Berta would say, Who will be next? I never thought she would be the one.

He pauses, then reflects on his childhood and the choices he made long ago that led him to the priesthood, and to the night of the kidnapping. He grew up in San Isidro Intibucá, a small village far from San Pedro Sula. He played on the street until late and he would meet friends in other barrios. Nothing bad ever happened. Maybe he was careless then. Maybe he is too aware of his mortality now. He does not think so. He thinks the country has changed. Even a poor priest is not safe.

Did you always want to be a priest?

No, a cowboy.

Father Cesar laughs. When he outgrew his fantasies of the ranching life, he decided to become a physician. As a child, he had seen people die of the most common of diseases because they could not afford a doctor. However, he had a competing interest: He had been drawn to the church since his first catechism class. He enjoyed leaving his village to attend religious retreats. He saw priests helping poor people and decided he wanted to be a priest rather than a doctor. It was a practical decision. The priesthood required less schooling and there was something appealing about reaching for something bigger than oneself, a spiritual ideal larger than his own life. He took his vows in 2004 and preached in a parish in Arizona. In 2009, Lenir Perez, owner of the Honduran mining company Minerales Victoria, announced that he wanted to buy two thousand five hundred acres, covering sixteen farming communities near Arizona in the county of Atlántida. One town, Nueva Esperanza, became the focal point of confrontations between pro- and anti-mining factions.

Perez offered a lot of money and many people took it and sold their land. Those who did not were harassed. Farmers received threats. Men in trucks drove through fences, tearing up crops, and Perez bribed officials to revoke land titles. Father Cesar spoke out against Perez from the pulpit and on the radio. In January 2013, he received his first death threat. A text message: Don't come too close to the mine because we will get you with a machete. He was afraid and stopped traveling outside of Arizona. People called him and said, Goons are talking about you and saying you are about to be done in.

Vicar Victor Camera, Father Cesar's supervisor, chastised Perez for creating strife and fear. The vicar saw with his own eyes the machinery Perez brought into Nueva Esperanza after he had said he would not bring in mining equipment without holding a community meeting first.

Do you think being transparent is to sneak in machinery on a Saturday escorted by the police? Vicar Camara wrote in an email Father Cesar showed me. *Have you chosen force and conflict? I hope that you ponder the consequences and that, above all, no human lives be put at stake, since no human life is worth all the gold in the world. Please know that with conflict there will be no winners, everybody will lose, including you.*

Perez responded: *It saddens me to see Honduras taken apart by businessmen, drug dealers, politicians, and environmentalists (communists and subversive curas[2]).* Perez also accused the church of cowardice for not opposing Espinoza's advocacy against the mine. He called Father Cesar *another sinner behind his robe.*

Believe me, I would like to open that mine hand in hand with the community, Perez wrote, *but I will not allow a Guatemalan [Espinoza] and the activists to destroy this country.*

In July 2013, Orlane Vidal and Daniel Langmeier, with the Accompaniment Project, a nongovernmental program designed to engage in peaceful protest in Honduras, came to Arizona to write a report on the mining operations. Vidal and Langmeier stayed with a family opposed to mining. Shortly after their arrival, they were held captive for two and a half hours by armed men, who, according to Amnesty International, worked for Perez.

The leader of their kidnappers told Vidal and Langmeier that they would disappear in the woods if they returned to the area. They were released at a bus stop in Nueva Florida, a town not far from Nueva Esperanza. They filed complaints with the authorities but the abductors were not charged. The abduction, however,

---

2   Curas is a derogatory term for priests.

galvanized the community. Activists met with local mayoral candidates and asked them to sign an anti-mining pledge. Honduran
law allows mayors the final decision on whether a mine can operate in their township. On August 20, 2014, upon taking office,
the newly elected mayor of Nueva Esperanza, Mario Fuentes,
shuttered the mine. However, the closure of the mine may be
temporary; Perez still owns the land. If a new mayor supports
him, the mine could be reopened, but even if it remains closed,
Father Cesar worries that some damage is irreversible. The waters
have been poisoned. He knows of several cases where women
have contracted skin diseases from washing clothes, and several
people who worked in the mines have cancer and metal in their
blood. When the mine was operating, miners did not speak of
these things. Those who said they were sick were fired and those
who stayed lost their jobs anyway when the mine closed. Some of
the unemployed blame Father Cesar for the lack of work. Perez is
accountable for these problems, not me, Father Cesar says. Perez
has different values than me. He is motivated by profit and power.
I try to understand that. I try to forgive him for that.

July 8, 6 p.m. *You have a telephone interview with Rodolfo Artega.
He does not want to meet with you because he is afraid you'll bring
unwanted attention to him. He lives in Palos Ralos in Siria de Valle.
It is far from where you'll be in San Pedro Sula. A mine called the San
Martin operated in the district of Valle de Siria not far from Arizona.
Artega lives in the district. The mine, owned by Glamis Gold Ltd., a
Reno, Nevada-based gold producer, started production in 2000. In*

2006, Goldcorp, a gold producer headquartered in Canada, acquired it. Goldcorp operated the mine through its subsidiary Entre Mares during the last three years of production. In 2008, a year before it closed, a report on the mine by the University of Glasgow found a number of serious problems with it: Leakage of cyanide from one of the main storage ponds where cattle graze, and where waters flow to local rivers; signs of substantial physical erosion of one of the principal mine waste management facilities; a flow of acidic water exiting the mine's perimeter and entering a nearby river; and exposed pit walls which would remain sources of wind-blown dust and contaminated runoff for decades or even centuries to come. On October 16, 2007, Luis Vidal Ramos Reina, director of forensic medicine at the Criminal and Forensic Sciences Laboratory in Tegucigalpa, released to the government a forensic report on the analysis of blood and urine samples of sixty-one people in Valle de Siria. The analysis indicated the presence of high concentrations of cyanide, mercury, lead, and arsenic. Furthermore, the report concluded that concentrations of lead exceeded World Health Organization acceptable levels by ten milligrams.

I have difficulty hearing Rodolfo Artega over the phone. Rural areas have poor service, he explains, shouting his voice hoarse as he recalls when representatives from the mining company, Minerales Entre Mares de Honduras (Minerals Between the Seas of Honduras), came to his small town of San José in Valle de Siria. At first, they said they would be taking soil samples. They mentioned exploration and extraction but the words meant nothing to Rodolfo and his neighbors. They were farmers, not miners, and had no idea what to expect. Then in 2000, men representing the mine told the people of San Jose that the town was going to be razed for mining and that they had to move to a new town about three miles away. Houses had already been built for them and the company would pay each family three thousand dollars. San Jose had been founded in 1880 and Rodolfo and his wife lived on land that had been passed down from his great-great grandfather to him. He refused to leave.

All of his neighbors left but Rodolfo hung on for twenty-five long days. San Jose became a ghost town, the unoccupied streets silent, stores closed, their shelves gathering dust. Only in his imagination did Rodolfo hear the bustle of life he'd always known. Mine representatives told him that if he did not leave voluntarily, a court would issue an order to remove him by force and he would forfeit payment for his land. The pressure became too much and Rodolfo gave in to their demands.

You cannot begin to know how hard it is to abandon your life, your house, everything you know and that is familiar to you, he tells me, his voice catching. I got sick but my disease was not of the flesh, but of solitude brought on by sadness. During the years following the relocation, Rodolfo and his neighbors began noticing problems. People got ill from the water with diarrhea and urinary tract infections and young women had frequent miscarriages. People are still sick today. They have thyroid problems, even cancer. Rodolfo feels bad for friends like Olga Velasquez who has five children, all of whom came down with skin diseases. She opposed the mine and was very vocal about it. Her eldest

son, Victor, would go out with friends and the police would stop
him and say, Oh, you're the son of Olga Velasquez. We'd hate to
see something happen to your mother. Victor became so afraid
for his life he decided to leave. He was just sixteen and crossed
illegally into the U.S. The Border Patrol caught him and sent
him to a detention center in the state of Washington. Before
he left, he told his mother, You need to stop your activism. Your
children are being harassed. Rodolfo tries not to dwell too much
on his problems. When he is by himself, he takes comfort in his
memories of the fruit trees and sugar cane fields of San Jose. He
remembers the small ponds and the cows that grazed nearby. In
those days, he would awaken at dawn, wash his face and hands,
and his wife would serve him a hot cup of coffee and he would
fetch the cows and milk them. Then he would hitch his oxen
and till the soil and plant corn and beans. That was his entire
day. During the rainy season, the crops grew. He felt happy and
content. He and his wife, Maria, married in 1985. Their first
children were twins but one died at four months. Four more
children followed. On weekends, the family went into town and
visited family. It was a happy, peaceful life.

They lived in an adobe house, white ceiling, a wood shingle
roof. Rodolfo had a clear view of the valley. It was full of trees
and very green. He could see two hills from his front door. One
has now been flattened by mining. From his new house, he can
see the one remaining hill. A warehouse that was once filled with
the mine company's dynamite stands where his house once stood.
Everything is so different, the landscape unrecognizable. When

Berta died, he lost all hope. He did not know her personally but he knew of her and how she stood up for people like him. Now he wonders, who is left standing? His foundation had been San Jose and these days Rodolfo feels unmoored. His new home is made of cinder block and has a prefab roof; the bare, concrete floor feels cold against his feet. He owns about half the land he once had and has no family other than his wife and children. An older brother, Sergio, won't speak to him. Sergio sold his land to the mining company and was happy to do so. You gave away your heritage, Rodolfo scolded him. In 2011, he felt their feud had gone on long enough and he called Sergio, but Sergio refused to talk. To this day, he defends the mining company. Rodolfo doesn't argue. He only wants his life back.

July 10, 10 a.m.: *Interview Pedro Landa in the town of Progresso, a forty-five-minute drive from San Pedro Sula. He is one of the most respected environmental activists in Honduras and worked closely with Berta Cáceres.*

On my way out of San Pedro Sula to Progresso, my cab driver asks why I'm in Honduras. I explain.

You flew here?

No. I came by bus from Guatemala.

Good country, Guatemala, he says. Honduras is a very dangerous place. Those who support the government are behind all of these big mineral companies. The government supports them and not us. We are used to people getting killed for no reason for defending their rights. This is not normal.

As I listen to the driver, I stare out my window at the faded billboards promoting Pepsi; a hotel, The El Rez Inn; and brands of
motor oil that are flitting by. Within twenty minutes, we leave
the freeway for a narrow, two-lane road. Street markets replace
billboards, and white sheets drying in the sun billow like flags.
Men in straw hats work in corn and sugarcane fields and birds
rise up around them. Buzzards circle hills pocked with shacks, and
families till the soil. Laborers wait for buses in the shade offered by
advertisements for Tampico orange juice and UNO gas. We stop
at a checkpoint and show our identification. An old man stands on
the side of the road with a sign: "I am blind. Help me out." Stray
dogs pebbled with ticks lie panting beneath trees. Pedro Landa
works in an office off a dusty road not far from the checkpoint.
A guard inspects my passport and lets me through a gate. I walk
across a rock-strewn lot and through the door of a squat, two-story building. Pedro waits for me on the second floor. I climb the
stairs and he motions to a bare wood table. He sits across from me,
folds his hands, hunches forward. His lined face settles into a pout.
Heavy circles hammock his eyes.

How long have you been an environmental activist? I ask him.

Twenty-five years. He was motivated in part by the destruction
caused by Hurricane Mitch in 1998. The storm created landslides
because mining companies had stripped the hillsides of trees and
plants. Without roots to hold the soil, the ground turned into a
mud-fueled tidal wave that wiped out entire villages, killing an
estimated seven thousand people. I mention my meeting with

Father Cesar. Pedro remembers when he was kidnapped. These days in Arizona things are very calm but the calm is a tense one, he cautions. No one knows what Lenier Perez might do next.

He pauses. I read a banner above a shelf behind him: *In Honduras we join the pact of dreamers in the movement.*

I myself have received every kind of threat, Pedro says. Phone, texts, face-to-face.

He counts off on his fingers:

2008: Mining companies brought workers armed with machetes and guns to a meeting about the need to limit mining licenses in which he was a participant. Police prevented a confrontation.

2010: Pedro traveled to Canada to testify before Parliament about the environmental impact of Canadian mining companies such as Goldcorp. The ambassador to Honduras was present. After he finished speaking, Pedro received a text: We know what you are saying in Canada. You are about to suffer consequences.

2013: Someone shot into his car after he left a meeting about the consequences of mining in Honduras. He fled the country for two months. He does not fear for his life as much as he fears for the lives of his family. The most difficult thing is when his seventy-eight-year-old mother asks him to stop being an activist. He has spoken to his family about retiring but they agree with him that if he did, he would betray his country and the memory of Berta.

Pedro counted himself one Berta's closest friends. They met in 1996 at a meeting of environmental activists. Despite all the pressure and her anxiety for her safety, Berta always had a smile. Every day, she wore jeans and boots, never a dress or skirt, and she treated people like a mother would her children. She carried tamales so everyone had something to eat. No matter what, she always made time for people to have a meal. She called her friends compas and compitas. A friend called Pedro at four o'clock in the morning to tell him of her murder. Her death was a declaration of war by the mining companies, he believes. Their message: We are coming. We are coming for all of you.

July 11, 3 p.m: *Visit nuns with the order Mensajeras de la Inmaculada, Messengers of the Immaculate. These nuns live right by the closed Nueva Esperanza mine and worked with Father Cesar. Arizona is two hours away from Progresso. After meeting the sisters, you have a telephone interview with Deputy Mayor Cesar Alvaranga of Nueva Esperanza. Like Rodolfo, he is afraid that meeting with you would create problems.*

The drive from Progresso to Arizona takes me past rows of palm trees and cows grazing in fenced pastures. Recyclers rest against their wagons, sacks filled with discarded plastic spilling from stuffed burlap bags. In fields beyond the palm trees, laborers cut grass with machetes near a dilapidated house where a family sits at a white picnic table near an empty pool. Pickups spew gravel on small memorials constructed for people killed in traffic accidents. Chickens peck at the markers, a dog runs across a vacant soccer field.

The cab driver leaves me at Nuestra Senora del Pilar, Our Lady of Pilar, Father Cesar's church. I follow a hallway to a room where a young woman sits behind a desk with a portrait of Berta Cáceres. I ask for the two nuns I am to meet, Sisters Presentación Aguilar and Maria de Rosario Soriono. The woman tells me her name, Olga

Hernandez, and says the sisters are on their way. She offers me a chair and I explain the purpose of my trip.

I am an activist with the sisters, Olga says. I want to protect the land. We have seen the mine destroy it piece by piece.

Olga has lived in Nuestro Esperanza for all of her twenty-nine years. She was just a child when Perez brought his mining company to town. Many rivers run in the hills of Nuestra Esperanza and all of Arizona and the people told him, This has been our land for centuries, but Perez showed no interest. He hired young men from town and paid them twenty-five dollars an hour, an enormous sum that would have taken them one week to earn harvesting crops. He bought the people of this town, Olga says. She knew a mother with five sons. The mother and three of her boys opposed the mine. The other two sons worked in the mine. One day, the mother stood outside the mine with the three sons who opposed it and protested while her other two sons held machetes and chased away demonstrators.

Other family divisions developed. Perez wanted the land of Olga's neighbor, Marcos Amaga, for an access road, but Marcos refused to sell. He was elderly and appointed his only son as heir and made him promise that he would never cooperate with the mining company. When Marcos died, however, his son sold the land to Perez and left town.

For more than a year, Olga tells me, people were afraid to go out in the evening. Mine security guards patrolled the street. They hurt no one. It was a psychological thing. Don't oppose the mine or else. During this time, Olga's cousin, a mine supporter, threatened her.

Watch out Olga, he said, You will end up chopped into little pieces.

Her cousin changed his mind later, when the mine laid him off, and he apologized.

This is all forgotten, Olga told him. Family is family.

The rest of the town, however, has not forgotten and life is not what it used to be. The people who supported the mine remain angry at the people who opposed it. Olga looks out at the land and remembers how it once was. The mining company flattened the mountains to extract the ore. She can see trees and plants flourishing again, but the mountains will never grow back. Nuestra Esperanza had been a safe place. As a child, she could play in the woods with a friend, especially when the moon was shining. There were parties on weekends, and everyone attended and shared what they had. She doesn't see that now. Today, relationships depend on politics. You spend time with people who agree with you and not with those who don't.

Sisters Presentación and Maria walk into the office just as Olga finishes telling me her story. She asks them for bus fare and leaves. The sisters face me, sitting side by side appearing tense, nervous. It is not me that makes them uncomfortable, Sister Presentación says. It is the subject of the mine. These have been difficult days.

Even before Perez came to town, Sisters Presentación and Maria were dealing with problems in Nueva Esperanza and the seventeen towns that make up the county of Arizona. Gangs, for instance. In Nueva Florida, not far from Nueva Esperanza, gangs extort families for hundreds of dollars and take their homes. Perez has been just one more problem. When he came to Nueva Esperanza, both sisters told the community: Don't be naive. Don't believe everything he offers. Keep in mind the cost of acceptance. Nothing is free. Every gift has a cost.

Perez offered jobs to some people and not to others, a dirty strategy to divide the community, Sister Maria believes. Money can make people talk. It can also make them complacent and shut them up. One community leader got a job with the mine and became very supportive of Perez. This person bullied people and stole from street vendors. He got cocky and believed the mine would back him up. If I'm sent to jail, I'll be out the same day, he boasted. He beat up one man and was arrested. Perez would have nothing to do with him. He's still in jail.

The sisters organized meetings in local parishes, interspersing their talks with biblical text. They spoke about creation and how man was called upon to protect nature, not destroy it. Perez never confronted the sisters directly. The meetings, however, were tense. Security personnel from the mine stood in the doorways of the churches where the sisters spoke, watching them and firing their guns outside. Of course they were afraid, Sister Presentación says. It was not physical terror, but psychological. Giving talks with armed men watching made her feel under siege. She found solace in her faith and in Berta Cáceres. Look at all Berta puts herself through for the people, Sister Presentación thought. Then Father Cesar received his death threat. Sisters Presentación and Maria were included in the same message: You and those nuns better not show your faces in this town again. The sisters didn't leave the grounds of the church for weeks.

I was very curious as to who would send such a message, Sister Maria says. I didn't think anyone in the congregation would do this. I paid attention, looked for a single gesture that might indicate who did this. Nothing gave them away.

We were so afraid, Sister Presentación interjects. We called our mother superior. Should we stay? we asked. She said, Look in your heart and make a decision.

They stayed but it was not easy. Even the church was divided. At one meeting, Sister Presentación read a paper about the dangers of mining and a church congregant interrupted her. Shut up, he said. Stop talking this nonsense. These lies. It's all bullshit.

She kept speaking until she had nothing more to say.

You lie, the man said. This is not true.

The sisters could feel the anger, the uproar in the entire community. Hatred possessing people and robbing them of all reason. Even today, even in church. Some families no longer attend Mass. Those who do sit in pews only with people who think like they do.

When I have no more questions, the sisters walk me to the street where I catch a cab back to my hotel in Progresso. After dinner, I call Cesar Alvaranga, deputy mayor of Nueva Esperanza. He grew up nearby and has known the valleys and hills and rivers and the singing birds of the town his entire life. There were only dirt roads when he was a child, and in some places not even that. The clear air did not have even a speck of pollution because few people owned cars. That has changed, of course, he acknowledges, but some things remain as they were when he was a boy. Even today, few towns have bridges. People cross rivers leaping from one rock to the next. In the rainy season, the rivers become so full, people must wait until the water recedes. This is the life people have known. When the mine came, people were confused. They had lived here for generations without any kind of disruption. The most dangerous year was 2013, a time filled with dramatic events. Cesar remembers Perez speaking to him and other anti-mining activists and trying to seduce them with job offers.

I'm not trying to buy you, Perez told him, but you can ask me for whatever you want and I'll give it to you.

Cesar said nothing.

On August 16, 2013, he received threatening text messages warning him to support the mine or die. The threat scared him but he continued his opposition and took precautions by moving out of his house and staying with friends for nine months. His wife urged him to abandon the fight. Farming comes first, she said. We can't live like this. He told her, Don't worry; everything will be fine. But she had had enough. I can't live in fear, she said. She took their five children and left him to stay with her family.

He still feels threatened. Six months ago a car with tinted windows followed him and he was very afraid. These people have money and the support of the government. They invested millions and don't want to lose it. Cesar calls his wife but she doesn't answer. He misses her and the children and the peaceful times and the mountains. The land was ideal for cattle and crops, a source of life for the entire population. It remains a source of life for Cesar, but only in his memories.

July 12, 8 a.m. *Take a bus from Progresso to the town of Choluteca (takes a little more than six hours) not far from Nacaome where you will meet Pedro Landa's sister, Miriam Landa, a nun with Hermanas of Our Lady of the Holy Rosary. She works to raise awareness about mining in Nacaome.*

I arrive in Choluteca at midmorning. The wide streets without traffic stand in contrast to the congestion of Progresso and San Pedro Sula. A Pizza Hut takes up most of a small shopping center across the street from my hotel. After I check in, I meet Sister Miriam on the brick patio of her convent. Flowers in large clay pots line a stone walk and a wide lawn spreads out before us, bordered by rose bushes. As we sip Cokes, Sister Miriam tells me her opposition to mining began in the 1990s when she was a young nun in Peru. She saw how engineers diverted rivers to support mines and how the rivers eventually dried up. She saw mountains leveled and farmland reduced to dust. In 2013, Sister Miriam was transferred from Peru to the convent in Nacaome. Her brother Pedro told her about the mining in Nueva Esperanza and the opposition by Father Cesar and the sisters there. The death threats they received shocked her, and she became determined to support them without knowing that her activism would be needed in Nacaome.

Two years before Sister Miriam moved to Honduras, a wealthy woman in Tegucigalpa, Maria Gertrudis Valle, claimed that a mine that had been closed for decades in the town of El Transito, not far from Nacaome, was on land that belonged to her. People would later tell Sister Miriam that Valle was like a ghost. No one saw her, only her representatives. By the time Sister Miriam moved

to Honduras, the El Transito mine had been reopened and dynamite explosions began rocking the town, as many as seventy a
day, frightening children and scaring chickens and cows. Families
protested and Sister Miriam joined them. The activists were very
organized. Twenty people at a time blocked the road to the mine
twenty-four hours a day while others watched the road from the
hills and from the steeple of a church. If someone tried to break
through the protesters, an activist would ring the church bell,
bringing everyone from town to reinforce the blockade.

Some of the miners told the activists, We're here to inspect
the trees. Protesters told them, Good idea. All of us will work with
you, and the miners left. One day, some miners did sneak in and
the activists refused to let them leave. The police had to bring them
water and food for one week until the activists released them.

The mine's supporters tried to bribe protesters. You can make
money if you keep quiet, they said. Other pro-mining people
intimidated activists by chasing them in their cars. Despite the
threats, the opponents of the mine continued protesting, and,
heeding public pressure, Maria Gertrudis Valle finally shuttered
it in 2014.

The struggle, however, continues. Miners will sneak into the
closed mine, especially during storms when they think thunder
will conceal their use of dynamite. These disturbances don't bother
Sister Miriam as much as the behavior of the mayor of Nacaome
and the police. They've targeted her, she believes. When she goes to
them on church business, they say, Oh, you were with those people
who protested and rioted. You are an instigator.

Sister Miriam talks to her brother Pedro daily and he encourages her to stay strong. Some priests have told her they don't like his advocacy. He can be very straightforward and blunt, she knows, and some people don't respond well to that. She fears for his life—look what happened to Berta. Sister Miriam met Berta once at a rally. She was very humble yet enthusiastic as she bustled around laughing and smiling. Then she was killed. Sister Miriam doesn't worry about herself. She believes Pedro's life has more value because of his advocacy and she prays for him every day. If one of them must die for the work they do, she hopes the killers choose her.

July 16. *Leave Honduras. Since Choluteca is near the El Salvador border, it is easier for you to take a bus to San Salvador and catch a flight from there to the States.*

As I stand outside my hotel and wait for a bus to El Salvador, I receive a call from Father Cesar. He has been thinking of our talk and does not want me to leave Honduras with the wrong impression.

What would that be? I ask.

That I have hatred toward Lanier Perez, he says. I don't.

Outrage better describes his feelings of how Perez and others came into the community and poisoned the land and divided families. Outrage is very different from hate and anger, however, Father Cesar says. Hate is personal. You hate individuals. Outrage is directed towards their actions. You act from outrage. You protest.

Father Cesar protests. Pedro Landa protests. Sisters Presentación and Maria and Miriam protest and will continue to protest just as Berta did, her spirit inspiring them and giving strength. Berta had the gift of words, Father Cesar recalls. She spoke with unusual clarity and was very direct. She told him and other activists, Let's prepare ourselves because many of us will die. I don't know which one of us will be first, but one of us will be killed.

Behind the Walls

Seventeen orphans died the year Hogar de la Casa Corazon de la Misericordia (Home of the Heart of Mercy) opened in 1995. Its founder, Sister Sandau Izabele Hernandez, could do nothing. The children were sick with HIV/AIDS when they arrived. She drove them to a private clinic for medicine, but it was too late. In that sad time, Sister Sandau buried the children in plots in the public cemetery for the unidentified dead. The children had names but were unwanted—they had died of a terrifying disease, and that put them on par with people whose names no one knew or cared to learn: gang members, victims of gangs, drug addicts, and homeless people. The cemetery stood on the south side of the industrial city of San Pedro Sula, Honduras, about a thirty-minute drive from the orphanage. Gangs controlled the neighborhood. Sister Sandau would visit the graves before nightfall.

Over the years, attitudes changed. In 2010, the Ministry of Health began an HIV/AIDS program at the public hospital. Now the orphanage's twenty-five children have their blood tested every two months, no charge. Every one of them is HIV-positive but healthy. Also in 2010, a private cemetery donated two hundred plots to the orphanage. It provides a sense of family, Sister Sandau believes, to know she can bury the children together rather than scatter them among the unclaimed, unnamed, and unwanted bodies in the public cemetery. Of course, she does not want to see any more deaths. She will never forget one boy, Angel. He was eighteen months old when he arrived at the orphanage, abandoned by his family because he was HIV positive. He grew to love nature and animals, especially cows, and he was very affectionate. Whenever he walked outside, he'd pick flowers. "Here you are," he would say to Sister Sandau, and give her a daisy. Eventually he got so sick that his doctor decided he could no longer help him. "Remove Angel from the hospital," the doctor said. "There is nothing more I can do."

"Tell us what you want to eat," Sister Sandau told Angel as she drove him back to the orphanage. "You can have whatever you like, no restrictions." Angel prepared a menu every day and Sister Sandau and her colleague, laywoman Maria Laura Donaire, fulfilled his every whim: ice cream, spaghetti, watermelon, hamburgers, anything he wanted.

Angel lasted two months. When he understood he was dying, he became very afraid and wept throughout the day. He was just a child. What did heaven mean to him? He fought for each breath. "Go," Sister Sandau told him. "Don't worry. Let yourself go." He'd stop breathing, rally, and come back gasping for air. He was nine and looked terrified like someone drowning. He struggled to live. Then one afternoon he let go for the final time. Sister Sandau held his hands. To this day she still feels his fingers around her own.

Sister Sandau is forty-eight. She grew up with both her parents, but they worked, and as a child she was often left alone. Her older brother would take her on long walks. "Oh, wouldn't it be wonderful to gather all the lonely children in the world in one place?" she would ask him. At sixteen, she joined the Sisters of Mercy, drawn to the order because of its work with orphans. As a novice, she volunteered in hospitals and earned a nursing degree. When the HIV/AIDS crisis broke out in Honduras in the mid-1980s, she noticed an increase in children exiled to the street because of their disease and began working at a house for HIV/AIDS-afflicted children. She realized one house could not provide for all the HIV-positive children in need. With the support of the Sisters of Mercy, Sister Sandau raised money to open Hogar de la Casa Corazon de la Misericordia.

Like the children in her care, Sister Sandau knows loss. Her younger brother was strangled and shot in 2009. He was driving a bus and some men, presumably gang members, stopped him and kidnapped him. His tortured body was found later that day on the street. Sister Sandau has no idea why gangs would target him, but thinks it may be that he refused to pay an extortion fee. A year later, Sister Sandau's sister was kidnapped. She has not been seen since. Sister Sandau cares for her sister's daughter, now six.

Gangs have made Honduras one of the world's deadliest nations. It is estimated that about twenty-three thousand gang members are involved in turf wars and almost daily shoot-outs with police. Sixty percent of the country's gang members are concentrated in San Pedro Sula. Within the city, gang allegiance is split fairly evenly: about fifty-one percent of gang members, some

1,034, belong to Mara Salvatrucha, known as MS, while the remaining 1,001 form part of another gang, Barrio 18. The capital of Tegucigalpa and San Pedro Sula have the highest murder rates in the world outside war zones.

I arrived in Honduras to interview Sister Sandau in June 2016 as a freelance journalist for the *National Catholic Reporter*. On my first night in San Pedro Sula, I ate dinner in an all but empty Chinese restaurant across the street from my hotel. In the morning, the desk clerk warned me against taking a bus to Hogar de la Casa Corazon de la Misericordia. As an American, I would stand out, she said, and attract the attention of gangs. She recommended a cab driver she knew, Juan Carlos Diaz.

Juan Carlos pulled up in a small white car about an hour later. He was crisply dressed in slacks and a polo shirt. He knew the orphanage. A very good lady, he said of Sister Sandau. He asked if I'd had a pleasant night. I said I had and mentioned how so few people were in the Chinese restaurant.

"What time did you go?"

"I don't know. About six."

"That explains it."

Cab drivers like himself, Juan Carlos said, pay a daily fee to taxi companies for the use of their cars. They usually earn enough money before noon to cover the fee. Whatever fares result afterward the drivers keep. Gangs know that by five or six drivers have a lot of cash. Most cabs stop operating before then to avoid being robbed. People who rely on them finish their business early too.

"In San Pedro Sula, the restaurants are empty at night," Juan Carlos said. "HIV is not the only thing that kills here."

MS demands an eighty-five dollar "war tax" from cab drivers weekly. Most drivers establish savings accounts to cover medical bills should they be shot. The savings also go toward a holiday tax of nearly two hundred dollars that the gangs charge the week before Christmas.

Every afternoon after work, Juan Carlos drives home using a different route so gangs can't anticipate his itinerary. He calls his wife and tells her he is on his way. She watches for him, raising the garage door at the exact moment he pulls into the driveway so he does not need to stop, get out of his car, and open the door himself. That would take too much time and attract attention. He never knows who might follow him. In 2012, before he began driving a cab, Juan Carlos owned a small clothing business. Two members of MS approached him one morning when he dropped his two daughters off at an elementary school.

"You have a house," one of them said. "You want to keep it?" He demanded an eighty-five-dollar initiation fee followed by weekly payments of fifteen dollars. They were children, Juan Carlos thought of the two gang members. Fourteen, fifteen years old at most and they rode bicycles. Of course, someone older had sent them, but not much older. The principal knew the boys because they had been students but dropped out. The one who did all the talking had asked the principal about Juan Carlos and he told them when Juan Carlos drove his daughters to school. It was tell them or get shot.

Juan Carlos knew a boy who attended parochial school. He belonged to MS. His mother asked Juan Carlos to pray for him. He's with the wrong crowd, she said. He disappeared and a while later the police found his body. He died when he tried to collect money in Barrio 18's turf. Eighteen years old.

Gangs often approach families and demand a child, a daughter most often, to use in the induction of new gang members. If a family refuses, they will be killed and their daughter kidnapped. Juan Carlos worries about his oldest girl. She is eleven, almost a teenager. The young men of MS may notice her. A handyman Juan Carlos knows and who used to help around the house disappeared for two weeks one month. When he returned, he looked awful, haggard and unshaven. MS had taken his daughter, he said. When they finished with her, they sent him a message. Come pick up your girl. She was dead, in pieces. The handyman wept. "My girl torn apart," he cried. "My girl torn apart."

He showed Juan Carlos a photograph of her before her death.

"Attractive girl," Juan Carlos said.

"Gangs have always been a problem," Maria Laura Donaire tells me.

She prefers her middle name and asks me to call her Laura. She has worked at the orphanage since it opened. She volunteered at another HIV home for children years before and it was there she met Sister Sandau.

"The children know all about violence," Laura continues. "They'll come back from school and say, 'On the bus we looked out the window and saw a dead guy.' or 'We saw someone shot.' or 'We heard a man was found dead on the street.' It's the talk of the day."

Despite the problems they pose, Laura believes the gangs respect the orphanage. Perhaps they know someone sick with HIV/AIDS. Perhaps they are afraid they'll get ill if they come too close. Whatever the case, gangs have never attempted to break in.

Not long after Laura started at Hogar de la Casa Corazon de la Misericordia, Sister Sandau noticed that the orphans sometimes returned home from school depressed, especially around the holidays. Their teacher might say, "Make a card for Mother's Day." But who would the orphans make cards for? They needed a parent, Sister Sandau realized. She told Laura to attend all school and sporting events, help the children with their homework, and to take them shopping.

"Do all the things a mother would do," Sister Sandau said. "You will be their mother."

For more than twenty years, Laura has filled that role. She has seen children come and go. One girl, Alva, about twenty, works as an accountant and attends college. She visits often and still calls Laura "mother." Another boy, Milton, moved out at thirteen. He works at a gas station and has an apartment. He also visits every week.

"Mama!" he shouts when he sees Laura.

When she takes the children shopping, a fruit vendor always stops her.

"Are all these boys and girls yours? Really?"

"Yes," she says, "all mine." She has to be careful where she and the children travel. Gangs post scouts at the entrances of every district with a banner of MS or Barrio 18. The scout will alert the gang of unfamiliar cars entering their turf. Laura and the children take buses. So far, the gangs have taken no notice of a middle-aged woman with a half-dozen boys and girls.

Laura insists she has no favorites among the children, however, a few of them have stolen her heart. One boy, Michael, was so small and malnourished when she first saw him, she didn't think he would survive. His mother had abandoned him to his grandfather. His grandfather didn't know what to do with him and turned him over to the orphanage. He had a skin infection from not being bathed. He drank one ounce of milk at a time. A year later, when his grandfather visited, Michael didn't recognize him. The grandfather took Michael from Laura and held him; Michael cried and the grandfather became furious. He did not understand the bond between Laura and the children.

Michael is nine now and doing very well—too well. He is the most mischievous boy. He also has problems at school, doesn't pay attention, and doesn't study. He will say he's doing homework, but when Laura looks in his folder she will find only blank paper.

Then there's Kenia. She had no birth certificate, nothing to identify her. Laura approached the mayor of Comayagua, her hometown, and explained the situation. He allowed her to register Kenia under her name, Donaire. Laura told him that although she was not her biological child, she was a child of her heart.

Laura met Kenia's mother when she brought Kenia to the

orphanage in 1996. Her mother was very straightforward. She worked as a maid and had to support three children and felt she could not afford Kenia. She said she would turn over her other children, too, but never did. She visited Kenia twice, and then Laura didn't see her again for three years until they ran into each other on the street one day. Kenia's mother invited Laura to lunch and asked about Kenia. She explained she had not visited because she was sick and busy with work. She needed stomach surgery. "I know my girl is in the best hands," she said.

Laura never heard from her again.

Kenia is now twenty and will leave soon. The children can stay at the orphanage as long as they want, provided they attend school. When Kenia finishes her studies at the University of San Pedro Sula, she will move out, like Alva the accountant.

Laura recalls one boy's mother who dropped by a year after she gave him up. She appeared weak and seemed very cold toward her son, maybe because she had no energy. Her son was too young to recognize her. She got very ill after she left and two of her sisters asked Laura if they could take the boy to visit her. She was dying, they said, but the orphanage, Laura explained, did not have permission from the courts to release him to the family, even temporarily. Instead, she shot a video of the baby and gave it to them. After the mother's sisters showed it to her she died. For a long time after her death, the boy called, "Anna, Anna." Perhaps that was his mother's name. Or maybe he was calling, "Mama, Mama." Did he sense she had died? Laura doesn't know.

No child has challenged Laura. No child has said, "You're not my mother." The other children tell new arrivals that this place is their new home and in this home, we call Laura "mom."

Sometimes, while the children attend school, Laura contemplates a mural of a tree on a wall near the kitchen. The leaves of the tree hold the names of deceased orphans. Their deaths were so sad. Laura was very attached to them, and to a six-month-old girl who also died. Laura and Sister Sandau went to the hospital to help care for her at the request of her doctor.

"Look after this girl," the doctor said. "She is very sick with HIV. Her mother died. We have too many patients for our nurses."

The girl recovered but then got worse. Laura would hold her and sing her lullabies. The girl sought Laura's breasts for milk. Laura tried to feed her with a bottle, but the girl rejected it. On her last night, the child appeared to be in agony. Laura told her, "Let go. You'll be in a better place. Your mother is calling you and you need to be with her." The girl was in pain a long time. Such a tiny little thing. Laura thinks the girl knew her mother was gone and was looking for her. So Laura repeated, "Let go. Your mother is calling," and the girl turned to her and died.

Kenia has lived at the orphanage longer than the other children and many of the girls come to her for advice. Eleven-year-old Dulce Rodriguez often speaks to Kenia. Dulce's grandmother brought her when she was four. Her grandmother told her, "This is your new home." After her first day, Dulce adjusted. She felt OK but she still missed her grandmother. Her grandmother visits twice a year. Dulce knows little about her mother; she died in childbirth.

Her name was Gladys Maribel Castillo Hernandez. Dulce knows nothing more.

"Maybe that is all you need to know," Kenia suggested. Although she never knew her mother, Kenia feels proud of her. Laura told her she was very brave and hardworking and that she loved Kenia very, very much. In moments of solitude, Kenia thinks about her and wonders: Is she alive? Is she OK? Laura has told her that she looks just like her mother. Kenia does not know how to imagine this. When she observes herself in a mirror she does not see her mother, only herself.

Over the years, Kenia has seen many children leave. Some were adopted. Others rejoined their families. One girl dropped out of school and ran away. It's sad to see them go. Kenia's best friend left to live with her family. They've known each other since infancy. Kenia hears from her from time to time.

When she was six years old, Kenia became friends with Johnny. Johnny had been abandoned by his family. He could not walk until he was five. In school, he would fall asleep. Kenia would wait until he woke up and they'd leave class together. One day, some children didn't want to be around them. They said they were sick. Kenia told Laura.

"Tell them they don't need to be afraid because you take medicine," Laura said.

Another day after school, Johnny wet himself and needed a diaper. Kenia changed him and calmed him down. That was a long time ago. It was the first time she had helped someone. No one asked her to change him, she just did it. She remembers when he died. He was sick and crying, and then one afternoon he stopped crying, stopped breathing. He was nine.

Kenia plans to be a journalist and cover health issues. She wants to live by herself for a while and be independent. It feels odd to think that one day she will leave the orphanage and Laura will no longer be there to remind her to take her medicine, eat the right foods, avoid the influence of gangs. She does not need to be reminded, but Laura can't stop being a mother. Kenia understands. She imagines her own mother would have behaved the same way.

At night, I follow Sister Sandau through the orphanage as she does a security check. She stops at the front gate. Locked. Interior corridors connect the orphanage's three buildings so no one has to walk outside and risk confronting a gang. She looks up, squinting through her glasses at the concertina wire stretched along the top of the walls. While the gangs have never approached the orphanage, they have stopped some of the children at school and offered them candy, snacks, anything to lure them into their orbit. Sister Sandau doesn't know what she would do if a gang member confronted her. Call the police? No, gangs pay off the police. The police are so corrupt, what good would it do to call them? She does not want to be shot, but it might happen. How long will she live? In Honduras, who can say? Only God knows.

"No one is safe," she says. If she had her druthers, Sister Sandau would work only with newborns. Infants are a blank slate. Older children come to the orphanage distressed. They've lost their family, friends, and home. Relatives rarely if ever visit them. They scare Sister Sandau with what little they know. They drink bathwater as they would bottled water. They don't think to change their clothes. They speak in slang. Long before they came here, they had been denied a proper upbringing.

Some of the children return to their families. These reunions do not always work. One time, a mother wanted to regain custody of her son, but the courts turned her down and placed the boy at Hogar de la Casa Corazon de la Misericordia. Over time, an uncle arranged to care for the boy and the orphanage released him. The uncle returned the boy to his mother. Months later, the mother was shot. Sister Sandau does not know what happened to the boy.

Looking in on the preteen dormitory, she sees twelve-year-old David Ulloa sleeping. He has been at the orphanage since he was two months old. Sometimes his grandmother and aunt visit but they haven't come by for a while now. He knows nothing about his parents. His mother died giving birth to him. At first, when Sister Sandau told him he was HIV positive, he didn't believe he was sick. He seems to understand now, and it scares him. "Can I live a normal life?" he asks. "Will I ever leave here?" He feels fine, yet he knows the virus could kill him. Sister Sandau tells him, "As long as you take your medicine, you'll be fine." Still, his eyes tell her he is afraid. Two of David's close friends, Carlos and Carla, left the orphanage to live with their grandmothers. David misses them. He told Sister Sandau he feels their absence. Like ghosts. They are here, but gone.

Sister Sandau glances in a dorm for children thirteen and older. Here Rebecca Pineda sleeps. She's twenty. She has been at the orphanage since she was five. Some of her aunts visit once a year but no one else. Her mother died years ago. Sister Sandau has no idea about her father. Rebecca told her that she worries about leaving, about facing the world alone. Something may happen. She may get hurt, get killed.

"I'll miss the love I get here," Rebecca said.

Sister Sandau finishes her rounds by looking in on her niece. Sound asleep. In the morning, she will attend school with the other children. Like many of them, she does not remember her mother, although Sister Sandau talks about her all the time. Perhaps one day this information will feel like memories. To the girl's questions about what happened to her, Sister Sandau says only, "God called her away." Sometimes she dreams of her brother and sister. They come to visit the orphanage and wait outside for her to open the gate, then disappear.

Kissing her niece on her forehead, Sister Sandau sighs. Hours from now, the sun will rise, and with it the possibility of new orphans. She receives very little notice. The police or a family just show up with a child. Some of the children will be older, others mere toddlers. Sister Sandau will embrace them all. They will call Laura mother, and will look to Kenia as they would an older sister. They will live and grow behind the walls, spared for now the troubles outside.

Call of the Narcocorrido

5 p.m., June 29, 2009

In the *PM* newsroom—across from faded purple- and brown-striped cubicles where reporters sit amid tacked-up centerfolds and layouts for the day's cover story of a man who had been shot, his body discarded in a ditch—two men, a photographer and assistant editor, listen to the strains of a narcocorrido drifting from a police scanner. The vague, shrill discord of accordions and a brass band echoes in the glass office until a burst of distortion shatters the ill-begotten melody and imposes a staticky silence. They know in the expanding quiet that someone will die tonight.

When and where the execution will happen, they cannot say yet. Perhaps in five minutes on a dirt lane beneath power lines heavy with dangling sneakers; perhaps in an hour in a van swerved to a stop, the spewed rocks and dust still unsettled even after the gunfire has ceased and neighbors will come to peer with accustomed caution through barred windows; perhaps after nightfall on the stony ground of a hill beneath sheets of laundry that, when billowed by winds, will rise like theatrical curtains to display the vast expanse of Juárez—its gated homes where dogs bark and loll in the heat, its tree-lined streets where kids play pickup soccer games, and the dirt lanes stretching toward barbed-wire fences that block entrance to the state of Texas just beyond the muddy band of the Rio Bravo.

They do know that the two-year-long drug war raging in this desert city of 1.5 million kills an average of nine people a day. The Mexican government sent in the army to help quell the violence. For two months, the number of violent deaths dropped dramatically. But in June, it spiked back up.

"Before, there were gunfights in the street with automatic weapons," said Juárez Mayor Jose Reyes Ferriz. "Now they kill with 9-millimeter handguns. Before, they drove around the city with AK-47s. They can't now. But they are still fighting. They fight all the way down to small-time distributors killing one another."

Were this not brazen enough, the competing drug cartels, La Linea (the local crime syndicate) and Chapo (an outside group vying for dominance), both monitor the same radio frequencies as the cops and journalists and broadcast the narcocorrido, a twisted version of classical Mexican folk music, as a warning to the authorities, ambulance crews, and reporters alike: *Stay away from where killings often happen or you might see something you wished you hadn't.*

"Every day I have nightmares," says thirty-four-year-old assistant editor Eduardo Huizar.

The scanner stutters into a firecracker staccato of electrical commotion, then the voice of a federale complaining to another officer: "No, not again." The corrido pierces the static in response, then disappears with an abruptness suggesting impatience. The photographer, fifty-seven-year-old Ernesto Rodriguez, glances at Eduardo.

"They are playing with us," he says.

The game has been a brutal one for Juárez journalists. Mexico is the deadliest assignment in the Americas and among the deadliest in the world. According to the New York-based Committee to Protect Journalists, dozens of reporters have been killed or disappeared since 2000. Many of the victims had recently reported on police ties to cartels. Others are suspected of working with the cartels, accepting drug money, but it's hard to be sure because the killings are barely investigated. Despite the fact that a special federal prosecutor for crimes against journalists was appointed two years ago, none of the murders of journalists—not one—has been solved. Some attacks target entire newsrooms—in at least two cases, grenades have been thrown at newspaper offices—but most single out individuals. Juárez reporters receive threatening mobile phone messages claiming to come from a drug cartel. El Diario crime reporter Armando Rodríguez Carreón was one. When he reported the threat to the Chihuahua state prosecutor's office, he was told he should leave town as there was no way of guaranteeing his safety. Rodríguez finally went back to work after a two-month exile and was gunned down on November 13, 2008, as he was taking his children to school. There were more telephone threats against journalists during his funeral the next day. The number of journalists leaving the region—and even the country—has soared.

Still, a handful of radio and television stations and four daily newspapers cover the violence. PM, one of those dailies, was founded in 2005 specifically to cover the growing violence in all its gruesome detail. The name is a promise from the editors to have copies on the street no later than noon (every day but Sunday) with graphic photos of the killings from the night before. Their front pages garishly display bloody bodies with smaller inset photos of smiling, nearly naked women with big breasts. Inside, more photos of bodies fill the pages—dead men and smiling, nearly naked women, including a centerfold. With a circulation of sixty-five thousand, it has become the most popular daily newspaper in the city. But even a tabloid that feeds off the mayhem takes precautions.

Like most Juárez journalists, PM reporters and photographers no longer use bylines in crime stories. Some writers at other papers tone down their language, using, for example, "armed men" rather than "gunmen." Some will not identify a cartel responsible for a murder unless a government official goes on record. Some media simply report the barest of facts, limiting their reports to news releases put out by authorities, with no analysis or investigation. In most places, journalists don't even report on killings they witness. However, the journalists at PM have vowed not to turn away. So on this humid June evening, two months after the Mexican Army entered the city, Eduardo pages through photographs of the dead, the faces he sees in his dreams, while Ernesto ventures out, every day between four p.m. and midnight to shoot the photographs that make those nightmares reality.

6:15 p.m.

Ernesto into his cell phone: Anything going on in the street?
Reporter on the other end: Tranquil.
Ernesto: Still?
Reporter: Still.

6:30 p.m.

Ernesto waits for the night's anticipated execution by settling behind his desk and reviewing his photographs from the evening before. No one dreams like Eduardo. He does his best not to think about what he sees. He downloads his photos:

A kid on his back. Tattoos. A leg turned sideways on the pavement. White tank top, socks, shoes.

Family of a dead man, sitting staring at the body covered by a sheet.

Shattered glass, two dead men in the front seats of a car slumped together cheek to cheek.

Blood-spattered yellow wall. Against it a woman, blue dress, black boots. Legs tanned from the sun. Paddy's Pub and Brewery logo on a shot-up, blood-splattered hat.

Sometimes the images stay with him. Like those two dead kids last year. Both shot in the head. White shirts, blood on their necks. Eyes swollen shut. Gold chains. A lot comes to mind. He is a parent and has grandchildren. Remember the woman, her head crushed by a bus? She was taking her son to school. Ernesto's wife took their kids to school. He shakes his head. Don't think.

7:15 p.m.

The police call a news conference to tout an arrest. Ernesto understands the PR value of a "perp walk": showing off the work of a police force known mostly for corruption. This year alone, eleven Juárez officers were arrested for carrying drugs in their patrol cars. A shooting between members of the Mexican Army and Juárez cops exploded in the streets when officers refused to take part in a sweep for illegal arms and drugs. Not even the mayor trusts the city police, so the army and federal police are here essentially to supplant local officers until a new force can be recruited and trained. About seven thousand five hundred soldiers patrol the streets, putting up roadblocks to search cars, raiding houses for weapons and drugs, and arresting alleged cartel members. A military officer now serves as police chief; others run sections of the police department and the city jail.

At the police station, the perp—a handcuffed twenty-year-old man accused of murder—stands in a corner, two masked officers on either side. Fluorescent lighting pours over him, illuminating his oiled and spiked hair. The officers parade him across the polished tile floor as cameras click and flash. Ernesto walks outside with the other photographers and waits for the next perp. Cool air floats down from distant mountains, gathers heat in the valley, and settles heavily around the police station. The waiting seems to last forever. Young women in short skirts walk past, and an officer asks no one in particular if they like women who dance on tables. Ernesto smirks and helps a TV cameraman look for a screw that fell out of his tripod, while other photographers discuss winners of the Robert Capa award. Time feels stalled by the humidity weighing on the lethargic city. Why isn't there anything yet? What does this quiet mean? Another slow curl of air drifts through the parking lot, followed by spitting static on Ernesto's police scanner, and then a voice that says simply, "Z 59"—code for a homicide by organized crime. Ernesto runs to his car, camera bag flopping against his hip, the other photographers fanning out behind him in the parking lot. The night makes sense now.

7:30 p.m.

Eduardo begins work at two a.m. so at this hour he sleeps. But his mind races—like Ernesto speeding, pulse throbbing, to the latest execution. Even before Ernesto arrives, Eduardo sees the dead in his dreams. Their shocked faces now his face. He sees himself executed or dying of a drug overdose; he sees his killer cut off his head. Blood rings his dreams.

7:45 p.m.

Ernesto steers with his elbows, in each hand a cell phone pressed against his ears. One phone connects him to PM reporters, the other with journos from other media outlets—TV2, El Diario,

Televisión Chihuahua, Televisión Juárez, Canal 44. He coordinates with them so they all arrive at the murder scene together. On this shift Ernesto has seniority. He knows the streets, the fastest routes.

"A killing, body in a car maybe," Ernesto says into both phones. "Have to confirm."

"You going?" a reporter on the other end asks.

"Yes, I'm going. Unless maybe they're just drunk and passed out."

"You think?"

"Kidding, man. Get there."

At one time they competed to be first. But then the cartels began threatening journalists. *How do you get here so fast?* an anonymous caller would ask. *Is the other cartel giving you information?* Now journalists arrive together to prevent being singled out.

Ernesto speeds down commercial streets beneath signs promoting restaurants (tacos y gorditas) and churches (centro de restauración dios de fuego) through a low haze of dust and smog when he catches the red flashes of police lights bouncing off squat, cinderblock homes. Soldiers mingle with the police, their presence a warning to the killers not to come back for an ambush. Ernesto parks, grabs his camera bag, and walks down a narrow alley taped off by the police. A glut of photographers converges on either side of him.

"Do we know how many bodies?" Ernesto asks.

"Just one," a photographer from El Diario tells him.

Ernesto reaches for his zoom lens. He peers through the view-finder, nose flattened against the camera. There, in shadows cast by streetlights, lies the body of a man in a puddle of muddy water. Someone thought he deserved no better. Ernesto begins shooting, his flash popping in the dark, washing the body in bursts of white light. He does not like what's happening in Juárez, but he enjoys taking pictures. Every crime scene has a particular challenge: Will the police let him take pictures? Is the body visible? Has it already been covered with a sheet? These questions occupy him, keep him focused.

A police officer kneels next to the corpse and inspects the ground. Ernesto waits for him to move. He has asked for other assignments. For a while he covered politics and was very comfortable. But then he was reassigned to the crime beat. He was needed for the crude reality he captures with his camera, the brutal artistry of his work. The cop stands, and Ernesto snaps the frame.

8:30 p.m.

In his pocket, the police scanner sputters. Ernesto lowers his camera, listens. The second narcocorrido of the night plays, stops. A cockroach scuttles near Ernesto's boots, antennae twitching, freezes.

"Z 59," a dispatcher says seconds later.

The music, this time, not a warning—or foretelling of doom—but a statement of fact. Another death, the smooth bone of completion, waits only for the cameras. Ernesto runs to his car, the music in his head drowning out the crunch of the insect crushed under his boot. A hymn to the deceased.

Midnight, June 30

Ernesto submits his pictures:

- Francisco Hernandez Gonzalez, 35. Shot eight times. On the street. Pistol. T-shirt hiked halfway up his chest. Bloated belly. Jeans, tennis shoes. Orange cones near the body indicate the number of shell casings found. Girlfriend shot in the foot. Not fatal.
- Twenty-five- to twenty-six-year-old victim. No name. Pistol. Shot five times. Twice in back of the head, once in the left temple, twice in the back. What's left of his face a ruined prism melting in moonlight.
- Parking lot of an Oxxo convenience store. Body of a man, twenty-five to thirty, inside a Ford Explorer, head hanging out the passenger window. As if asleep. Car still running. Eight shots. Crowd of young people. Laughter, drinking. Babies bawl. Rotating police lights bruise trees purple. An old man walks past, his cane tap, tap, tapping as he goes without pausing.

12:30 a.m.

Ernesto drives home, eats with his wife. She always waits for him. Concerned. She watches TV news and sees the murders. Knows the dangers of his job. She's always alone. Nervous, afraid. *How's everything?* she asks him. He reassures her. *OK. Three dead tonight.* Slumped in a chair before the TV, he lets loose the adrenaline rush of the evening. A gradual draining of energy that leaves him deflated and adrift until he sleeps.

1:30 a.m.

Eduardo leaves for the half-hour drive to work. His wife has asked him to get a different job, but there wouldn't be any options. Juárez once had a strong economy but no one comes here now. They are afraid of being killed or extorted by the cartels. Eduardo has had no trouble with the cartels. Still he worries. They killed Armando after all. If they killed him, they will kill anybody. Who's next? When he drives at night, Eduardo fears he might see something and the killers will chase him and shoot him. When he comes to a red light, he slows, coasts through the intersection without stopping. He looks left and right with the hypervigilance of a bird, not allowing his eyes to linger on any one thing too long. Police sometimes pull him over, but always let him go. They understand. Some *PM* staffers move repeatedly to avoid being identified. *What is the point?* Eduardo wonders. *The cartels know everything. They can get information. They know who we are, where we are.* Especially Eduardo's supervisor, *PM* editor Alejandro Tellez. He receives threats from the cartels when they don't like a story or a picture.

One time, a caller complained that *PM* photographers never took photos of Chapo graffiti. "Write some," Alejandro said. The next day a caller told him where the cartel had sprayed graffiti. "As long as I see it published," the caller told him, "you're no longer at risk." Alejandro sent two photographers. When they arrived, he received another call. "Are your photographers in a white car? One tall, one short? We're looking at them. No police will come. Take all the pictures you need." Since then, Alejandro wears a bulletproof vest.

Eduardo marvels that Alejandro would continue to work at all. It is like a guerilla war. The invading cartel has spent a lot of money to dominate the Juárez drug trade. The local cartel has a lot to lose. Neither one will give up. Eduardo warns his kids, *Don't tell anyone I work for a newspaper. Don't bring friends to the house unless I know their parents. Don't tell anyone when we go out.* They usually don't have visitors. They usually stay home.

His brother used to teach English to elementary school students. The local cartel demanded money otherwise it would start killing kids. The school closed. It turned out not to be the cartel, but a group posing as the cartel. The real cartel cut off the heads of the extortionists for using their name. Bad people killed by bad people. *It's still killing*, Eduardo says. Now his brother sells burritos on the street.

2 a.m.

Eduardo studies the evening's photographs so he can write headlines. He has used all the verbs he knows for *killed*. Eduardo hates to admit it, but after a while it just becomes another body. It gets more difficult when the cartels call. They know when the paper goes to press. Sometimes they wait until the last minute. Then they phone in with a body, forcing Eduardo to redo the design. He cannot say for certain it is the cartels, but who else would call? They are very professional with precise information. They want to be the cover story.

Are we part of the problem? Eduardo asks himself. Alejandro says: No. We show the reality. This happens on a daily basis in Juárez. We can't pretend it doesn't. We give the truth. We don't elaborate. Still Eduardo wonders, *Are we advertising for the cartels?* These questions haunt him. He looks once more at Ernesto's photographs, clears his mind of distractions. He can't help what he dreams. But awake, he has a paper to get out.

PM, Tuesday edition, June 30

Front page: 116 MINORS ASSASSINATED IN 18 MONTHS
Page 2: EXECUTED IN PARKING LOT
Page 5: ELIMINATED!

Noon, June 30, San Rafael Cemetery
Wind sends dust devils across rocky ground, swirling scraps of grass, pink images of the Virgin Mary sold by vendors. Backhoes rumble. Holes are dug and filled, first with the discarded water bottles of the diggers (portable radios tuned to El Paso rock stations), and soon the nameless dead. *Fosa común,* the common hole. Two bodies in a trench, numbered 13618348 and 41349, both killed June 16.

Then the named dead in a section set aside for cartel victims:
Manuel de Jesus Perez Urbina
02 June 09
Enrique Morales Samudio

14 June 09

Maria Elva Rivera

02 June 09

Faustino J. Perez Martinez

05 June 09

Sergio Antiglares

14 June 09

Crosses as erect as sentries dot burial mounds eroded by the wind. Empty bottles of Tecate lay piled beneath sun-faded photos, one after the other, smiling. The handiwork of assassins begets cross after white cross far into the horizon. Heat-distortion, a low haze. No pity. Eduardo's nephew lies here, dead of an overdose. Also a sister-in-law and his father-in-law. You talk to a mechanic, a shopkeeper, they'll tell you about a brother, a sister who has been shot. Eduardo has had friends, neighbors killed. In some way, he's always dealing with death.

4:30 p.m.

No music this time. Just a federale on the scanner announcing a homicide downtown. Almost immediately, Ernesto's cell phones begin ringing. Rumors fly. Other photographers tell him the dead man is the popular local labor leader Géminis Ochoa. Ernesto can't believe it. Ochoa helped poor vendors get permission to set up stalls downtown. He denounced police corruption just days ago and now he has been shot. Was it the police? Or a crime of opportunity? Maybe his enemies knew the murder would be blamed on the authorities. Someone other than Ernesto must figure that out. He grabs his camera. An agitated crowd of three hundred people has already gathered downtown in the hot blaze of afternoon near the patina-stained statue of General Vicente Guerrero. The police unfurl rolls of yellow tape. Ernesto parks his car and runs to a cluster of taco stands across from where the body lies sprawled, face-first on the pavement at the bottom of the steps of a pawn shop, blood pooled beneath it. Police drag away a weeping woman who tries to reach the dead man. Smiling children jostle with their parents to glimpse the corpse. A man rushes toward the prostrate Ochoa from the other side, cursing the police as murderers. The police pin him down.

"You left him to die," the man screams. "You always leave them to die."

"They only know how to kill people!" a woman shouts.

"Viva El Che! Viva Géminis!"

The laughing curiosity of gawkers switches to a sudden rage, as if the crowd had been waiting for just this moment. Tempers snapping like crossed live wires. Uncoiling in one motion, the crowd rushes the police, and Ernesto rolls with it, staying on the edge so as not to get trampled, keeping his shutter clicking as more police and soldiers converge on the sudden rampage.

"Respect a man who loved so many people!" they shout. "You only know how to kill people!"

The dead man lies alone in his blood, a single woman kneeling beside him in that pool, head bowed, her hands reaching out to the body.

The outrage spends itself as quickly as it began. Perhaps from the heat. Perhaps from grief. Perhaps from the sense of futility that incessant corruption breeds. People stop cursing and recede like an ebb tide, as if propelled backward by invisible hands. Muffled weeping, the undercurrent of their defeat. The police tape off more areas, forcing the crowd to move farther away. A vendor hawks fajitas. Beside him, a man displays used shirts on a fence. An elderly woman on a bicycle asks why the road is blocked and mutters at the inconvenience. The coroner's van arrives.

"Will there be peace?" a man asks no one in particular.

Ernesto lowers his camera. "It will take a while," he tells the man when no one else answers him.

"They'll never find who did this."

"I know," Ernesto says.

6 p.m., July 1

Eduardo rides with the Mexican military to see Juárez through their eyes. While he waits for the comandante outside the police station, he overhears a woman tell an officer about a man who tried to extort money from her. He told her to "invest" her money with him or he would cut off her hands. The police arrested the man, but now tell her they have no evidence to hold him, and he will be released in fifteen minutes.

"I will lose my hands," the woman says.

Eduardo watches her walk away, head up, arms at her sides. She could be his mother. Two pickup trucks filled with green-uniformed Mexican soldiers pull up to the curb. The comandante sits in the front passenger seat of the first vehicle and waves Eduardo over. He gets in the backseat as the comandante explains that tonight they will patrol downtown and nearby barrios where a lot of drug dealers work. They will stay close to Avenue 16 de Septiembre, a main drag.

"I know this area," Eduardo says. "It's very rough."

"Let's see what it's like tonight," the comandante says.

They drive west through downtown, meandering to unpaved side streets that lead into western Juárez, the oldest part of the city, the land increasingly rocky and uneven. The sky turns gray, then orange as the sun sets, making the dry scrub grass look ablaze. To the north, the Wells Fargo Bank of El Paso and the Camino Real Hotel turn golden.

"We are trained for war," the comandante says. "We like helping the community, but sometimes the people don't help. They go under the tape, ruin the crime scene. They want to hug the dead."

Over the radio, the dispatcher announces a suspected suicide attempt with a knife.

"A knife?" the comandante asks. "Not a gun?"

"Cutting their wrist," the driver says.

They drive farther, down dirt roads gouged and pitted from heavy rains. Lurching in his seat, the comandante receives a report of a stolen car that was abandoned nearby. He tells the driver the address, but few of the streets have names. The driver asks boys playing soccer for directions. They point downhill. But that road turns into a dead end. The driver asks a man selling tacos if he knows the address. He points the way they had come. The driver switches on the siren, but no cars pull over for him as he races back.

After forty minutes, they find the right spot. Families stand outside their homes as the soldiers deploy on the street. A woman carries water in buckets, the child beside her in pants cinched tight by rope. Dogs bark, restrained by heavy chains. The comandante follows a path up a hill, slipping on the loose stones. When he reaches the top, he sees the remains of the stolen car. A white 1998 Nissan Altima. The seats have been ripped apart and the dashboard removed. The rear doors stand open. The comandante looks inside. Nothing. A soft wind blows. Trees stand in shadows beneath a darkening sky. The hum of generators mixes with the buzz saw sound of cicadas and makes the air sound alive. The comandante opens the trunk: Nothing. No bodies.

"We see a lot of abandoned cars," the comandante tells Eduardo. "They are used for robberies. A gang then dismantles the car. Or maybe someone stole it for parts."

They walk back down the hill to the pickup. Another report comes over the radio: two gunshots called in. Then the dispatcher changes that to a man who has been shot three times. After a few seconds, the dispatcher alters the report again to a mugging, no shots fired. Nothing. The comandante wonders about the quiet. Why has he not seen clusters of young men on street corners? It can be like that—one sector calm while another explodes.

"I feel good serving here, but you see how complicated it is," the comandante tells Eduardo. "Juárez is like a monster. It keeps mutating."

5:30 p.m., July 4

The music plays. Ernesto runs to his car.

Homicide No. 1: Meraz Binaga, 52, shot in stomach and left thigh.

5:55 p.m. El Gran Hero district. Gray skies. Graffiti-smeared wall.

Scene: "Luis, get down," a woman tells her son perched on a fence. A dog pisses.

"Is it a man?" Luis asks.

"I don't know," his mother says.

Soundtrack: On Ernesto's car radio, Ringo Starr sings "Photograph." 92.3 FM, The Fox, El Paso.

Homicide No. 2: Victoria Justinian, 45, in a black Toyota Corolla. (Like my car, Ernesto says to himself.)

7 p.m. Nine shots fired.

Scene: Victoria's left arm flops out from beneath a sheet on the gurney. Gravel clings to her fingers. In an apartment, the sound of a washing machine swishing, then water pumping. Rinse cycle. Funeral directors call the scene: Are they dead, how many shots? What is the name? The directors will call the family, offer services.

Soundtrack: Peter Gabriel, "Sledgehammer."

Interlude.

Ernesto stops at a gas station. Chats with the attendant. Across the street, a carnival. Children wave to him from a Ferris wheel. A rainbow constellation of colored lights.

Homicide No. 3: Antonio Gonzalez Salazar, 40. Beneath a light pole.
8 p.m. Four shots.
Scene: *I want to be* Elías Calles district. A baby sits in a stroller beside a hollowed-out, abandoned building, no roof. A house-lined road stretches downhill, empty. A colleague from *El Diario* asks Ernesto to let him take his picture.
Soundtrack: The Eagles, "Hotel California."

Homicides No. 4 and No. 5: Around the corner of a church, Aztec Iglesia. 9 p.m. Two dead. Guadalupe Lopez Ortega, 29, and Armando, 25, no last name. Ten to twelve shots fired.
Scene: A woman holds up her son for a better look. A man sells tacos within the crime scene. Businesses in the area include McDonald's, Office Depot, and Abarrotes las India. Ernesto orders four tacos and two quesadillas.
Soundtrack: Heart, "Barracuda."

Homicide No. 6: 10 p.m. Very far, not worth the drive. Scene: Ernesto returns to the office, downloads his photos. "I ate too much," he says to no one. Soundtrack: The Rolling Stones, "Beast of Burden."

5:30 a.m., July 6

Eduardo lays out the paper (his screensaver: a woman in a bra and black panties).

Page 3: Two dead, domestic dispute. Fight between neighbors.

Page 4: A person killed on Saturday.

Page 5: A killing in Colonia Granjero district. One dead.

Page 6: A man shot to death in a barrio outside the city. Cutline: *At point-blank range and without mercy.*

3 p.m., July 7

Ernesto dresses for work in a gray polo shirt and jeans. He remembers when student protests were the only problems in Juárez. Social leaders, agitators against the government. Maybe gangs, but no guns. Chains at most. Never this type of assassination. You could walk the streets, no problem. Have no fear, calm.

The last two years have been intense. Dangerous. In May, he was threatened by a group that came from the south of Mexico and tried to extort him for one hundred dollars a month. He moved to El Paso for four weeks. They knew things about him. They knew the kind of clothes he wore. They had a unit prepared to assassinate him. They were exploiting the violence, using it as cover to extort him. When he left Juárez for El Paso, they stopped calling.

One time at a Juarez gas station two men approached him. They wore suits and had short hair. They noticed his PM identification credential. One of the men showed Ernesto the day's PM. Did you take this picture, he asked Ernesto, indicating the photograph of a dead man on the front page. That's my job, Ernesto said. If I do this to paper, the man said twisting it, it will drip blood. Who tells you to get to crime scene so fast? Nobody, Ernesto said. We have a police scanner. Next time you get there first you're dead, you die, the man told him.

6 p.m.

Eduardo lives in a newly opened, gated community of small, brown adobe-style houses. Many of the front yards still resemble construction sites with nails and scraps of lumber and plastic sheeting strewn about. Most of the young families here, like his own, have three to four children. In five years, Eduardo believes the neighborhood will change for the worse. The kids won't be as young. They won't find work. They'll come under the sway of gangs. He must build a wall around his house while he still has time. It will be very bad, that's for sure.

5 p.m., July 8

Ernesto drives a rutted lane that runs beside the Rio Bravo. A small crowd gathers around a muddy bank where bones were found. Ernesto nudges his way through, and looks at the small shape in the ground.

"Alligator or chicken," a policeman says.

"Very slender head, ribs, legs," another officer says.

"Dogicide," Ernesto jokes.

"Even a dog isn't safe in Juárez," a man says.

Ernesto walks back to his car. The scanner sputters to life. He listens to a narcocorrido play its mournful warning. He settles in his seat, begins checking in with the other reporters, and lets out a long sigh. If he retires in two years, he will receive a pension worth 80 percent of his salary. He doesn't feel strong enough to wait and retire at sixty-five with his full pension. Staying focused gets harder and harder for him. Age, stomach problems—it frustrates him. His feet hurt in the heat. He can't climb walls to get the best shot as he did when he was younger. He should get an operation on his stomach, but he refuses. He doesn't like the idea of being put under anesthesia. He has seen too many bodies, laid-out and lifeless. When he does retire, who knows? He might start a restaurant. Or maybe not. Something always happens in Juárez. Bar fights, shootouts in parking lots, cops sealing off streets. But what else can he do? For now, Ernesto will wait and listen for the music.

Crossing Over

Across the courtyard and at the far end of an empty basketball court, I see the diminutive figure of a drenched man standing in the rain on the roof of a three-story dormitory.

"El tren!" he shouts. "El tren!"

Two Honduran men beside me, Elias Enamorado and Oscar Velas, look up. The rain pounds on an aluminum roof above our heads, clattering like horses' hooves and falling in curtains.

"El tren!" the man shouts again, his voice barely discernible above the storm. "El tren!"

Elias stands, shaking with anticipation and indecision. He considers whether he should chance it—run out the front gate and down a dirt road to a highway, cross it, and hurry through alleys until he reaches a set of railroad tracks, the train barreling down. After a long moment, he sits.

"Too much rain," Elias says, staring at his hands. He's twenty years old but looks much younger. "The train will be back in two or three days. It will be a good time to ride it then. If there's no rain. It's too easy to slip off in the rain."

"Much too dangerous," Oscar agrees.

"I have to get to the United States," Elias says, raising his voice above the clamor of the storm. "I cannot live like this forever."

I am staying at a shelter for migrants fleeing the violence in Central America. The shelter is named La 72 after the killing of seventy-two migrants in August 24, 2010, in San Fernando Tamaulipas, Mexico. It stands off a brown dirt road in Tenosique in the Mexican state of Tabasco, not far from the highway that cuts through the center of town and the railroad that carries "el tren da la muerte," the death train. The ominous name refers to Mexican freight trains that roll across the country, and that migrants use to reach the U.S. The train is also called "La Bestia," the beast, and "El tren de los desconocidos," the train of the unknowns. Sometimes the train stops at towns, sometimes it does not. Moving or not, thousands of migrants seek to board despite the risks that come with leaping onto a moving train. Many fall off and are maimed or killed under the speeding wheels. Despite the dangers, migrants at La 72 take turns watching for the train from the roof of the men's dormitory, the tallest building here. El tren! becomes almost a battle cry, rousing the migrants out of the stupor of long, hot days to grab their few things and race for the tracks.

When La 72 first opened, it offered a few beds behind a chapel. Today it sees as many as four hundred to one thousand migrants a month, depending on the season. Franciscan priests administer the program and support migrants during their passage through Mexico with food, shelter, and protection. The staff often submits more than one hundred applications for humanitarian visas to Mexican authorities. If a migrant family does not receive a visa or work permit and loses its appeals, it has twenty days to depart Mexico. However the law does not say which border a migrant must use to leave. Many travel north with the hope of entering the U.S. and applying for asylum.

Murals depicting Che Guevara, and the Virgin of Guadalupe with a Zapatista bandana around her face, among other images, cover the shelter's cinder-block buildings—a men's and a women's dormitory, a kitchen, a chapel, and administrative offices—that make up the now-sprawling complex.

A volunteer, Orlando Martinez, from San Pedro Sula, Honduras, watches the front gate. He thrusts his chest out when he walks, falling into the rocking gait of a sailor. Gold caps on his front teeth, and a thin beard frames his face. His smile is not one of warmth, but rather a reminder that he won't be trifled with.

"I first left Honduras for the United States when I was twelve," Orlando tells me. "The last time I got deported from there was 2014. And there were two times before that. First time, 2001. No papers each time. I'm forty-five. I worked in Baltimore installing AC downtown. I did forty-nine months in Houston for returning illegally to the U.S. in 2014. I'm trying to get work papers and stay here in Mexico but there're no jobs here."

Migrants, Orlando has found, show up and ask for shelter at all times of the day and night. He has them sit on a bench inside the gate and wait for an intake worker. The questions are brief: Where are you from? Why did you come here? Who came with you? Have you experienced any violence? Would you be subject to violence if you returned? Most migrants answer yes to the last two questions

Oscar suggests I speak with people individually rather than in groups; no one will talk to me otherwise because they will worry about who might be listening, good guy or bad guy? Coyotes get in here, Orlando cautions, and try to take advantage of the migrants. He has never seen one but he has his suspects. A single man with six children. Where did he get all of those kids? Groups of men who claim not to know one another and yet they all have the same story. Who are they? Sometimes these guys leave and stay in a hotel and try to meet with migrants outside the gate. They promise to take them to the United States and charge them hundreds of dollars only to abandon them once the money has changed hands.

"I'm afraid to stay here," Oscar says. "Coyotes try to make you leave and go to the U.S. They kidnap you just to force you to go. They call your family and tell them to pay for your travel or they say you will never be seen again."

I came to La 72 by way of Chiapas, a Mexican state south of Tabasco, to report on a visit by Pope Francis for the *National Catholic Reporter*. The pope arrived at ten o'clock in the morning on February 15, 2016, in San Cristobal, the capital, and spoke at an outdoor stadium. From there, he drove in a motorcade to a downtown cathedral where I waited to cover that portion of his trip.

Hundreds of people, myself included, gathered ahead of time in a plaza and stood for hours. Some men held signs identifying themselves as Honduran migrants and I presumed they anticipated words of support from the pope. If they did, they were disappointed. Few, if any of us, even saw the pope enter the cathedral through a concealed side entrance. In the plaza, flat-screen monitors meant to show his speech instead played advertisements for action films such as the Will Smith science fiction flop *After Earth*, while the loudspeakers aired gospel hymns but no words from the pontiff.

About an hour after he arrived, Pope Francis emerged from the cathedral, waved to all of us who had hoped to hear him, and then left in his motorcade; the crowd dispersed, and within a short time street vendors and shoeshine boys began plying their trades as if this day was no different from any other. The signs held by the Honduran migrants stood aslant in trash cans. I returned to my hotel. The next morning, I caught a bus for the six-hour ride to Tenosique.

Only a few passengers got on with me. The bus wound its way through mountains patchy with farm fields and streaked with dirt roads that from a distance resembled little more than trails. Wind rocked the bus and the pounding noise of construction rose up from valleys where road crews labored. A heavy fog settled in at the higher elevations, cocooning the bus in a gray mist that lulled me to sleep.

When I woke up, sunlight had burned through the fog and dense woods thick with palm trees reduced the highway to a narrow strip of asphalt. Women balancing baskets on their heads walked along the road, followed by scampering children and yipping dogs, and the bus passed through cleared areas in which isolated restaurants, little more than shacks with picnic tables, stood in the sun, shined by the vanquished mist, and worn fences held cattle in stunted pastures, and beyond them mountains rose and disappeared in the few remaining clouds.

The bus dipped into a valley and passed a school. Girls in white blouses and pink dresses ran into a parking lot and watched us pass. Pickup truck drivers leaned against the hoods of their vehicles eating tortillas; burros and horses plodded past them bearing bundles of wood, and men with machetes hacked at the growth alongside the road.

In a town with no signs suggesting its name, a Pemex gas station stood empty beside a pharmacy and rows of vendors selling cantaloupes. Pregnant women negotiated the jammed sidewalks, sometimes crossing the street and resting beneath trees that divided the highway's northbound and southbound traffic. Small businesses flipped past our windows, Dolores Asada Taqueria, Buenvedo Restaurant, Miguel's Internet, and I had almost fallen asleep again when the truck before us hit a dog. The dog laid on its side without making a sound, its tail moving in circles like a stalled motor, its head raised, showing its teeth as it strained to move, and we rolled over it and everyone inside the bus made a collective gasp except for the driver who continued without pause, the back of his head revealing no more of his thoughts than the expressions of the people outside revealed they had seen anything shocking.

Just before we reached Tenosique, we stopped at a police checkpoint. The driver opened the doors and a female officer peered inside. Pressured by the U.S., Mexico had increasingly militarized its southern borders to prevent Central American migrants from entering.

"Buenos dias," the officer said.

The bus driver nodded.

The officer stepped aboard and asked each passenger for identification. Other officers lingered outside, joking and laughing, not a raucous laugh, but the laughter of people who found some innocuous statement to be quietly amusing, the humor breaking up the monotony of their day until they had sucked it dry, and then they stopped laughing and their boredom returned and they once again began waving cars over to search. Faded posters of the pope hung off a utility pole with a broken streetlight, the bulb drooping downward, suspended by wires like the tendons of a broken neck.

The officer on my bus told a man and a woman to get off. She stood a few inches from them and did not raise her voice. She seemed almost pleasant, her expression calm as she escorted them outside. After a moment, the man slunk back on and retrieved his suitcase from an overhead shelf. He appeared embarrassed. The humiliation of being paraded off before his fellow travelers expressed in his sad eyes, like a student called before the principal in front of his classmates. Reduced to the status of a child. Degrading for the rest of us, spared but feeling vulnerable. We gave him furtive glances and then looked at the floor and said nothing, shamed by our silence and our gratitude that we were not him. He stepped off and vanished into the afternoon as if he had never existed. The driver closed the doors. Some of us sighed aloud. Five minutes later, we crossed a bridge into Tenosique.

"Were they Honduran?" Elias asks me about the couple the officer took off the bus.

"I don't know."

"They probably were," Oscar says. "If you don't get out of Honduras, you're dead. That's why people come here. The violence there is too much."

From one of his pockets he pulls out a scrap of paper on which he has drawn a crude map, a route to the U.S. a black line squiggling near the creased edges.

"Maybe I'll hire a taxi and drive out of Tenosique," he says examining his map. "The police would not expect a migrant to hire a taxi."

"You think too much," Elias tells him.

Near the entrance of La 72, a mural of Mexico has been painted on the wall of an administrative office. Black lines track routes north into the U.S. through Texas and Arizona. A legend explains the symbols on the map.

Pistols indicate places migrants have been assaulted.

Cups and plates mean that a town offers free food.

Triangles denote shelters.

Money in the shape of a U.S. dollar bill warns of human traffickers who demand cobre de cuta, quota charges, usually one hundred dollars.

I stand before the map surrounded by the men and women who are considering their next move. One at a time, starting at Tenosique, (a pistol, cups and plates, a triangle), they roam the map with their hands moving north; Palenque, (a pistol, cups and plates, a triangle, a dollar bill); Turra Blanca, (pistol, triangle, La Prono, cups and plates); Oritaba, (a dollar bill); Mexico City, (a triangle); dragging their fingers from town to town toward the U.S. border, and I ask them to tell me their stories:

Karen Trouchez, twenty years old, with her two-year-old daughter, Allison: "I ran a convenience store in Santa Barbara, Honduras and my husband worked construction. The gangs wanted one hundred dollars a week from us. One guy came to our house at six in the morning and he said, 'Pay the rent or I will kill you.' Young guy. Eighteen, twenty years old. He had two guns. We left last week by bus. It was very sad to go. My mother cried. She told me, Don't leave, but I told her I have to try to find a way to take care of my daughter. But sometimes I want to run back and see my family. There were many migrants on my bus— you recognize them because they stay in the back of the bus and have many bags filled with clothes, and many children. We want to go to the U.S. My husband lived there for twelve years. The first time he was deported was in 2002. He has been deported four times. I'd like to be a cook. I enjoy cooking and I could do that and have my daughter with me."

Dania Marisela Salina, twenty-eight years old, with her six-year-old son: "I lived in Chulateca, Honduras. Three times I saw people killed. Young men took them out, shot them in the back of the neck. They saw me and took me by the hair. Be quiet, they said. They threw me down and beat me. 'Go now,' they said. 'Get out of our country or we kill you.' I've been here one month. I came through Guatemala, walking and hiding, running from the police. I worry about my family. My dad was in a gang. He'd rather stay in Honduras and die by the gun than leave."

Freddy Cruz Bolina, forty years old, sitting with his wife, Marina Elizabeth Hernandez Gonzalez, and their infant son, Dylan: "I had a little restaurant in San Miguel, Honduras. For three years I paid the gangs four hundred a week. Then a gang guy told me to pay an additional two hundred a week for or they would kill me. I couldn't afford that. My wife and I talked into the night about the gangs. 'They'll come for you,' she said. We left our house at four in the morning and took a bus to San Salvador. We rode another bus to Guatemala and then to the border with Mexico. We walked here."

Nelson Ávila, twenty-eight years old, San Pedro Sula, Honduras: "I was sixteen when I crossed for the first time, in 2004. I took La Bestia from Chiapas, Mexico to Topochula to Vera Cruz. I worked there one year in construction and carpentry.and saved money for the U.S. The next year, I took a bus to Monterrey. I got on La Bestia again to Nuevo Laredo, Mexico. I walked across to Laredo, Texas. Immigration agents look for a lot of people, not one kid and they didn't see me. I had a friend in Laredo and I stayed with him for one month. Then I called my father in New Orleans. He said, 'Wait one more week and I'll have a coyote pick you up in a truck.' There were seventeen of us. The coyote drove us to Houston. My father was going to pick me up there. Then a tire blew. The coyote says, Everybody out. Wait thirty minutes. I'll get it fixed. I thought, OK. I waited two hours. When he came back, he said, 'Everybody, let's go.' Then the police came. All of us were from Honduras and El Salvador but I told the police I was from Mexico so they sent me back to Nuevo Laredo. The next day, I crossed again and called my father. This time, I said, no coyote. Send me money. He sent me one thousand dollars. I bought a used Mitsubishi for eight hundred dollars and drove to Houston and connected with my father. From Texas, we went to New Orleans where he lived. I stayed there for ten years, got married and had a daughter, two years old now. We had an apartment downtown I loved New Orleans. I liked the food, fried rice, dirty rice, shrimp, all of it. I'd eat at restaurants built on boats. Beautiful, man..In 2015 I was in the parking lot of my apartment, walking to my truck when four cars came at me on all sides. Immigration. Do you have papers? No, I said, and they handcuffed me. I was deported one week ago."

Paola Regalado, sixteen, San Pedro Sula, Honduras: "I left because gangs tried to kill me. They murdered my parents. My mother was killed eight years ago; my father was killed four years ago. They were both caught in the middle of a gang war. Walking home and got shot. I was brought up by my grandmother. They wanted me to become the girlfriend of an MS guy. I said, No, and they chased me, cut my right calf with a machete. I dream of my parents. They are in the sky and look down at us. In my prayers I tell them I'd to be a nurse or a doctor and save lives."

"El tren! El tren!"

Elias starts running for the gate but Oscar stops him.

"It is headed south, not north," he tells him.

"How do you know?"

Oscar points at the man on the roof of the men's dorm. He waves his arms for people to stop. El alto!" he shouts, "Va por el camino equivocado!" Stop. It's going the wrong way.

Elias lets out a long sigh and sits down.

"Why did he say anything?"

"He made a mistake."

"Stupid man."

"I'm thinking I'll take a bus to Villahermosa," Oscar says, referring to the capital of Tabasco. "And from there go north."

"You should get on the train with the rest of us," Elias says.

"I have to decide if that's how I want to go."

"You think too much."

"Do you have Facebook?" Oscar asks me. "I will friend you so you know if I make it or not."

"OK."

"What do you think of the Baltimore Orioles?"

"So-so."

"They were good when I lived in Baltimore. What about the Dallas Cowboys? They were my favorite football team."

"I am thinking of working in Tampa," Elias says. "I have a friend who was working there and made good money."

"This fool," Oscar says, pointing to a man seated at a table next to ours, "had an ice cream cart in Houston. One day, he stopped his cart in front of the city's immigration office. A guy comes out, 'Sure, I'll buy ice cream,' he says. 'Give me a chocolate cone and your papers.' Was he stupid or what? Who would stop in front of an immigration office to sell ice cream?"

The man turns around, an embarrassed smile on his face.

"I got deported," he tells me. "I had the chocolate cone but I didn't have the papers."

"Stupid," Oscar says.

At night, Oscar sleeps on the groud outside the men's dormitory to avoid its sweat-filled, congested heat. He stares at the sky buttoned with stars. The tip of his cigarette flares like a firefly. Drying laundry perfumes the air. Oscar considers a faded photo of his wife and three daughters. They stand beneath a palm tree, squinting against the sun, heads tilted to one side. Oscar hated leaving his family in San Pedro Sula but he hated living there too. When someone gets killed—if you're lucky—the police show up three hours later. They don't care. If you don't get out, you die. He left once before, in 2010. He crossed into Texas and caught a bus to Rockville, Maryland, where his father, an uncle, and two brothers lived and he took a job in an Italian restaurant. The owner, an Iranian guy, died recently, his death announced on Facebook. Nice guy. He didn't mind when four years later Oscar returned to Honduras. He was lonely and missed his wife and kids. He took a United Airlines flight to Tegucigalpa without anyone stopping him. No one asks questions when you leave the U.S.

Oscar could not find work in San Pedro Sula. A little more than a year later, he told his wife, I'm leaving. She wanted to go with him but he said it was too dangerous. He hugged her and their daughters and they stood in the door and cried as he walked out. He caught a bus for Guatemala and from there took another bus to the Mexican border. Then he hitchhiked to La 72.

Elias spends his evenings by the railroad tracks. He gets the jitters at La 72, feels caged. The train should come again soon. Usually every two to three days but it's impossible to predict. Elias plans to be a cook in the U.S. He has always worked in kitchens. A San Pedro Sula hotel employed him as a chef. He left that job for another and another, but no matter the job the salary remained too low. Five, six dollars a day, the work always temporary. He talked to his wife and six-year-old son before he left. They didn't like the idea of him going. What if you die? his wife asked him. Don't go. He said OK to end the conversation. His wife thought he wasn't leaving, but he had only decided not to discuss it with her. On his last day at home he felt sad because he had not told his wife and young son he was leaving. He waited until they were asleep and then he crept out of the house and caught a bus to Guatemala and crossed into Mexico. Mexican police asked for his ID and he told them he was sixteen and returning to his parent's home. In Mexico, no one is required to carry ID until they reach eighteen. Go and take care of your mother and father, the police told him. Elias dreams of living in Tampa. He hears it's beautiful and that many Spanish-speaking people live there. He hopes to save money and send for his family. A man without work, he believes, is not a man.

"El tren! El tren!"

This time there is no rain. This time the train is traveling north.

Elias and I and everyone but Oscar sprint to the front gate, a mob hurrying down a dirt path to the highway and across it toward a cluster of restaurants and vendors and we dart between them until we reach the tracks. The migrants fill their pockets with rocks to throw at Mexican immigration officers should they show up and try to arrest them. We see the shine of a locomotive's headlight rolling toward us, and the light grows larger and larger, and Elias, chest thrust out, his face and hair pulled back by the draft of the train, runs alongside it until it screeches to a stop and he and dozens of other men and women scramble onto freight cars, pulling each other up. Elias climbs to the top of a tank car and waves at me, and for no good reason I am reminded of a childhood friend who, after he scored a soccer goal in a high school game, ran to the sidelines and asked his father to take a photo of him. The boyish grin on his face was the same as the one now spread across Elias's face, and I can see how Elias convinced the Mexican police he was just sixteen. But the memory of my friend holds tragedy. Afflicted with depression, he died by suicide when he was forty-two. I wonder, given its dangers, if the train is a form of suicide for Elias. A desperate do-or-die effort to achieve his dream of the good life in Tampa.

"Bueno suerte!" I shout. Good luck.

I have no idea why the train stopped. The migrants tell me some kind-hearted engineers stop for them. Others stop merely to take a break. After thirty minutes, the train starts forward. It picks up speed, metal against metal, hurtling past those of us who stayed behind, its immense length diminishing into the distance until gone. I wait, and when I can no longer see or hear it, I wander back to La 72 where I find Oscar sitting alone, his worn map spread on his knees. I sit beside him.

"It's easy to ride the train, but what lies beyond it?" Oscar asks, but I'm uncertain if he's talking to me or thinking out loud. "What hope do we have?"

"I don't know."

"It's kind of crazy," he says.

Facebook,
March 27, 2016
Oscar Velas: Malcolm, I am back in Honduras. A man was shot here in the street yesterday by MS. In the head. Where are you?

Facebook, March 27, 2016
J. Malcolm Garcia: I'm in Chicago. What happened? Why are you back?

Facebook,
March 27, 2016
Oscar Velas:
I was caught in Veracruz. I will try again.

This is Not a Love Story

Marlen believes her husband, Josue, lost his mind before they left Honduras.

"His life made him crazy, I think," she says.

Marlen and I sit across from each other at the Instituto Madre Assunta, a Tijuana women's shelter run by an order of missionary nuns. One hundred and twenty women and children live here. Marlen shares a room with three of her kids, ranging from six months to eight years old. Their father, Josue, stays with her two teenage boys from a previous marriage in a men's shelter a few blocks away. The nuns told Marlen the boys were too old to live at the institute. Sometimes, she and Josue and the boys run errands for the nuns or Marlen might meet them for lunch.

"It is difficult to be away from my children," she says, "but I have no choice."

On this day in February 2016, Marlen has been at the shelter for three months. Her black hair falls to her shoulders and a resigned look crosses her face, eyes wide, staring at nothing. Thirty-six years old and two months pregnant with her sixth child. She leans back on the couch and rests her hands on her stomach.

Delivering the baby could kill her, she says, because she has epilepsy. If she has a seizure while giving birth, she might die. Yet Marlen has taken the extraordinary measure of leaving her country while pregnant, five children in tow, because staying at home could have meant death for her family.

I think of the stories my mother told me about her father. How he was pursuing the American ideal by taking advantage of his ambition and his family's wealth. How he left Spain to study law in New York, where the family owned a home. He had been accepted at Syracuse University but did not speak a word of English and required a tutor his first year. He earned a law degree. His is an immigrant success story, but eased with money.

I grew up instilled with the American immigrant success story: Work hard, study hard, and anything is possible in America. My brothers and I did not speak Spanish growing up. English only. We live in the United States, my mother said. A roof over our heads, three meals a day, school, and jobs, all of this and more we accepted as our due. You're Americans, my mother told us. Our last name was the only attachment to Spain we had, and it was increasingly distant.

When the institute's director introduced me to Marlen, she asked about my last name. "Garcia?"

she said. I told her both my maternal and paternal grandparents came from Spain. My mother's father moved to New York; my father's father left for Cuba and later Florida.

"Ah, España," Marlen said.

She was impressed that my mother's father became a lawyer. Marlen never completed school. Something that paid more than the five to six dollars a day she earned as a maid would be nice. I don't say anything more about my maternal grandfather. Separated by class and money, he would have had no sympathy for Marlen. There is no comparison between his story and hers, except that as he once had, she, too, dreams of going to America.

"Tell me about Honduras," I say. "Your life there and why you came here."

"We're here because of what happened in 2009," she says.

She describes to me how a group of Honduran politicians and military officers that year ousted the democratically elected president, Manuel Zelaya. The stated motive was to prevent Zelaya from changing the constitution so that he could run for reelection and hold on to power. Critics of the coup, however, warned that Honduras was moving toward a military dictatorship. No matter the motive, the years since the coup have been marked by a huge uptick in violence, including the slayings of labor activists, environmentalists, peasants, politicians, and journalists.

"After the coup, the military men wanted Josue's land," Marlen says.

"Why?"

"Because they had the power to take it. Let him tell you his story."

Thirty-six-year-old Josue meets me outside the men's shelter and says he'd like some coffee. He wears blue jeans and a button-down white shirt over a T-shirt. He speaks quietly, picks at his mustache. We walk together up a hill, to Calle Galileo and stop at a restaurant and order coffee.

Josue met Marlen one afternoon outside his mother's house in 2005. She was very humble, and did not look at him directly. He liked that. She dressed simply, too, and was a member of the Jehovah's Witnesses. They married that same year.

When the problems started in 2009, Josue and Marlen were living in an apartment in Colón, Honduras. He worked in the fields. He had attended school long enough to learn how to write his name, but he had always planted crops, even as a boy. He belonged to a cooperative of forty-two farmers. They grew coconuts and sold coconut oil, a good group of men providing for their families, but there were many jealous government people who wanted the land for themselves.

At first, the government people were polite when they asked the farmers to sell, Josue recalls, but he and the other farmers remained firm and told them, No, we're not selling. Then the government people stopped being civil. They shot Josue's brother-in-law, the president of the cooperative. Then they started killing the rest of the farmers one by one. Josue took Marlen to her mother's house where he told her to stay until he came for her.

On October 12, 2009, Josue received a court summons. The document had no official seal and did not define the complaint against him. Many of his friends had been killed and he assumed that now the government people wanted to kill him. Let them come and shoot me, he thought. He would not go to them to die. He ignored the summons. Two weeks later, he received another summons and tossed it.

One day toward the end of November, Josue stood among

a group of farmers when a truckload of soldiers drove onto their land and started shooting. Four farmers fell dead. Josue and the others ran. Panic consumed him and his breath became uneven as he fled; everything seemed crooked and he stumbled as if he were drunk. The soldiers arrested him and the other farmers and put black hoods over their heads and screamed at them and jabbed them with their guns and shoved them into the trucks. They were taken to a jail in San Pedro Sula and locked up for the night. The next morning, they appeared before Judge Rafael Diaz, who demanded to know the president of their group. Josue answered that he had been named president after his brother-in-law's death.

"Renounce possession of the land," Diaz told him.

"That is not possible," Josue said. "The land was given to us. We have documents proving it's ours. We can't just give it up."

Diaz said he had documents, too, and he gave Josue papers to sign, relinquishing the land, but he refused. Diaz sent them all back to jail where they were held for two months until a journalist friend of one of the farmers started making inquiries. On a January morning in 2010, a guard woke them up at two o'clock and told them they were free, but Josue and the farmers sensed a trap. That hour of the morning no one would be on the street to see them assassinated. They refused to leave until daylight.

About half a dozen journalists were waiting for them when they emerged from the jail. Josue spoke about their arrest. He mentioned Diaz and the government people who wanted their land and he spoke of the farmers who had been murdered. A journalist's phone rang, interrupting him. When the reporter got off, he said a source told him that the police had gone to the house of Josue's twenty-year-old brother, Carlos, and killed him. Josue took a bus to the house and saw where Carlos had been found strapped to a chair, tied and handcuffed, beaten and burned. The next day his uncle called. Another brother, Victor, had disappeared and his corpse had been found in La Ceiba Atlantida, a port city on the northern coast of Honduras. Just like Carlos, Victor had been tied to a chair, tortured, and left on an empty street. Police at the scene recognized Josue and turned him over to the military. Soldiers put a black hood over his head and took him to a dilapidated house in an isolated place. They sat him in a chair nailed to the floor and took off the hood.

"Oh, so this is the famous farmer who stands up to the military?" an officer said. "So you are president of a farmers group and you think you own your land?"

"No, you confuse me with someone else," Josue said.

"The dead guy is not your brother?"

"No, he's not my brother."

The officer stepped back and the soldiers started beating Josue in his chest and groin. When they stopped, the officer told him to sign some papers, but he refused, and they beat him until he passed out. Josue woke up in a ditch and felt someone rifling through his pockets and he moved and the would-be thief shouted in surprise. He might have been a criminal, but also a good man because he called for help. An ambulance took Josue to a Red Cross hospital. His older brother, Rafael, saw him on TV when a newscaster showed his picture and asked any viewer who recognized him to notify the hospital. An hour later, Josue was discharged into Rafael's care. Marlen met them at Rafael's house and hugged Josue. He screamed in pain and pushed her away and told her not to touch him. Rafael helped him to a bed. Marlen stayed in another room.

In the morning, Rafael advised Josue to give up the land. They'll kill you, he said. Work with me. Josue began spending his days behind the counter of his brother's shoe store with Marlen and slowly he began to heal. He told jokes and held Marlen's hands and soon she was sleeping in his bed. He suffered from nightmares. Sometimes he would wake up and ask her, Did you see that? Did you hear that? and Marlen would shake her head and tell him to go back to sleep.

Weeks passed, then months and years. The horrors of 2009 were behind them, Josue and Marlen thought, but then one February day in 2015, while Marlen was out of the shop, a gang member of MS walked in.

"You are a valuable person," he told Josue. "The military is looking for you. I won't kill you right here because of your children. I've never had any trouble with your family. I'll give you an opportunity to leave the country. If you are still here in two days, I will kill you, your family."

"Why now after so much time?" Josue asked him.

The young man shrugged.

"I don't ask questions," he said. "I take orders."

That night, Josue told Marlen, "We must go," but Marlen did not want to leave. She was pregnant with their fifth child. Why would MS want to kill Josue? Was this one of his nightmares? Was he confusing a bad dream with life?

"We have to go!" Josue insisted.

He suggested they travel to Mexico and then try to make their way into the U.S. Marlen had an Aunt Julia in Tampa. Maybe she could help them. Before they left, they dropped off their children with Marlen's mother. Josue promised to return for them as soon as they found a place to live. The next day they took a bus to Guatemala and from there to the Mexican border. They walked eight hours until they reached the migrant shelter, La 72, where Marlen and Josue applied for asylum in Mexico. Their application was approved in a matter of months. In May, they left La 72 for Casa de los Amigos, a shelter for migrants in Mexico City. Once there, Josue returned to Honduras for their children but Marlen's first husband would not let him take the two older boys. He returned to Mexico with their two younger children.

In May, Josue and Marlen tried to enter the U.S. from Matamoros, Mexico, across the Rio Grande from Brownsville, Texas, but border agents stopped them. They weren't eligible for asylum, the agents explained, because they had been granted asylum in Mexico, and so they returned to Casa de los Amigos. Four weeks later, Josue noticed two men in the shelter watching him. He followed one and overheard him talking on the phone.

"He is here," the man said, "with his wife."

"Who are you calling?" Josue demanded when the man hung up.

"None of your business."

"What do you want?"

"What I was looking for. And I found it."

"What?"

"You."

Josue began shaking and then he passed out. Sometime later he woke up in a hospital where a nurse told him he had fainted. He told a doctor about the man in the shelter and the doctor gave him medication to help him sleep and advised him to see a psychiatrist. You might have post-traumatic stress syndrome, the doctor told him. You may be having hallucinations. The next morning, Josue left the hospital and he, Marlen, and their children returned to the U.S. and again requested asylum. This time, border agents held them. The next day, a bus carried Josue and other migrants to a detention center in Miami where he was held for four months before he appeared before an immigration judge in October 2015.

"Everything you say is credible about why you left Honduras," the judge told him, "but you have asylum in Mexico. You can't have asylum in two countries."

The judge ordered Josue deported to Mexico the next day. He lived on the street in Mexico City rather than risk running into the two gang members at Casa de los Amigos. He got in touch with Marlen's mother and Marlen's two older sons in Honduras and Aunt Julia in Tampa but none of them had heard from her. Gangs wanted to recruit them, the boys told Josue. He spoke to their father and he agreed to send them to Mexico with some money if Josue would try to get them into the U.S. Two weeks later, in November, Josue and the boys reunited in Mexico City and left for Texas, but a border agent told Josue that if he crossed he would be deported again and the boys would be sent back to Honduras. The agent told him about programs in Tijuana for migrants. Josue called Marlen's mother and Aunt Julia.

"If you hear from Marlen," he said, "tell her I have the boys. I'll be in Tijuana."

While Josue had been in Miami, U.S. Customs and Border Protection officials had placed Marlen and her two children in a Houston immigration detention center. She did not know Josue had been deported. Her fifth child, a girl, was born August 8, 2015. A little Texan, Marlen called her.

One December morning, four months after her daughter's birth, she called Aunt Julia and expected her to say what she had said in previous calls, that she had not heard from Josue. However, this time Julia had some news. Josue was in Tijuana, she said, and gave Marlen his phone number. When Marlen told Josue he was the father of a baby girl, they both cried with joy. After fifteen minutes a guard told her she had to get off the phone. She hung up and offered to drop her appeal for political asylum if she could return to Mexico and see her husband. The guard said he could not make that decision, but the next day immigration officials agreed to send her to Tijuana.

Now, three months later, Marlen wants to return to the U.S. She would like to work in a pizza restaurant or some other service industry job but she worries she will not be let in. Worse, border agents might take her American-born baby. If she must, she will enter the States illegally with her children. The two oldest boys can meet her in the U.S. or remain with Josue. She would miss them but they are old enough to make decisions for themselves. One way or another, Marlen won't stay in Tijuana. She wants her sixth child to be an American citizen.

"Josue has too many mental problems," she tells me. "I can't stay with him. I will go without him. Is there nothing you can do for me?"

I don't answer. The story of Marlen and Josue should be a love story, a story of how they fought against all odds and won. But it isn't. Josue is no longer the man she married. Honduras is no longer the country she knew. Mexico is not the place she wants to be. She looks at me for a long time. I am an American. In her eyes, I represent the status and good fortune she wants for herself and that Josue can no longer offer.

"No," I tell her finally. "I'm sorry, but there's nothing I can do."

I see Josue as a normal man with a harrowing story, but I can't speak for what goes on in his head, how the traumas he experienced come back to haunt him, or how that feels to Marlen. A psychologist friend of mine described mental illness as the natural reaction to unnatural circumstances. I suspect that would provide little comfort to Marlen, but I do know Josue would not want her to go. He hopes to rent an apartment for them. The part-time jobs he finds bring in just sixty-seven dollars a week. He would work more but his right knee aches and he can't stand for long. Worried about running into the wrong people, he does not go out except to work and visit Marlen. He sees his dead brothers in the faces of his children and dreams of them when they were alive, and he dreams of beatings. He wakes up and runs out of the shelter until someone stops and calms him.

To leave your country, he thinks, is like being born again. Leaving the womb and emerging into something new and confusing and dangerous. He finds the Spanish spoken in Tijuana hard to understand. The accent doesn't make sense to him. Some words are different. On his way to work, the police stop him as if they know he is not a Mexican. In Honduras, he had plans for his land. To build his own house, raise a family. He lived a tranquil life before all the trouble started.

On my last day in Tijuana, I see Josue and Marlen standing together outside the closed gate of the institute. Marlen looks happy, and had I not spent time with them, I would not know they are plagued by ghosts. I imagine that one day, or perhaps over the course of several days, the ghosts had relented and they got together to buy food for the shelters and they forgot themselves and their problems and loved without caution and Marlen became pregnant again.

Josue rests his right hand on Marlen's stomach. She watches him. He leans down and cocks his head to one side as if he might hear the baby and Marlen smiles. They are happy at this moment to be a husband and wife expecting a baby whose own children may say of them as I say of my grandparents, I am descended from immigrants. In moments like this nightmares and visions no longer torment Josue, and Marlen has no plans to leave him. They are no longer a Honduran couple on the run living under the radar and seeking refuge and talking to a writer who has nothing to offer them other than questions that remind them of what they have been through and of the impossible choices they face. In this moment, they are eager parents with a future traveling north to the United States.

No Overtime

I tell Rosa about a time when I was down on my luck as a free-lance journalist. I wasn't getting any work, and my bank account was all but depleted. Desperate, I took a job as a groundskeeper at a Chicago country club.

"I worked with twelve Mexicans. One other guy and I were the only gringos," I say. "I saw how the Mexicans were treated."

Rosa offers a polite smile and looks at her watch. She has to be at a Tucson taco factory in an hour. She has worked there a little more than a year and earns about four hundred dollars a week. Only two months earlier, she had been in sanctuary at the Southside Presbyterian Church, a small religious community of about one hundred sixty worshipers less than a mile from down-town Tucson. The church offers weekly prayers for refugees fleeing violence. Its members routinely search for migrants who have lost their way in the Arizona desert or have been abandoned by the people they paid to bring them to the U.S.

Rosa and I are meeting on a cold January morning in a clut-tered office of the church. We can see our breath and a volunteer flips on a heater. Rosa stayed at the church in a small room with a bunk bed, a miniature refrigerator, and a microwave for fifteen months while she appealed a 2014 deportation order that had started with a traffic stop for an incorrect lane change. Her U.S. worker visa had expired. She'd gone to the church because under most circumstances Immigration and Customs Enforcement and Customs and Border Protection avoid detaining people in religious institutions, schools, and hospitals. A 2011 ICE memo designated such areas as "sensitive locations."

In November 2015, after Rosa spent four hundred sixty-one days in sanctuary, her attorney worked out what she would describe only as a confidential agreement with the Department of Homeland Security to spare her deportation. ICE maintains that Rosa was never a high priority for removal. Still, Rosa worries she might be stopped again.

"Nothing is certain," she says.

Despite her concern, Rosa appears far more relaxed than the photos I'd seen of her while she lived at the church. Her wan face stared into the camera with disbelief. Now, she sits before me in blue jeans and a red turtleneck, her brown hair streaked with blonde highlights, a smile on her face.

We had arranged to get together at four in the afternoon. Then Rosa asked to meet in the morning. She apologized—her work schedule was always in flux and she found it difficult to get away without losing hours.

"We were paid minimum wage at the country club," I tell her. "We'd start at five in the morning. The boss said he would provide opportunities for overtime. These opportunities came every day and we worked twelve, fifteen hours a day. No one turned down the overtime because the hourly pay was so poor. Just eight dollars. We put in brick walks, sewer pipes, cut down trees, along with the union workers. I don't know how much the country club saved with us. For six months I did this seven days a week."

Rosa laughs.

"You were lucky. I get no overtime," she tells me. "On Monday, I worked twelve hours. I came home and was called back two hours later and worked another eight hours. Twenty hours in one day with just a two-hour break."

I knew then that there was nothing comparable between my spell of bad luck and her life.

After Donald Trump won the 2016 presidential election, I wondered how I should respond. Trump had demonized Mexican immigrants before his run for the presidency and continued to throughout the campaign. Gary, the other white guy at the country club, voted for Trump. He rarely spoke about politics. He liked NASCAR and chewed tobacco. He had lost all of his teeth and took pills for high blood pressure, high cholesterol, gout, and his heart. He dyed his gray hair and mustache black, and was at least fifty pounds overweight.

"Mexicans are stupid and lazy," he told me.

He never explained how he reached this conclusion. He just repeated it over and over when I asked him why he felt that way, or he would rattle off a list of complaints. He didn't like the Mexicans using the microwave during break to warm tacos and Tupperware filled with rice and chicken. He didn't like them speaking Spanish. He didn't like how they sat together. He didn't like what he considered their casual attitude toward work, how they joked and talked as they cut grass, weeded, trimmed trees, and performed any number of tedious tasks. He didn't like it that they weren't citizens. I don't think Gary represents all of white America that is suspicious of immigrants. I don't think they are all as extreme, ignorant, and bigoted. But he was the white guy in my life then who was running down Hispanics, oblivious of my family's connection to Mexico.

"My cousins are Mexican," I told him.

Gary backed off.

"Well, that's different," he said. "They're your family. They're not like these guys."

He had a point. My cousins are as conservative as Trump, and like him, have nothing good to say about migrant workers.

With capitalism, I've heard my cousins say, you have winners and losers. The losers cannot be allowed to enter countries illegally no matter their need. Rules must be followed to prevent chaos. My cousins come from wealth. They are financially well off, were educated in the U.S., and have dual citizenship. They don't follow rules; they follow their pedigree. They make their judgments of others from the great financial divide that separates them from the people they condemn, a few of whom I came to know at the country club.

After some thought, I decided to drive from my Kansas City home to Tucson. A friend knew people there who were involved in the sanctuary movement. They had provided shelter for a Mexican woman, my friend told me, Rosa Robles Loreto. I made some calls and arranged to meet her.

In early January 2016, I packed a duffel bag and headed southwest on Interstate 35 to U.S. 54, then south. I drove through country traveled by Mexican and Central American immigrants on their way north, through blighted towns they have helped save from desolation, through communities never fully recovered from whatever calamity had struck them. I saw small western Kansas towns like Liberal thriving today thanks in part to the influx of Mexican families employed by meatpacking plants, farms, feedlots, and oil field service companies. Beginning in the early 2000s, these immigrants had reopened businesses and filled schools with their children, jump-starting communities in the Midwest that had been close to dead.

About halfway between Dalhart, a north Texas town that barely survived the Dust Bowl, and Tucumcari, New Mexico, I stopped at an Econo Lodge in an empty town with no name I saw on my map. Boarded-up storefronts with faded help wanted signs looked out at a vacant street turned to mud in places. Deserted homes absorbed the silence, their broken windows latticed with cobwebs.

"Garcia?" the Econo Lodge receptionist said when I asked for a room. "How'd that happen?"

"How do you mean?"

"Well," he said handing back my ID and credit card, "we've got a lot of people with your name here now, but you sure could pass as white."

The next morning, I continued south on U.S. 54. Murals of Mexican men with thick black mustaches and large sombreros filled the sides of old brick buildings until I got on Interstate 10 heading southwest and for hours saw only desert that finally unfurled into high rises that guided me into El Paso. After a quick nap at a Motel 6, conveniently situated among Mexican and Chinese restaurants and a Denny's, I went to see Carlos Marentes, founder and director of El Centro de los Trabajadores Agrículturas Fronterizos, The Border Farmworkers Center.

Farmworkers lingered in the dark hall. Sunlight filtered into a large, bare room where a man sat by himself on a stool watching the news on TV. It was a cool winter day, the desert heat still subdued. I leaned against the front desk and waited for Carlos. The center reminded me of my time as a social worker in San Francisco before I became a reporter. I'd start my day sitting by the front door of St. Vincent de Paul. Homeless people stood in line for coffee and I signed them in. The issue then, in the mid-1990s, was not migration but NIMBYism. Help the poor, but not in my backyard.

A lean man with short gray hair and wearing a blue work shirt and jeans came out of a back room and shook my hand.

"I'm Carlos," he said. "Coffee?"

He showed me a chair and poured me a cup before I could answer. Carlos came to the United States from Mexico in 1977 and got involved in the farm labor movement a short time later. In 1980, he began organizing agricultural workers in El Paso. That effort led eventually to the opening of the center to help migrant families with food, shelter, and other day-to-day needs.

I saw only a few workers that day. Carlos said they would begin drifting in around March for the April onion season. In July, the chile harvest would start and draw the most farm workers. They stay through December and the start of the pecan harvest.

In the summer and early fall, Carlos will shelter about one hundred men and women a night. They'll sleep on the floor, wrapped in blankets but dressed for work including their boots. They wake up and stumble from the floor to a coffee machine and then to the buses that carry them to the fields.

Most of these workers are about fifty-five. Younger workers often leave for New England, where they face less job competition. The older workers stay close to Mexico, visiting family on days they take off. Sometimes Carlos sees them rummaging through photos in their wallets and on their cell phones, looking at spouses and children, parents and siblings left behind, exuding a desolate feeling that mingles with the smell of sweat and coffee and cigarettes.

The older workers have been harvesting for years in New Mexico's Luna and Hidalgo counties not far from El Paso. They might travel an hour to three hours on the buses depending on the location of the field. They pick by hand and use plastic buckets. The landowner determines how the workers will be paid, by the day or by the pound. Some days last longer than others. Carlos rifled through a pile of pay stubs: $38.78. $53.96. $58.

"You work today and you don't know for how long but you go out anyway," Carlos said. "You don't know what might happen tomorrow. Maybe there's no work. Maybe you're deported."

"I came to Arizona only to work," Rosa tells me.

In Mexico, she had been a bank teller full time and earned forty dollars every two weeks. She and her husband, Gerardo, would take vacations in Tucson to visit his aunt. While she was there, Rosa babysat part time and made one hundred dollars in five days. When she became pregnant with her first child, she asked Gerardo, How will we provide for this baby in Mexico? They applied for U.S. worker visas and moved to Tucson in 1998. Rosa cleaned houses and brought in more than twelve hundred dollars a month. Gerardo worked as a landscaper. When it was time to have the baby, they returned to Mexico. She now has two boys, thirteen-year-old Gerardo Jr. and ten-year-old Emiliano, both born in Mexico. Rosa thought she would be accused of using her children to receive welfare if she delivered them in the States. She wanted to be a mother, yes, but she also wanted to work.

It makes her sad that people think she came here to receive benefits and take jobs from U.S. citizens. I think she means it makes her angry, but I may be wrong because I hear in her voice a kind of despondent confusion that she would be thought of in this way.

"They say we are all killers, robbers," she tells me.

Occasionally, yes, she is sure a Mexican immigrant does a bad thing, but not every one of them. They are not all awful people. She has been told by Americans that they could not work the hours she does at the taco factory. Twelve, twenty hours, no way, they say. They don't need to. They're citizens. They can work somewhere else.

The Mexican men and women at the country club all had work permits. Most of them stayed in Chicago with family who had come to the States before them. A few had been employed by vineyards in California. What English they knew, they learned on the job.

My first days after I was hired, I'd follow the Mexicans out to a tool shed every morning for our job assignments. Cut golf tees, pick up dead branches, trim hedges, clean sand bunkers, whatever it might be.

When I would grab a rake, one of the Mexicans, sometimes Anarbal, sometimes Santos, would say, No, no, mister. That's mine. OK, I would say and take another one. That's my rake, Miguel or Raul would say. For every rake I chose, someone, Antonio or Lydia or whoever, took it from me until I was left alone in the shed with the last rake.

I wondered what was behind their behavior. Were they picking on me, the new guy? Were they asserting seniority? Were they worried that the country club would replace them with gringos? Did they think, What will happen to us?

I never asked and I did not complain. I knew I would only look weak if I ran to the supervisor. I pushed back another way. I hung out with the Mexicans in the morning before we clocked in and I ate my lunch with them during the afternoon break, speaking what little Spanish I knew. I asked about their lives. I told jokes. I talked about the trouble I'd had finding work as a journalist. They nodded at this because they understood what it was like to be unemployed.

"Muy difícil," they murmured among themselves. Very difficult.

There was no one particular moment when things changed. The harassment just eased until it stopped. One afternoon while we were eating lunch, a woman asked for our supervisor. She approached several Mexicans. They did not speak English and pointed to me.

"May I help you?" I asked.

"It would be nice if someone here knew something other than Spanish," she snapped.

"May I help you?" I repeated.

She told me water was spilling into her yard from one of the country club's drainage pipes. I passed her concern on to the supervisor and mentioned her complaint about everyone speaking Spanish.

"Well, if club members gave us the money to hire people at a decent hourly rate, we wouldn't have to hire Mexicans, would we?" the supervisor said.

His comment didn't surprise me, but his blunt assessment did. He stared at the floor for a moment and then shook his head. He told me to help Anarbal trim a hedgerow.

Anarbal grew up on a farm in Chiapas. He followed friends to Chicago in 1995. He had worked at the country club for more than ten years and spoke English better than he gave himself credit for. After work, he cooked at an Italian restaurant every evening but Sunday and rarely got home before midnight. He came to work in clothes stained with grease and tomato sauce, his eyes half open, face drawn.

I found Anarbal in the tool shed. He called me Mister although I had told him my name several times; he had difficulty pronouncing

Malcolm. Mister spared him the trouble. I didn't mind. Grabbing a pair of shears, I followed him to the front of the country club. A hedgerow stood parallel to the entrance. Club members drove past us as we began cutting errant twigs. Anarbal trimmed judiciously. He stepped back, examined his work, and made adjustments. He raked fallen twigs into a pile and scooped them into a bag. I hacked at the hedgerow as if I were in a knife fight. I didn't care how the bushes looked. I resented being here, resented this mindless drudgery. I wanted to tear them out by the roots. I wanted to stomp them into the dirt, kick and scream, and rip them to shreds. I threw my shears. Anarbal grabbed my arm.

"What are you doing, man?" he said.

I didn't answer. I knew I would leave, score a freelance gig eventually, and get on with my life. Anarbal wasn't going anywhere. He may not have wanted to, I don't know. He let go of my arm and said nothing more, but I knew he expected me to respect his job.

Many of the farm laborers at El Centro de los Trabajadores Agrículturas Fronterizos don't have work permits and consequently are hostage to low wages because they have no legal recourse. Landowners send buses to the center to pick up the workers at midnight. They leave about an hour later and arrive at the fields while it is still dark. The landowners bring them early so they can start harvesting at sunrise. They wait without pay and watch the flight of bats. Some farmers refuse to take workers who carry their own water. They want the workers to buy bottled water from them at jacked-up prices.

Since she left the sanctuary, Rosa has remained in Tucson. She never travels outside of the city. Never. She lives with a kind of disquiet that follows her like a shadow, a daily worry the intensity of which comes and goes. She accommodates this fear day to day, but she does not allow it into her home. There she focuses on being a good wife and a good mother to her boys. She lives in the same situation as all other undocumented people, even if she is not a priority for ICE. She hopes the critics of migrants are humane despite their angry words, and that they will not do the things they say.

"I don't want to be deported," her younger son tells her one night.

"It is not just us," she tells him. "Have faith."

"Faith in what?" he asks her.

Rosa has overheard her children tell their friends, If your family gets in trouble, find a church. You have rights. The right to look for help. You have that much.

The father of a boy they knew was deported. He tried to return and got lost in the Arizona desert near Douglas.

"Was he found?" I ask.

Rosa doesn't know.

When she prepared to move into Southside Presbyterian Church in August 2014, Rosa consoled herself by thinking it would be only a matter of days before she returned home. She bought food to provide for her family while she was away. In the church she lived day to day. Her lawyer was negotiating with ICE but it was taking longer than expected. Days turned into weeks. Weeks turned into months. Rosa hated the wait. She cooked meals for her family. Her husband stopped by after work on the way home from his landscaping jobs, then hurried off with the food to take to their boys. Her children visited on weekends when they had a break from homework and Little League. Between visits, Rosa would call and text them.

Each time her family left after visiting her, Rosa's sadness deepened. It was hard to believe it had come down to this: to stay in the United States, she had to be separated from everyone, including her family. She worried that the publicity around her case would lead to their deportation. She paced in her room, felt desperate for them.

Why stay? she recalls asking herself. Because Tucson was home now. Because living here provided an opportunity for her husband and children that Mexico never could. Because she had done nothing wrong.

Rosa says she had looked into becoming an American citizen, but she had no special skill to offer and knew no American who would sponsor her. She and Gerardo made a life for themselves anyway. They worked, they raised a family.

"How was that a crime?" she asks me.

I had no answer.

She talked to other people in sanctuary around the country once a week for support. Volunteers with the church stayed with her so she would not be alone. Some of them spoke only English. She didn't mind. She liked having them around.

Rosa helped at the church to stay busy. She cleaned bathrooms, prepared meals for the homeless. She listened to the stories of men and women sleeping on the street and thought, Well, I have it good here, and for a moment forgot she was in sanctuary. Other days when everyone left, she became aware of the silence. She thought of her family, how cut off she was despite having a phone and the company of volunteers, and she wept.

Rosa's tears would not have moved Gary. He had been at the country club for almost forty years. He had never worked with Spanish-speaking people before until his supervisor, Joel, began bringing on Mexicans in 2005. Two of them, Oscar and Antonio, had been with Joel at another country club for twenty years. They worked hard and accepted minimum wage, Joel told Gary. Gary called Antonio "Tony" and Antonio would correct him.

"You're in America," Gary told him. "You're Tony."

When it suited him—that is, when he wanted to get out of a particular job—Gary would remind anyone paying attention that he was the senior employee. He was convinced Oscar and Antonio wanted him to retire so they could claim seniority. Gary had no plans to leave.

"I'm not putting down no sod, get one of the Mexicans," he'd say. "I'm the senior employee."

"Cállate, tortuga," the Mexicans told him. Shut up, turtle.

When he pulled the hood of his sweatshirt over his head and tightened it, pinching his heavy face into pockets of fleshy bulges and wrinkles, Gary did look like a turtle. Antonio and Oscar laughed. Gary did not speak Spanish and didn't know they were laughing at him. He sat on a mower and watched them, the other

Mexicans and me lay sod until he clocked out. He was fifty-eight and lived with his widowed mother. He had never married, never moved out of his parents' house. He never had to face the world alone as Antonio, Oscar, Anarbal, and the other Mexicans had. He had never needed overtime.

As I got ready to depart El Paso for Tucson, Carlos told me about a young Mexican man who got up at midnight one morning to harvest onions. He arrived at the field three hours later and waited until seven o'clock when there was enough light to work. By that time, so many workers had arrived that the field was harvested in less than three hours and the young man was back at the center by one o'clock. He earned just under twenty dollars. That night he was up again at midnight and boarding a bus for another field.

No matter what happens politically in the United States, Carlos told me, most workers do not think their lives will change. No matter what they do in Mexico, no matter how hard they work, they will remain poor. Consequently, they will keep coming into Texas and elsewhere. They will work about ten months and then many of them will return to their families in Mexico. If they are deported, they will simply cross back. Some will make it, some won't. Most will, or others will take their place because the landowners in Luna and Hidalgo counties need them.

"Who else will pick the chiles, onions, lettuce, and cabbage?" Carlos asked me.

On the day Rosa's lawyer told her that he had reached an agreement with ICE and she could leave the church, she felt lost. She had become a local cause célèbre and the experience was disorienting. She saw signs on the street—*We Stand With Rosa. Keep Tucson Together*—and cried. People she did not know stopped her and told her how wonderful it was that she was out. They recognized her from news reports, they told her. When she got home, she sought the silence she had known in the church until she could collect herself and control the emotions overwhelming her.

These days, she lives a cautious life. If she sees a police officer, she watches him and follows all the traffic laws. She understands ICE is not looking for her. Still, she remains aware. She knows people who have been deported and they don't return. To cross the desert is really hard. They call from Mexico and tell their families, Stay in Tucson. The cartels in Mexico are too strong. Drug traffickers compete with one another for control of Tijuana and Ciudad Juárez, and the states of Durango, Sinaloa, Guerrero, Chihuahua, Michoacán, Tamaulipas, and Nuevo León. Mexico is very dangerous now, the deported people tell their families in Tucson.

Rosa stops talking, glances at her watch. She needs to leave for work. Eight hours today, maybe more. She doesn't know. I will follow her out and leave Tucson for my Kansas City home, driving until dark. I'll be fast asleep in a motel when Rosa gets home, when the farm workers get up, when the Mexicans at the country club start at dawn.

Rosa shakes my hand.

"No overtime," she reminds me.

Desert North

Sarah Roberts and I load a Jeep with bottled water, canned beans and tuna, and medical supplies and leave Tucson taking Interstate 19 south to the ramshackle, off-the-grid town of Arivaca, about ten miles north of the Mexican border and a little over thirty miles northwest of Nogales, a port of entry. We continue for another hour into the Sonoran Desert and park. Before we begin walking, Sarah leaves a jug of water by the Jeep.

"For someone in need," she says.

We carry more water and canned food with us in backpacks and follow a dry stream to a broken dirt bank and climb over to a trail and slog uphill into the brush. Just 10:30 this April morning and already a simmering, unfriendly heat. Sarah assumes that temperatures should reach the nineties today. In the summer, it will be much hotter, more than one hundred degrees some days. The U.S. National Park Service recommends that hikers drink one half to one full quart of water every hour in extreme heat. No way can the people we hope to help today carry that much water.

The U.S. Border Patrol estimates more than six thousand five hundred migrants have died near the U.S.-Mexico border since

1998. Increased law enforcement has led, some advocates think, to migrants taking more obscure and dangerous routes north through increasingly barren and uninhabited terrain. Their suspicions are well-founded. The 1994 Border Patrol strategic plan put forth a strategy deliberately designed to make migration more difficult and potentially deadly.

"The prediction is that with traditional entry and smuggling routes disrupted, illegal traffic will be deterred, or forced over more hostile terrain, less suited for crossing and more suited for enforcement," the report reads.

In 2002, more than two hundred migrant men and women were known to have died in Arizona deserts. Sarah presumes many more lost their lives, but their bodies were never found. That year, she and other immigration activists and people of faith formed Tucson Samaritans, a group of more than one hundred volunteers who go out into the desert seven days a week to assist migrants. They leave food, water, socks, and medical supplies along known and suspected travel routes.

"We can offer food, water, medical attention," Sarah tells me. "That's not violating the law, but we can't harbor, transport, or further their illegal presence in the United States. One time, we came across a migrant who asked, 'Where is Chicago?' We explained how far we are from Tucson, let alone Chicago. We showed them a map where they were. But we didn't give directions. That would be considered furthering an illegal presence."

Sarah grew up in Ohio, raised by socially conscious parents. In high school and college, she met "social justice types" involved in migrant rights. Later, she spent part of her college years studying in Spain. In the early 1980s, she chose to earn a nursing degree in Tucson where she had friends and she never left.

It was as a nurse at Carondelet St. Mary's Hospital-Tucson that Sarah met Janet, a migrant in her mid-twenties from Chiapas. Her mother had cancer and Janet wanted to work in the U.S. and pay for her mother's medication, but she broke an ankle when she crossed into Arizona. Left behind by other migrants, she tied discarded clothing to her knees and hands and crawled and hobbled north for four days. In the evening, she'd look at the sky and see her mother's face. When it rained she drank water from puddles. At one point, she reached an empty, unlocked house. Framed photos of men in military gear hanging from the walls made her uneasy and she left and made her way to a road. A passerby picked her up and took her to a hospital. Because she was not in the custody of the Border Patrol, the hospital released her after she recovered. She now lives in Idaho and Sarah still hears from her.

We follow a trail into Wilbur Canyon, part of the nearly one-hundred-twenty-thousand-acre Buenos Aires National Wildlife Refuge. We pause by a mesquite tree and find a rolled blanket beneath it. Sarah nudges the blanket with a stick, wary of snakes and scorpions. Ants scurry over a comb, a crushed tube of toothpaste, a toothbrush, a small shampoo bottle, and empty Red Bull cans. Red Bull and other energy drinks hold off exhaustion but also contribute to dehydration. Near the cans, a water jug painted black so it won't reflect the sun, and a pair of torn slippers with soles made of thick carpet to avoid leaving tracks.

Sarah points to a large, round, barrel cactus. It grows at an angle and points south. Migrants use it as a kind of compass. Walk in the opposite direction from where the cactus faces and you'll be headed north. A thin, acidic fluid runs through the plant and can make people sick, Sarah cautions. Cutting into it exposes a prickly pulp good to eat but full of small stickers. You must clean it first. Samaritans have pulled thorns from the mouths of migrants who bit into the cactus desperate for water.

Another compass point: Baboquivri Peak, a distant, solitary rise of barren rock in the Baboquivri Mountain Range. A telescope, part of the Kitt Peak National Observatory, glints in the sunlight to one side of it. The range runs north to south. As long as migrants keep the telescope to their left they'll be heading north, Sarah says.

I squint at the peak and the land between us and realize that I could stand here an hour and not see anyone or anything other than cactus and mesquite.

"Amigos," Sarah shouts. "Somos Americanos con comida y agua. Estamos con una iglesia." Friends, we are Americans with food and water. We are with a church.

No response.

"No tengas miedo. No somos policías," Sarah shouts. Do not be afraid. We are not police.

The echo of her voice fades and a breeze rustles the knee-high, pale grass. Birds call, flit past. Pebbles roll down an embankment. The sky remains motionless, cloudless, and empty.

One year, two Samaritan volunteers saw vultures in an otherwise vacant sky. Should we stop, they asked themselves. Perhaps it was intuition, Sarah says, but they walked toward the spot where the birds circled to a gully and heard a man calling out who had injured his legs and could no longer walk or stand. He was from Honduras.

"Tenemos agua y comida, suministros medicos." We have water and food, medical supplies.

Nothing.

Sarah and I resume walking.

"We see less usage of the water we put out overall," she says. "Maybe fewer people are crossing. Maybe it's the Trump effect and the active destruction of rescue supplies by the Border Patrol. They puncture water bottles and confiscate food. I have found slashed water bottles and bottles filled with a red liquid. Dye or poison? I don't know. I've also found notes: We hope you die. It might be the cartels controlling the flow of migrants. We don't know. Sometime they just stay hidden unless they need help."

In 2009, Sarah received a call from a young Guatemalan man in Oakland, California, whose fiancé, Credencia Artine Gomez, had crossed into the U.S. that summer, part of a group of migrants, but was left behind when she became ill. The young man, Ismael, had planned to send for her once he was settled and had not known she had crossed. His father was in the Guatemalan military, and Ismael fled the country when groups critical of the military threatened him. Credencia, he learned later from the migrants who had come over with her, had wanted to surprise him.

"I just want to find her body," Ismael told Sarah.

Guatemalan migrants who had entered the U.S. after Credencia told him they saw her remains by a power line pole in Ironwood National Monument Park west of Tucson. She was wearing a dark red sweatshirt and jeans and had long, flowing black hair, and a tattoo on her left wrist. Sarah and three other Samaritans looked for her body but did not find it.

How far from the power pole? Sarah asked Ismael after the failed search.

Ten minutes west maybe, he guessed.

Sarah went out again with another migrant aid group, Humane Borders and found Credencia's body by a dry creek just as Ismael had said, not far from a power line. Had it rained she might have had enough water to survive. Her body had decomposed and been dismembered by scavengers.

Sarah flew to Oakland to tell Ismael. He was so distraught, she recalls. He'd lost the love of his life and didn't know what to do. He told her he had met Credencia when they were thirteen. They knew they wanted to be together even then. He would always see her walking home from school or playing basketball. They were both athletic. She was eighteen when she died.

"Their lives are a form of resistance, I think," Sarah says. "I've seen how people find the strength to not give up. There is so much sadness but despite everything, they keep coming."

We walk a little farther and find a mesquite tree with six bottles of water and five cans of beans. A Samaritan drop site. I read greetings scrawled on the containers: *Buenas suerte.* Good luck. *Ten un viaje seguro.* Have a safe journey.

Sarah tells me to leave one of the bottles we brought, and hands me a Magic Marker.

"Write something on it."

"What?"

"Bienvenido," she suggests. Welcome.

Butterflies

Early morning, April 2017. I drive from my Kansas City home to Texas, to meet with thirty-three-year-old Marleny Menchu Gaspa, a Guatemalan woman held at the T. Don Hutto Residential Center outside of Austin.

The center holds mostly Central American and Mexican women caught entering the United States illegally. It is named after Terrell Don Hutto, a cofounder of Correction Corporation of America, now called CoreCIVIC, which operates several private prisons and detention centers, including Hutto. Before it contracted with U.S. Immigration and Customs Enforcement in 2006, Hutto had been a medium-security state prison.

Grassroots Leadership, an Austin nonprofit that advocates on behalf of Hutto detainees, arranged my visit. Before I left Kansas City, I spoke by phone with Mimi Lawrence, a Grassroots volunteer. She described Hutto to me as a place with high walls, guards, metal doors, scanners.

"Airport security stuff, the whole bit," Mimi said.

Mimi began seeing Hutto detainees in 2014—her "amigas," as Grassroots volunteers refer to the women. Before each visit, she checks the ICE website. If she doesn't find a detainee's name, they're gone. She can only guess what happened. Asylum, transferred, bonded out, or deported.

Mimi recalls one detainee, a Honduran woman who wanted to be a teacher, interrupted her studies to flee gang violence. Very sweet person, twenty something. On one visit, Mimi mentioned that her husband had been hospitalized for knee surgery.

I'll pray for you, the woman said.

She gave Mimi a prayer book and a friendship bracelet. Mimi can still picture herself sitting on a bench outside her husband's hospital room, the prayer book in hand.

"What happened to her?" I asked Mimi.

"She didn't make it," Mimi says. "She got deported."

The Center stands just outside Taylor, Texas, population 14,000, about an hour north of Austin. The wire fence surrounding the white, block buildings suggests a housing project. More than five hundred women live behind Hutto's walls. I walk inside and a guard asks me to sign in, remove my shoes and the contents of my pockets. I step through a body scanner, just as Mimi described.

The guards are friendly. They comment on a storm that recently drenched Taylor and all of Austin. But I still feel their distrust. Their work requires a level of suspicion that casual conversation can't conceal.

A guard escorts me into a large, brown carpeted room. Heavy blue chairs occupy the center. Dim lighting scarcely illuminates the pale walls. Three plexiglass cubicles, designed for legal consultations,

take up one side. Near one cubicle, a boy and a girl, the children
of a visitor, play with Legos. I sit in one of the chairs and wait for
thirty-three year-old Marleny, the woman I have come to see. The
facility's policy prohibits me from bringing in a pad and pen for
notes. After we speak, I will hurry out to my car and jot down what
I remember.

Marleny walks through a door. She wears blue sweat pants and
a T-shirt. She sits across from me, hands clasped on her lap.

"Can you adopt me, can you help me?"

She smiles. Joking. Acknowledging the impossibility of her request.

The next day, on another rain-soaked morning, clinical psychologist John Rubel greets me at the door of his suburban home, not far
from Taylor. He worked at Hutto, but left because of what he considered to be the administration's interference with his work. After
making himself a double espresso, he joins me at a table. When we
begin talking about the facility and the women detained there, he
answers my questions with a slow deliberation. Sometimes he says,
"Golly," when reaching for an answer.

John worked at Hutto from 2013 to 2015. He never imagined himself at a detention center. Originally, his plan had been
to graduate with a marketing degree and work in his father's water
well business in upstate New York. One day, a professor suggested
he enroll in a personality theory course, to help him understand
the individual impulses that influence markets. John followed his
advice and found he enjoyed the writings of Freud so much that he
switched his major to psychology.

After completing a graduate degree at Chicago's Forest Institute of Professional Psychology in the mid-1980s, he accepted an internship with the Federal Bureau of Prisons.

We have a slot, an administrator told him. We'll send you to a federal prison in El Reno, Oklahoma.

Where's that? John asked.

Go south, he was told.

After twenty-six and a half years, John retired from the Federal Bureau of Prisons and set up a part-time, private practice. Three years later, in 2013, a colleague told him that Hutto had an opening for a clinical psychologist. John considered it. There was one drawback: he didn't speak Spanish.

You might want a bilingual psychologist, he told Hutto administrators.

They disagreed. Most of the healthcare staff didn't speak Spanish, either. John could hire an interpreter. He accepted the job, clueless, he admits, about immigration issues and the detention system.

It surprised John to learn that private prison companies house more than half of the detainees in the U.S. Detainees have no constitutional right to a lawyer, because they are not citizens and are not facing criminal trial. Many do not speak English, have no criminal record, and have committed no wrongdoing other than entering the U.S. without a visa. That in itself is a civil violation, not a criminal offense.

Like immigration detainees in other centers across the country, the women at Hutto are held like prisoners while not being considered prisoners. In his years working for the Federal Bureau of Prisons, John had never experienced anything like this. Most of the detainees were in their late teens or early twenties. John felt he had entered a high school, except all the young women were locked up.

"Like a prison," he says.

During my visit at Hutto, Marleny tells me that she grew up on a coastal farm in Guatemala with six brothers. She and her brothers helped their father harvest tomatoes and corn. When they weren't working, they played marbles and flew kites.

A 2007 flood ruined their land. Neighbors became ill from drinking dirty water. They developed rashes. Marleny's family could no longer grow crops. She was twenty-three, young and eager, and desired a better life. She told her father she wanted to live in the U.S.

"We will live simply and get by," her father insisted.

Eventually, he conceded that the farm had no future. It made sense for her to leave. Marleny traveled north by foot and by bus through Mexico. She crossed deserts. She saw mirages of cities. Near the Texas/Mexico border, she noticed that mesquite trees had been trimmed to reduce cover. Twice, border patrol agents caught her and sent her back to Mexico. She crossed successfully on her third attempt and made her way to Houston. From there, she took a bus to Los Angeles, where an aunt lived.

Her aunt had legal status. She wanted Marleny to work in a neighborhood bar that needed a waitress. Marleny refused; she didn't like bars and the people who frequented them. Her aunt insisted. It would be a job. Marleny still said no. Her aunt put her out of the house for the day to break her resistance.

At a nearby park, Marleny found herself sitting beside a woman who knew of a Hindu restaurant that needed people, but it was too far to walk. To earn money for bus fare, Marleny made tostadas and sold them door-to-door. In this way, she met a Guatemalan man living in the same building as her aunt. He worked as a fruit vendor. He was not a U.S. citizen. After a while, Marleny moved in with him. They had two children, a boy and a girl.

Marleny and the children's father lived together until 2011, but their relationship was unravelling. Marleny's father was sick with cancer, so she returned to Guatemala by bus to care for him. She took the children with her.

Seven months later, her father died. Marleny stayed on to help her mother. She began a relationship with a man who became physically abusive. She worked and saved money to leave him and return to the States.

In August 2016, Marleny bought a ticket to fly her children to their father in LA. She would cross into the U.S. by herself. But her daughter refused to leave without her. Her son flew to California alone.

In October, Marleny and her daughter took a bus to Hidalgo, Texas, a port of entry. She told U.S. Customs and Border Protection officers that she was fleeing her abuser and requested asylum. An officer told her she would be placed in detention. Her daughter, an American citizen, would be removed from her care.

"I'll return to Guatemala," Marleny said. "Don't take my daughter."

"Too late," the officer told her. "You're with us now."

Marleny held her daughter for what felt like hours. Then an officer gripped her from behind while another pulled her daughter from her arms.

Momma, help me, the girl cried, Marleny recalled. Tell them I want to be with you.

Marleny collapsed in tears. She was bussed to Laredo Detention Center, where she applied for asylum. In November, she was transferred to Hutto. Authorities released the girl to Marleny's aunt in LA, who turned the girl over to her father. As the biological parent, the father is entitled to custody and guardianship of his children, regardless of his status. Unless ICE detains him, he can remain in the U.S. with his children.

Marleny tried to hold her family together with phone calls, but her daughter's father told her he didn't want to hear from her.

Our daughter gets upset when she talks to you, he said. She wets the bed.

The father recently put a block on her calls.

"What if I don't get asylum?" Marleny asks me during my visit. "What if I'm deported? I'll never see my children."

She cries. A guard brings her Kleenex. I watch her wipe her eyes but I can think of nothing to say. Finally, I thank her for her time. I wish her good luck. Before I leave, I see a guard scan her with a wand, presumably to check if I slipped her something. Then Marleny stops at a door, opens it, and I no longer see her.

At his kitchen table, John tells me that every woman he counselled at Hutto had experienced something awful prior to their detention. Sexual assault was common. As part of their initiation into gangs, young men allowed gang members to rape their girlfriends. Gangs also extorted families.

Other detainees experienced the horrors of the road. A *coyote* kidnapped one detainee and raped her repeatedly for seven days. One teenage detainee saw a friend cut in half after he fell off a freight train in southern Mexico.

None of the women came to Hutto directly. They were first detained in temporary cells in south Texas ICE stations that the women called "*hieleras*," or ice boxes, because of their frigid temperatures. Immigrant rights groups accuse U.S. Customs and Border Protection of deliberately keeping the temperature low to pressure detainees to agree to deportation.

If a woman decided to fight her removal, she might spend 10 to 12 hours on a bus bound for a detention center without any idea of her destination. Single women without children landed in Hutto. They stayed about six to eight weeks before an immigration judge decided their case.

At Hutto, prison jargon interspersed with normal speech. Detained women made up the "population." They had "uncontrolled movement" within the "facility." At certain times of day, they stood for a "headcount." They had "access" to a gym, art, and ESL classes, and other various indoor and outdoor "activities." At night, they slept in two person, 9 x 12 cells. No bars, but the doors could be "secured."

Stress took its toll. Hundreds of confined women who didn't

know one another had to get along. They confronted a legal system they didn't understand. They worried about their families back home. They agonized about being deported. Their health suffered. Twenty year old women complained of chest pains, loss of appetite, headaches and nightmares.

After his first two weeks counseling at Hutto, John concluded that he could not hold individual therapy sessions for so many detainees. He developed group therapy programs instead. Participation was voluntary.

Come once a week while you're here, John told the women. I can help you manage your emotions, show you how to handle your fears and all the stress you're under.

He facilitated three groups a day, five days a week. Eight to ten women attended each group. They sat in a circle, introduced themselves, and said where they came from. Honduras, El Salvador, Mexico, Guatemala. In one exercise, John asked yes and no questions. Whoever answered yes entered the circle. John asked, "Who has children? How many of you have parents who are still alive? How many of you worry about your children back home?"

Almost all of the women responded by stepping into the circle "You have a lot in common," John told them. "You're not alone."

In another exercise, John showed the women an ink drawing of a caged butterfly.

"Is this you?" he asked. "Do you sit in a cage all day?"

A few women nodded yes.

He offered a second drawing. It showed dozens of multicolored butterflies fluttering around outside the same cage.

"Get out of your cells." John said. "Take care of yourself."

He distributed pictures of butterflies. Yellow, brown, black, red, green and many other varieties.

"If you were a butterfly, which one would you be?" John asked.

The women picked.

"Why that one?"

"It's free."

"I like the color."

"It's big."

"It's beautiful."

John gave each woman a picture of the butterfly they had chosen.

"I think butterflies are strong," John told them. "They are also fragile and delicate. They can also travel long distances and survive. I think people are a lot like butterflies."

Some of the women got tearful. They had come to the U.S. with hardly anything. What little they owned, border patrol agents took away. Now they had this, a flimsy piece of paper, a picture of a butterfly.

John never knew how long a woman would participate in group. One day they attended, the next day, they vanished. He received no notice about where they might be or why. The absent woman aroused fears of deportation among the remaining women.

"Maria is gone." John said. "Let's stand."

He held a carving of two hands in prayer.

"For those of you who want to pray, touch the hands. Turn your thoughts over to the God you believe in."

At least twice a month, a detainee received bad news, usually a death in the family. How do you deal with a sudden loss while locked up? John asked himself. How do you say what you need to say to a dying person from your cell in Hutto?

One woman lost a son to a gang. Shot, murdered. It was gut-wrenching to see her. She stayed in the Hutto medical clinic isolation room for a few days just to be alone and grieve.

Some of the guards showed little patience for her tears.

"Go to your room," they said. "You can't be in the common area. You're upsetting people."

Sometimes in group, John asked the women to consider their options should they be deported. Did they fear for their safety? What would they need to do to say alive?

How do you want to die? he asked. He was deliberately provocative, to get the women to release their anger. Would you fight back? How do you want to be remembered? As a fighter?

One group participant, Violeta, a Salvadoran woman in her twenties, told John she had no family or friends left in El Salvador. Her father owned a small convenience store. Violeta and her older brother worked for him. A local gang demanded money, and when the family couldn't pay, the gang murdered Violeta's father and brother. Violeta and her mother found their bodies one afternoon when they returned home from shopping. A gang member watching their house shot Violeta's mother. Violeta escaped through a back door.

Violeta told John she believed the gang would hunt her down

and kill her if she returned home. She said she'd kill herself if she was deported.

"I'd rather die in Hutto," she told John.

He placed her on suicide watch.

A typical suicide watch rarely lasted more than three days. Violetastayed in a cell by herself for almost seven. She wore a smock she could not use to hang herself. She ate food without utensils.

John met with her and together they considered alternatives to suicide. She believed suicide was a sin. What would be the consequences if she killed herself? John asked. She did not want to go to hell, she told him.

"Where could you live other than your village?" John asked.

Violeta said she had a friend in another part of El Salvador. The killers would not know she was there.

Options. That was what John wanted her to find. Options to giving up.

After one week of therapy, John removed Violeta from suicide watch. She met with him several more times before an immigration judge denied her asylum claim.

"Send me a note," John told her. "Let me know how you are."

He wrote his Hutto office address on the back of her picture of a butterfly. He never heard from her. He hadn't expected to, not really. Why would she want to remember detention?

John considers his time at Hutto the most clinically challenging and emotionally taxing work of his career. It drained him. However, despite the challenges, or perhaps because of them, it was also his most satisfying professional experience. The groups succeeded. Suicide watches declined as did outpatient psychiatric and other medical care. The women got more active and involved in other center activities: basketball, volleyball, art and ESL classes.

However, administrators at Hutto didn't see the success. They didn't ask John, How can we support you? Instead, they questioned his methods. Why are you doing this? Why are we spending so much on interpretation services? They didn't say, You can't do groups anymore. Instead they told him to change the schedule because it took too much time. As a result, he held fewer groups. John resigned in 2015, about two years after he started.

"The mission of the U.S. Immigration and Customs Enforcement Health Service Corps is to provide care equal or equivalent to the community standard of care," John says. "It doesn't say, 'We treat only crisis and prevent suicide.' The mission is mental health treatment. It doesn't say, 'We can help you but you have to wait several weeks for a group.' I think that's immoral."

John offers to drive me through Taylor to Hutto. Although I've already seen it, I agree to go to the center again, to stare at its walls and reflect on my conversations with Marleny, Mimi, and John.

We get in John's car and drive past housing developments and shopping centers, part of Austin's expanding suburban sprawl, until we reach Taylor. Empty 19th Century storefronts take up much of its downtown. Luxury Inn & Suites advertise nightly rates. Flashing lights illuminate Zapatas Restaurant. Near it, a Quick Way Grocery and ACE Dental of Taylor.

When we reach Hutto, we circle the parking lot and John notes that barbed wire no longer lines the top of the former prison's walls. John pauses by the granite sign, T. Don Hutto Residential Center, and I lean out the window to snap a photo.

The dictionary defines 'residential' as "designed for people to live in/providing accommodations in addition to other services/ occupied by private houses." Hutto's use of the word accomplishes two contradictory goals: accuracy and deception. Residential sounds better than prison. Hutto's past use, however, leaves no doubt to its purpose today.

As I take my photo, I imagine Marleny behind the walls. I wish I'd had my interview with John before I met her. I might have brought her a picture of a butterfly. Or let her choose one from a series of pictures, as John had. I'll never know which butterfly she would have chosen or why; beauty, strength or fragility? She is a prisoner but not a prisoner, held in a prison no longer called a prison.

I turn to John. He is staring out the windshield and I notice the slightest shaking of his head.

"There has to be a better way to treat these women," he says. "Are they a threat? I didn't think so."

Hello, I Do Not Come Violently to Your Country

Please help me
I'm still the same
Lost in a different world
So close
But
So far away
Maybe,
if I close my eyes it will all disappear
No
Still here
Great big wall
Please
Somebody
Anybody
Help me

–Excerpted from the poem "Lost In A Different World," by Felix Alvarez

December 12, 2018

Despite everything—dropping out of the Army, brawling and drinking his way behind bars, and then, after serving three years in a Utah prison, being deported to Mexico—fifty-five-year-old Felix Alvarez sees each day as an opportunity to observe the desperation of his fellow human beings and determine from the hard-won lessons of his own bruised life who among them he can help. So I am not surprised when, out of dozens of Central American migrants, he zeroes in on one Honduran woman with an infant outside a tent on a Tijuana street in what he dismissively calls a bar district—*the hookers are another street over*—and recommends I talk to her, ignoring my suggestions of other people—*No, I don't like his look; No, he's busy with his family; No, they look half asleep*—not because he thinks she would be a good interview (How would he know?) but because he understands a homeless woman with a small girl in a country not her own is a woman in need, more need than he experienced after his expulsion from the U.S., and he sees me, a reporter, as the necessary bridge to begin a conversation that will allow him to hear her story and, if he can, offer her assistance.

What is your name? I ask her.

Ariché Ferrer Gomez.

Her voice rises barely above a whisper. Rumpled clothes and stuffed animals tangled in blankets clutter the interior of her damp tent. A church group, the name of which she does not know, gave Ariché the tent, its multicolored panels catching the afternoon sunlight that waxes it and other tents in a hot glare before it vanishes behind clouds which float above apartment buildings protected by gates that, despite their stylish design, indicate nothing less than a fearful desire to keep out those who lurk on the periphery of the camp: the intoxicated Mexican women wearing platform shoes and wigs the texture of straw; the skeletal, tattooed young men with shaved heads, lounging against cars, arms folded, their hooded stares following each passerby; the outstretched bodies of inebriated dope fiends, their legs swollen from drugs cut with something toxic, Felix explains, the skin splitting like torn cloth. And through this maze of destitution and implied violence, Ariché followed other migrants here to Cinco de Mayo Street, where local authorities opened the Benito Juarez Sports Complex, with its worn baseball field, playground, and two outdoor basketball courts, to about five hundred migrants.

City workers built showers and arranged portable toilets beneath an old scoreboard. Charitable organizations issued clothes and food from pickup beds, and police, alternating between vigilance and boredom, lingered on the edge of the emerging, makeshift village while more migrants arrived in Tijuana seeking asylum in the U.S.

Immigration opponents north of the border soon took notice. In California, hate crimes against Latinos increased by more than half. A headline in the *New American,* a right-wing magazine asked in October 2018: "Will Migrant Caravans Kill Your Child—With Disease?" During that year's midterm elections, President Donald Trump warned of an impending invasion.

The number of asylum seekers jumped almost 70 percent from 2017 to 2018. Nearly 93,000 people cited a credible fear of being targeted because of their race, religion, nationality, political opinions, or social group, the first step in winning asylum. That was up from nearly 56,000 migrants who asked for asylum in 2017. Only a limited number of people can apply for asylum in a single day. In Southern California, at San Ysidro, the nation's busiest port, sixty to one hundred asylum claims per day are processed. Meanwhile, as many as 5,000 migrants remain stranded in Tijuana, stuck on a waiting list. Only 10 percent of the requests are granted.

Far from the political posturing in Washington, the mild winter weather that had for months settled over Southern California and Tijuana turned cold and wet. It rained for several days the last week of November and the downpour turned the sports complex into a swamp; the migrants relocated to Cinco de Mayo Street itself, abandoning soiled clothes and children's toys in mounds of drenched refuse that fouled the air and still remained after the rain stopped, moldering in the heat beneath blue skies, when Felix and I showed up this morning one week later.

Another shelter in an old dance hall across town recently opened with accommodations that Mexican officials declared would include a roof and a dry floor. Felix has heard rumors that the government wants all the migrants on Cinco de Mayo to relocate there. Ariché does not know about the new shelter and does not appear to care. Her blank expression suggests she has lost the capacity to feel, that what emotional fortitude she once had vanished some time ago, leaving only this blank slate of an inscrutable twenty-three-year-old. Her tent stands between two families. The men, preoccupied with their wives and children, pay little attention to her, but their presence provides her with a modicum of security. Without them, she explains matter-of-factly, she would have had to find a boyfriend among the migrants for protection.

Where's your daughter's father? I ask.

My husband, Roberto, was murdered in May, she tells me.

In August 2018, he had left their home in the La Mosquitia region of Honduras to buy food and never returned. The killing, police told Ariché, was a case of mistaken identity. A member of MS 13 wanted to retaliate against someone who, unfortunately for Roberto, looked just like him. The police advised Ariché to be careful; the gang would likely come after her next. Why, she wanted to know, if it was a mistake? You'd be a trophy of war, the police said.

Ariché stayed with a friend for five weeks. She did not leave the house, lost track of the days of the week. Then her father told her about a large group of people leaving for the U.S. from San Pedro Sula. She left La Mosquitia at midnight by bus and three hours later joined about two hundred people waiting for buses to carry them north into Guatemala. From Guatemala, she and the other migrants walked into Mexico. She slept outside and thought of Roberto and cried. In the morning, men helped her carry her daughter, Leticia. Ariché developed blisters, cut them with a knife, and resumed walking. She waded muddy rivers and lost a sack of clothes and her ID, she climbed hills and fell, holding Leticia, and other migrants pulled her up, and she brushed off her squalling daughter and trudged onward. In this way, six weeks later, she reached Tijuana. She has yet to apply for asylum in the U.S. She doesn't know where to go. And what would she say?

I just want a room and a job, she tells us, and to live unafraid.

Felix whispers to me, I'm going to give her five dollars, in a tone of voice suggesting I should do the same. I dig into my pocket. A man leaning out of a tent watches us. We walk away and I slip Felix a five and he cups it in his hand and then we turn back and I ask Ariché another question as if that was the reason for our return.

What kind of work do you do?

I have a teaching certificate, but in Honduras you need to know someone in the Ministry of Education to get hired by a school, so I never taught—I cleaned the houses of rich people.

I shake her hand and then Felix does the same, slipping her the two fives.

Papa, Leticia says, looking at Felix.

Ariché smiles.

She calls all the men here, "Papa," she says.

Felix grins and tells Ariché he'll not forget her. He intends to speak with a pastor he knows about offering her shelter. The pastor takes in homeless people, Felix tells me. Ariché would have a room, people around to help with Leticia, and she'd be off the street. He doesn't think she has a chance for asylum because she has no proof Roberto was murdered. If the pastor agrees to take her, Felix will return here to see if she's interested. She may not be. Here on Cinco de Mayo Street, she belongs to a group of Central

Americans who have experienced what she has. At the church, she would be alone among people who would have no idea what it's like to abandon your country. It's hard. Felix knows.

When I moved to San Diego in 2018 to write about families fleeing the violence of Central America, I inquired about a translator. I understand enough Spanish to get by but I'm not fluent. Contacts I had in Tijuana recommended Felix because his English and Spanish were excellent and—as a deportee— he needed work.

Felix was born in Culiacan, Mexico, more than fifteen hundred miles south of Tijuana on Mexico's Pacific coast, but he grew up in California. He barely remembers when his father left Mexico for the U.S. in a 1949 Plymouth that he sold en route to pay for a smuggler. Two years later, when Felix was six, his father paid another smuggler to bring his wife and son. They rode in a Ford station wagon and Felix sat on his mother's lap. No one stopped them at the border and the smuggler drove straight through to East LA. Felix and his mother joined his father in a house behind his paternal grandmother's home. He remembers how they shared a thirteen-inch, black-and-white TV.

Felix's father gave him military toys and helmets to play soldier. When Felix was older, a pair of Bad Boy Heritage Boxing Gloves replaced the toys. He was thirteen when he first saw his father punch his mother. The old man was playing poker in their house and losing. He asked Felix's mother for money from her purse. When she refused, he threw a cup at her. Then he smacked her. At night, Felix's parents argued. Sometimes his mother would call to him and no matter how deep his sleep, he'd wake up and run to their bedroom and pound on the door, yelling, Are you OK, Mom? and the fighting would stop. His father would shout, Yes, everything's fine, but Felix would not leave until his mother told him she was unharmed.

In high school, Felix boxed and played racquetball at Belvedere Community Regional Park. His friends called him "Hubba Bubba," the brand name of the gum he chewed. His old man said he would disown him if he joined a gang and he would tell Felix to strip when he came home from school to see if he had tattoos or needle marks from drug use. He never did, but he felt pressure to join a gang. At Montebello High School, Felix fought two to three gangbangers at a time to prove his independence. When he was fifteen, a kid with the Mara 18 gang shot at him as he walked off a school bus. He ran home and his father drove him to an aunt's house, where he stayed until his father was confident the gang had not followed him. Felix transferred to another school, Baldwin Park High School. He still remembers the address: 4949 Bogart Street.

At eighteen, he saw for the first time the be-all-you-can-be recruitment ads for the Army. The images of guys jumping out of helicopters impressed him. That's for me, he thought. He had a green card and a recruiter told him he would become a citizen after boot camp. He enlisted in 1982. No one mentioned his status again. He assumed, wrongly, that his enlistment had made him a citizen.

After he graduated from basic training at Fort Knox, Kentucky, the Army sent Felix to Fort Lee, Virginia. Six months later, his mother asked him to come home.

Take care of me, she told him over the phone. Your father's beating me.

I can't just leave, Mom.

I need you, she repeated.

Felix asked one of his NCOs for an emergency leave. You can't do that, the sergeant said. Felix insisted.

It's my mother, he pleaded.

Finally, the sergeant advised him to request dismissal from the Army by claiming he could not adapt to military life. Felix followed his advice and received a general discharge under honorable conditions, which meant that his performance as a soldier had been satisfactory but that he had failed to meet all expectations of conduct. Upon appeal, his discharge was later upgraded to honorable.

At home, he broke up fights between his parents, pulling his father off his mother. But as he gained the upper hand, his mother would strike Felix on the back of the head with a pot, a water hose, a newspaper, whatever was within reach.

You're fucking up my life, he told his parents.

I didn't tell you to come home, his father snapped.

Felix started drinking. In 1998, drunk, Felix stole a Datsun 280Z, assaulted the cop who pulled him over, and received a three-year prison sentence. At the time, Felix did not know about a 1996 law that called for the deportation of immigrants convicted of crimes that meet the definition of an aggravated assault and who serve a sentence of at least one year. Upon his release in 2001, immigration authorities deported him to Tijuana. He lived on the streets for three years until he connected with a group of deported veterans who had established a support house. In 2010, he entered California, got caught, served three years in prison for illegal entry, and was deported again in 2013.

Felix knows what it's like to be Ariché. Well, he doesn't know what it's like to be a woman, but everything else about her, he gets. He felt lost in Tijuana, dropped into a world unlike anything he'd known. When Ariché speaks, her accent alerts anyone listening that she did not grow up in Mexico, that her Spanish is not Mexican Spanish anymore than the Spanish of Felix's East LA neighborhood is the Spanish of Tijuana. He was just a child when he moved to California, a few years older than Leticia. His parents wanted a better life. So does Ariché. Hundreds of people are fleeing Central America. Why? He answers his own question: For the promise of America. And yet they are no more wanted than he.

That's some profound shit, he tells me.

December 19, 2018. Five o'clock in the morning, San Diego. My cell phone rings.

Malcolm, this is Felix.

(groggy) Hey.

She's not there.

Who?

Ariché. I went back last night to tell her the pastor would meet with her but she was gone. The police are clearing the street and taking everyone to the new shelter.

Everyone?

A few are left.

OK, I'm coming.

OK.

Two hours later, Felix meets me on the Mexican side of San Ysidro. He tells me that two young men were found hanged in a downtown apartment. He suspects gang involvement. The Sinaloa cartel and a newer group, the Nueva Generación Jalisco, have been battling for control of the city's street drug sales. At night, in an apartment he shares with another veteran, Felix hears gunshots and car crashes and assumes it's cartel members battling it out. Recently he has been receiving phone calls from a private number. No one answers when he picks up. What's that about? he asks me.

In 2005, he sat in a Tijuana bar one night when a young woman started chatting him up. He told her he was a deported vet. You know how to use guns? she asked. Of course, Felix replied. I'd like you to meet someone, she said, and introduced him to stocky man in a leather jacket who said he had a job for him. Come with me and I'll give you a gun and then I'll tell you what I want you to do. Felix thought about it. He was broke and two years into his deportation, but he wasn't going out with some dude he didn't know. Give me the weapon first, Felix said. The man refused. Forget it then, Felix said. The man left with the woman and he never saw them again.

One thing about Tijuana, he says. If someone wants to kill you, they'll kill you. The fact that I'm not dead means no one wants to kill me. So I'm not worried.

He may not be, but this morning he is hypervigilant. Cutting through the bar district, he points to a guy he believes is following us and jerks me off the street and into an alley. The man, wearing ill-fitting, dirty clothes, stares at us but keeps going in another direction.

A dope fiend looking to roll American tourists, Felix says.

We continue walking, stepping over the bloated limbs of passed-out junkies, making our way between taco stands to Cinco de Mayo Street, where I see that the tent village has been reduced to half its size. A flea market has taken over the space once occupied by tents. Felix notices young men gathering in groups among the remaining migrants. They had not been doing that before, he comments. Now they've been here long enough to know they should stay together for protection. Soon, he believes, they'll be a gang, or others will assume they are, and then the fighting between Mexicans and the migrants will start.

The young men saunter beneath the same walled-off apartments and barred windows and flapping laundry lines I saw when we met Ariché. No movement of any kind among the drying blue jeans or on the balconies between which the laundry lines extend or inside the apartments. Even among the parked cars nothing stirs, as if the cars have been abandoned to the cats curled between the tires. The camp, or what remains of it, however, bustles with journalists roaming between tents shooting photos and video.

Several stop and take pictures of Felix and me, presuming wrongly that we're migrants. It's a hot story. Any photo will do if the subject looks the part. With our long gray hair and beards, our faded jeans and shoulder packs, Felix and I fit the profile.

Cigarette? a man asks Felix.

Felix digs into his coat pocket and gives him a smoke. Another man comes up beside him and demands to know what we're doing. We explain that I'm a journalist and then he tells us to give him a dollar. Felix cusses him out and photographers converge on what they presume will be a fight but the two men raise their hands and back off. The photographers follow them.

Looking for a family to speak with, I observe a man standing in front of a tent with a young woman and baby boy. The man has on a brown T-shirt and jeans that hang loosely off his thin body. His toes poke out of torn sneakers. The woman tugs at her faded sweatshirt and pants as if to make them fit better. They ignore the activity around them, standing apart from the other families, squeezed up against their tent, sorting clothes. Felix asks the man if I may talk to him and he agrees.

My name is Ikal Espinoza, he says.

We shake hands. He speaks a little English and answers some of my questions without Felix's help. I ask him why he has come to Tijuana. As we talk, the commotion of the camp occasionally intrudes.

I am here because of the high risk of life in Honduras, he says. In Honduras you live with fear. Any day someone can enter your house and kill you.

Ikal introduces us to his wife, Aurelia Maria Flores, and their son, eighteen-month-old Eric. Until recently, Ikal and his family had lived in San Antonio de Cortés, in northwestern Honduras, with his father and mother. His mother kept a garden of purple, white, and pink flowers; and birds called from papaya, avocado, and banana trees as Ikal walked through forests collecting wood for cooking. In 2017, a member of MS 13 killed his two nephews, Miguel and Rafael. Ikal doesn't know why. Twenty-four-year-old Miguel worked as a security guard in a metal factory and was shot walking home. Rafael, just four years older, was murdered in front of his house. Ikal had been in the living room listening to a reggae CD when he heard two gunshots. He looked out a window and the shooter saw him and ran. Rafael lay on his stomach, blood spreading out from beneath him. Ikal didn't move. He had no intention of going outside. Who would? He called the police.

Ikal pauses in his story and I overhear a man behind us speaking to a videographer.

No one has to tell you to leave, the man says. You just know you can't go back because of things you've seen. Where will you live? I had a house. I lost it. I just left it. It was a poor house with a dirt floor, aluminum walls. I was sad, but we have only one life, not two.

In early September 2018, a neighbor who knew the shooter told Ikal he had been released from prison and that he intended to kill him because Ikal had seen him shoot Rafael. Ikal and his family left that day and joined a group of migrants gathered in the western town of Corinto near the Guatemalan border. Ikal carried Eric on his shoulders. Sometimes people offered them rides, sometimes they caught a bus, but mostly they walked. Guatemalan police stood on the roadside but did not interfere. Ikal felt happy, his worries lifting with each step. He had the energy that comes with meeting a goal, like an athlete pursuing a medal, and he held up his arms as if he had won a trophy and laughed. At first his goal had been to escape Honduras. Now it was to reach the United States.

Ikal's mood changed when he entered Mexico. The country seemed so big, the distance to the U.S. border daunting. He felt small and overwhelmed. I'm in Mexico now, he told himself. I've left my home. He thought of his elderly parents and how they did not even know how to use a cell phone. How would he communicate with them? He began to cry and then composed himself and continued walking; he and his family arrived in Tijuana six weeks later. They stayed in the Benito Juarez Sports Stadium until the November downpour and then moved to the street with everyone else, wedging cardboard beneath their tent to keep it dry. He applied for asylum and was put on a waiting list, number 1,425. As he waits for his asylum interview, Ikal looks for work. He will take any job, provided he can bring his family with him because he won't leave them alone on the street. At night, he dreams ugly dreams. The previous night, he dreamt he fought off a man with a machete. He does not understand the source of this dream. At other times, fully awake and for no apparent reason, memories of violence fill his mind so completely that he feels as if he is back in Honduras.

When he was fifteen, he saw a headless body. The police

wrapped the corpse in plastic. An elderly woman examined the man's bare feet. That's my son, she said. The body lay close to a park. The mother didn't cry, but Ikal knew she suffered inside by the expression in her eyes.

He remembers Pepe, a young man he saw shoot another young man, Elvis. Ikal knew Pepe's father. He would sit on the porch of his house and they would exchange pleasantries whenever Ikal passed by. One time, Pepe's father complained of being hungry and Ikal gave him beans. He was a humble old man and he held the bag of beans with both hands as if they were something fragile.

On the day of the killing, Elvis was walking home after getting off work at a metal factory. Pepe noticed him and got up from the porch, Excuse me, Papa, he said. Then he turned to Ikal. You're going to see how I kill a man. Pepe stopped Elvis and gave him a banana. Elvis took it and Pepe shouted, Who told you you could have that? and shot him. Pepe laughed. Ikal felt as if the bullet had struck him. He sucked in his breath and his heart leaped and he vomited and ran. Ikal had attended school with Elvis. He was a simple, poor man, just nineteen. Black hair, maybe one hundred seventy pounds. The police shot Pepe a few days later. Ikal doesn't know the details. Until he left Honduras, he continued to see Pepe's father on the porch, but the old man no longer spoke to him or anyone.

Felix appreciates the story of Pepe. He assumes Pepe's father was somewhat like his own. Pepe might have turned out OK but he probably had a screwed-up family. Like father, like son.

Dad, my life could have been so different, Felix had told his father after he was deported. His father made no comment, but he would come to Tijuana and give him money when he could. He died in 2010.

A girl brushing her teeth bumps against me. She rinses her mouth from a bottle of water, spits. Some distance away, a woman screams from the bed of a pickup parked on Cinco de Mayo Street.

Calm down! I'm just handing out clothes, as a glut of migrants converge on her. Photographers close in, snap, snap.

I'm going to talk to the pastor I know about Ikal, Felix tells me.

OK.

I'm going to help him out.

He looks at me expectantly.

I take out my wallet and give him a few ones.

This is the last time, I say.

Felix gives Ikal the money and then asks if he has a cell phone. They exchange numbers.

December 26, 2018. Ten p.m. San Diego.

My cell phone rings:

Malcolm, this is Felix.

Yeah?

They closed down Cinco de Mayo Street. I went there tonight to give food to Ikal. They've moved everybody to the dance hall.

Have you heard from him?

No. But he must be there.

OK. See you in the morning. Eight o'clock.

I meet Felix at a taxi stand near downtown Tijuana. We ask a driver to take us to the dance hall on the city's east side, about a half-hour drive.

These people come to Mexico and bring problems and conflict, the driver complains. Hondurans beg for money. They steal and fight. We have our own poor. How come we take care of Central Americans? I came from Mexico City when I was twelve. I worked. I made my way. Why can't they do the same?

Have you met any migrants? Felix asks him.

No, the driver says, but I know the way they are.

He drops us off at an intersection amid a cluster of shops near the dance hall. Felix buys five beef tacos and soup to give to Ikal and some candy for Eric. Exhaust fumes from trucks and buses mingle with dust, and the clanging bells of food carts pushed by elderly men and women compete with the noise of car horns. We make our way to the hall, a large, white stucco building at the bottom of a hill. Beneath an arch, a man distributes fliers from the Mexican government offering fifty thousand pesos, about twenty-five hundred dollars, to migrants willing to return home. We wave the man off as he thrusts a flier at us and enter a large plaza where I imagine vendors gathered and sold T-shirts and other souvenirs of the bands that played when the hall was open.

Now, tents on wood pallets fill every available space. Graffiti adorn sheets of cardboard: *Kill ICE*; *Canada, I'm still waiting for you to take me in*; *Escaping death is not a crime*; and I as I read the angry scrawl, I overhear men and women speaking with representatives of Save the Children and other NGOs:

I'm from El Salvador. There is no work. I have three children. I had to leave to take care of my kids. Every day there is stealing and death. Gangs take people off the bus and kill them.

I lived near the capital where gangs are in charge. Even the cops, they are corrupt. I hear firecrackers and wake up. I think it's gunshots.

MS 13 was going to kill my son because he wouldn't join them. They beat him in May and again in August. We left with just what we had on. Gangs have total control.

Nearby, men sit in a circle playing cards and shooting dice, and they, too, talk about why they fled their homes:

There was no going back. We walked six, eight hours a day with calluses on our feet, sometimes without food or water, in the sunlight, in the dark. At night it was cold. People fought over sweaters and jackets. I found a sweater that was dirty but I wore it until I found another one. It was dirty too, but warmer.

Their conversations mingle with a kind of desperate commerce as families sell necklaces and wristbands made from string beside tables where women and children offer apples and bananas for twenty-five cents.

Felix and I enter a maze of pathways between tents, almost like streets dividing neighborhoods with some sections dubbed Little Honduras, Little Guatemala, Little El Salvador until by chance we see Aurelia and Eric. Felix calls to them. Turning, Aurelia smiles. He gives her the bags of food and candy and we follow her into the dance hall to find Ikal.

Before she knew Ikal, Aurelia had been married to a man who left her for another woman. In those days, she cleaned houses close to her home and never saw violence, although it still affected her. Gangs had killed her twenty-six-year-old nephew. His mother heard about it on the news. She had had dreams that he would be shot.

When Ikal told her, We have to leave, she brought only diapers and baby food. In Mexico, people offered them rides, but so many migrants would converge on a car that the drivers often didn't stop. Cattle trucks were much easier to catch because migrants who had leaped on ahead of Aurelia and Ikal would reach down and pull them aboard.

Aurelia has heard stories about children being separated from their families and worries that Eric may be taken from her if they reach the U.S. She left a four-year-old son from her first marriage, Pedro, with her mother, who advised her not to take two small children on such a long journey. Pedro stayed because Aurelia's mother thought he would be easier to care for than eighteen-month-old Eric. Aurelia misses Pedro. She tries not to think of him too much or her heart will break and she'll go back.

We find Ikal standing below a second-floor balcony where towels and clothes hang off a railing above his head. No light. Varying shades of shadow spread throughout the dance hall and it takes a moment for my eyes to adjust. A jumble of chairs and tables stand in one corner; a disc jockey's booth juts out from a wall. Around us, men and women emerge from a confusion of tents, snaking their way out of narrow openings, being careful not to stumble into one another, hair askew, sticks of deodorant in one hand, combs and toothbrushes in the other.

Ikal tells us that the police rousted him and the remaining migrants on Cinco de Mayo Street at about two o'clock in the morning. They were allowed to take their clothes but nothing else. They climbed into pickups as garbage trucks descended and cleared piles of abandoned tents and toys. Ikal prefers the shelter to the street but he does not feel entirely safe. On Christmas Eve, people partied. One drunken woman fell off the balcony. The police came but left. Ikal and Aurelia stayed in their tent holding Eric between them. Ikal overheard women propositioning men. At midnight, Mexican soldiers walked through the hall and told everyone to sleep or go to jail.

A man in a windbreaker, polo shirt, slacks, and shined leather shoes approaches us. His carefully groomed mustache has been trimmed to a thin line. I presume he represents one of the NGOs until I see an insignia on his jacket for Mexico's National Institute of Migration. He does not introduce himself. He requests my ID in a demanding voice that suggests he deems me suspect for reasons I can't imagine. I show him my press badge. He examines it, uses his cell phone to look me up on Google. Finding my byline, he returns my ID, spins around, and walks away, the sound of his shoes clicking evenly against the floor. As Felix and I resume talking to Ikal, he glances repeatedly in our direction.

Ikal ducks into his tent for a manila envelope. He withdraws a police report that, he says, proves he would have been killed had he stayed in Honduras. Do we think it will be enough for asylum? Felix and I examine the paper: *Mr. Ikal Espinoza, entity 0507-1976-00356, filed a complaint on Twenty-Two December of the year Two Thousand and Seventeen for the crimes of death threats and intrigue, alleged to have been committed by Mr. Pedro Torres, who according to other complaints, operates a gang of criminals who have caused serious damage to families near our municipality, San Antonio de Cortés, Honduras, cases [the police] are still investigating.*

Nothing in the document confirms that Ikal was in danger. He registered a grievance against a known bad guy, nothing more. I return the paper.

I don't know, I say.

Felix tells him about the pastor he knows.

You would have a room and a safe place to leave Aurelia and Eric while you waited to apply for asylum, he explains. In the meantime, you could look for work.

Ikal likes the idea.

You should call him, Felix tells Ikal, just to introduce yourself.

He gives him a slip of a paper with a phone number. Then we hear the click of the immigration officer's shoes grow near as he approaches us again. Without a word he snatches the paper from Ikal, reads it, and looks at Felix with an arched eyebrow. Felix explains about the pastor.

What's your name? I ask the official.

He ignores me, lets the paper slip from his fingers to the floor. He brushes his hands as if he'd held something dirty.

You should look for work, he tells Ikal. The Mexican government won't put you up forever.

I'm applying for asylum, Ikal responds.

You have a five-thousand-to-one chance to be accepted.

You can't say that, Ikal snaps. You're not God.

The official smirks and walks off. Felix picks up the paper and returns it to Ikal.

I'll talk to the pastor, he tells him.

January 3, 2018, five a.m. My phone rings.

Hello.

Hey, Malcolm, guess what?

What?

Guess?

What?

Ikal crossed.

He what?

He crossed, man. He's in LA. I called him to see if he'd spoken to the pastor and he told me he crossed! He didn't tell me much, he was too excited.

Can you call him again?

Yeah.

I'll be over.

Eight o'clock?

Yeah.

I meet Felix in Parque Teniente Guerrero, a city park with manicured lawns, shaded walkways, a playground, fountain, and picnic areas far from the bustle of downtown. Sprinklers have just shut off and the grass gleams in the sun. Evangelical preachers speak into microphones, their voices distorted by static. A man walking a pit bull veers off the sidewalk and goes behind the bench where Felix and I sit. I don't think anything of it but Felix is certain the man wants to listen in on our conversation. We stop talking until he strolls out of earshot. Then Felix calls Ikal and we ask him how he got to LA.

It began with the Mexican immigration officer. He had angered Ikal. No, not angered. As a Christian, Ikal, says, he doesn't get angry. But he didn't appreciate being spoken to in such a condescending manner. He was also worried about the holidays. If people had been drinking on Christmas, what would they be like New Year's Eve? He thought long and hard about that as he and Aurelia ate the food Felix had brought them. When they finished, Ikal made a decision: We're leaving, he said. They took only water and diapers for Eric. Catching a bus downtown, Ikal asked the driver for advice on where to enter the U.S. He suggested Playas de Tijuana, a neighborhood on the border. There, along a metal barrier, Ikal searched for an opening. An old man told him of a spot where workers had not completed a repair. Ikal followed the old man to a hole and crawled through, sliding down a concrete embankment. He called for Aurelia to follow.

About fifty yards away stood another fence. Near it, a Border Patrol Jeep idled. Ikal knocked on the driver's window. He explained in halting English to the surprised agent that he had fled Honduras for the welfare of his family.

I do not come violently to your country, he said.

The agent told Ikal and Aurelia to sit on the ground and take off their shoes, presumably, Ikal thought, so they would not run away. The agent spoke in a kind but firm tone. He knew only a little Spanish and gestured to make himself understood. Then he got on the radio and started shouting. In a few minutes another Jeep arrived to pick them up.

The second agent took Ikal and his family to the Otay Mesa Detention Center, an Immigration and Customs Enforcement facility in San Diego. Ikal stayed in a cell apart from Aurelia and Eric but he could see them when he left his cell to be questioned. He thought the ICE agents were polite. They did not speak Spanish. He explained as best he could why he had left Honduras.

Two days later, an officer escorted him out of his cell and asked him to sign forms that were in English. Ikal did not know what they said but he signed them. This officer spoke Spanish and explained to Ikal that he and his family were being released to a church-run shelter in Los Angeles. He and Aurelia would be required to wear ankle monitors. That afternoon, a representative of the shelter picked them up.

My wife and I, we are just amazed, Ikal tells us, his giddy disbelief apparent in his voice. We're in the United States. It's a reality.

He looks forward to finding a job, a home. He understands he still must make a case for asylum before an immigration judge but he is convinced the judge will believe him just as the border agents did. From his first night in Otay Mesa to his evenings now in LA, he sleeps without waking. He tells us he left his nightmares at the border.

Felix and I catch a bus for Playa de Tijuana, known locally as La Playa. We laugh, imagining the shock of the border agent when Ikal knocked on his window. Felix believes that helped his case because by turning himself in, Ikal showed he was an honest man.

Remember how he told that immigration guy, You can't say that, only God? Felix asks me. He had a look in his eyes. Words have power, man.

At La Playa, I see the wall that confronted Ikal stretch downhill into the Pacific Ocean surf. Heaving, white-capped waves crash against it and seagulls rise in currents above the mist. The wall, composed of iron rods set at right angles with spaces in between, stands about twelve feet high with coils of wire mesh layering much of the top. Artists and advocates have painted sections of the wall with images of butterflies, rainbows, children flying balloons, and an upside-down American flag. *Freedom doesn't work unless we're all free*, reads one piece of graffiti. *Immigration is not a crime. There's still hope for you, America. No ICE. Trump, we want you out.* Felix shows me where he and other deported veterans signed their names.

Walking beside the wall, we watch workers laboring on one section where I could see a hole. Is this where Ikal crawled through? I wonder. Maybe, Felix says. He's happy for Ikal. He would like to think he helped him reach the U.S.—the food he gave him didn't hurt. Hard to make a risk-filled decision on an empty stomach, right? He'd sure like to be where Ikal is now. Why him and not me? Felix asks himself. He had joined the military. OK, it didn't work out, but he joined, that should count for something. He was a badass but that was a long time ago. He did his time. His lawyer told him he didn't have a chance to reenter the U.S. Not with an assault conviction. Why not? He's not the same person he was then. How long has he been deported? Sixteen, no, seventeen years, not counting the time he did in prison when he was caught trying to cross in 2010. Yeah, seventeen years. Man, all this time later, day by day, he's still dealing with it.

Felix doesn't know what he'll do. Maybe volunteer at an old folks home. He did that when he was in high school and earned extra credit. He's growing old, might as well size up some places. He may need one. He would still like to know what happened to Ariché. Maybe he'll look for her.

We both stare through the slats at a barren stretch of California coast. A security corridor fifty yards wide stands between the wall and a second, taller fence. I wonder if Felix imagines his East LA home. I don't ask and he doesn't say.

Dead Sites

In the early hours of a Tuesday morning, an old man drives a Jeep out of Tucson and onto Arizona Highway 286 toward the desert and the first of three sites he'll visit where the remains of migrants were found. He has made this trip once a week for the past six years. Three crosses, four feet tall and two feet wide, each a different color—blue, blue-green, and rust—rattle in back. Heat from the sun warms the vehicle, and the woman in the passenger seat, Alicia Baucom, cracks her window to shrieks of air still cool from the night. A second Jeep carries a man and two women who, like Alicia, have volunteered to help plant the crosses. Flat land covered with cactus and scrub juniper slanted by wind unfurls into distant, bare mountains peaked against the dome of blue sky slowly revealing itself two hours after dawn, and as the Jeeps rush down the highway, also known as Sasabe Road, the old man, seventy-three-year-old artist Alvaro Enciso, asks Alicia the names of the dead migrants.

The one found in 2006 is unidentified, she says. The man discovered in 2015 has a name, Valentine Guzman Flores. Thirty. Found December 29 near Three Points. Skeletal remains. Cause of death unknown. The third was found in 2017. His name is Felipe Vargas. Also thirty. Found near Sasabe on June 8. Hypothermia. Dead less than a day. Coroner said he was fully fleshed.

The first two could have died long before their bodies were found, Alvaro says.

He hunches over the steering wheel and makes no further comment and Alicia doesn't speak either. She has been helping Alvaro just five months, replacing another volunteer who broke down after he and Alvaro found a migrant's body nearly a year ago. That volunteer sought counseling. It was one thing to hear about people dying in the desert but it was quite another to see a body.

Alvaro collects information on dead migrants from the Pima County coroner's office. Last year, the medical examiner recorded the remains of 127 dead migrants. Before 2000, the bodies of fewer than five migrants on average were found each year. However in 2001, the number soared to 79 and then to 151 the year after that. The number of annual migrant deaths since then has remained well above one hundred.

As he follows the highway, Alvaro notices workers laying asphalt, shoveling it off the back of a truck, filling the air with fumes as a roller inches toward them, and two Border Patrol agents lean against pickups and watch the men work. They are either chasing someone, Alvaro says of the agents, or they've given up. They don't move as he passes them, heads down staring through dark sunglasses at the steaming asphalt.

Alvaro often encounters Border Patrol agents. A few times he's tripped a sensor and they converged from nowhere to check him out. He explained his purpose and showed them his crosses and they were cool. He had no problem with them and doesn't now. They have a job to do; some are good, and some are bad. If they see someone in the middle of nowhere, they get suspicious. Alvaro understands that. He shoots the shit with them, complains about the heat. Many of them aren't familiar with deserts because they were raised outside of Arizona. They've seen earthworms but nothing bigger, and worms don't bite. Rattlesnakes do. They worry about snakes.

Alvaro recalls the spring of 2017 when the Border Patrol could have been a problem. He and some volunteers found a man in the desert walking south toward Mexico. He was delirious and thought he was headed north to Phoenix. He had no food or water. Alvaro considered his options: he could call the Border Patrol, give the man something to eat and drink, or leave him to his fate. He could not, however, transport him. If the Border Patrol stopped him, he could be charged with harboring. But the man needed medical attention. How was he to say, I can't help you, to a desperate man? Sometimes, he reasoned, laws have to be violated. The volunteers had their own car and drove the man to a safe house. Alvaro doesn't remember his name but was told later that he ate eleven pancakes, three sausages, three cups of fresh fruit, two glasses of orange juice, and five pieces of toast his first night. He had come from Honduras and it took him two weeks to recuperate. When he left, the staff gave him directions to Phoenix, but he didn't make it. The Border Patrol picked him up.

Alvaro had been unaware of migrants dying in the desert when he moved from northern New Mexico to Tucson in 2011. He started walking migrant trails and imagined himself crossing borders on foot. The idea appealed to him as something romantic: people entering the United States seeking the opportunities he had. He noticed all sorts of debris, rusted cans that had held sardines, sausages, beans, and other food migrants had brought with them. He collected the cans and accumulated a huge mound of them to use in his art. Every can told a story of the person who had eaten from it. He didn't know if the stories had happy endings, but a can was there for him to imagine a life.

Two years later, he took a four-hour orientation with Tucson Samaritans, a group of more than a hundred volunteers who go into the desert seven days a week to assist migrants. The presenter showed a map of southern Arizona covered with red dots. Each dot represented a spot where a migrant's body had been found. From 2001 through 2018, the remains of over three thousand migrants have been recovered in southern Arizona. No estimates have been offered for how many have not been found.

Alvaro wondered what happened to those people. He searched those locations for anything that gave substance to those who had died. He lay on his back and stared into an unrevealing desert sky and felt only the emptiness of his surroundings, a nothingness that had absorbed suffering and death.

Alvaro felt a bond with the dead through his own sense of not belonging. He was not a gringo, but he didn't consider himself Hispanic, either. He rarely hung out with Spanish-speaking people, and when he did, he assumed a different character than when he spoke English. Who was he? He had been born in Colombia. He had left everything he knew—his family, his country—to live in a place that was and was not his home. He began contemplating how, as an artist, he could convey the quandary of his existence with the experiences of dead migrants caught between the countries they were leaving and their visions of America.

As a first step, Alvaro snapped photographs of what he called "dead sites," but a photo could not capture the absent bodies of migrants. He hired a woman and had her wear a black dress and drove her to the desert to be photographed. He shot beautiful pictures of her against the sparse landscape, but a woman in a black dress, a strikingly mournful figure, said nothing about the people who had perished. He made sculptures of red dots, but they weighed too much to transport to the dead sites. Next, he sprayed red dots on the ground like graffiti, but the dots alone conveyed nothing.

The idea of building crosses came to him as he combed through books about Roman history. The Romans, he read, crucified many people, not only Jesus. They left them exposed to the sun and elements until after they died. The same, he believed, was happening to migrants. Through its immigration policies, the U.S. government was forcing them to follow the most difficult routes north to kill them. Where the two pieces of a cross intersected formed the nucleus of an encounter between poor peasants of the south and the American giant of the north, and the encounter was fatal. Goliath won.

Alvaro understood that not everyone would agree with his

overtly political symbol. However, he was not seeking approval but laying a philosophical foundation to buttress his ideas to mark the dead sites with crosses. Absent politics, a cross would also have meaning, not as a Christian symbol, (Forget religion, Alvaro tells the volunteers. Death is very democratic. Death has no interest in faith.) but as a secular, geometric one. A cross consists of vertical and horizontal lines. Alive, people stand erect. Dead, they lie flat. Life and death exist in the same image.

As a child, Alvaro learned to accept absence. He grew up in a shanty in Villavicencio, Colombia, a frontier town where men earned a living raising cattle and selling marijuana. He did not wear shoes his first five years at school. In the evenings, he gathered dead birds from cockfights for his mother to cook, or he would walk to the slaughter-house and collect blood to eat with his rice because they could not afford meat. His mother had few soft edges. She warned him against daydreaming. Dreams, she said, wouldn't deliver him from poverty.

Alvaro never saw his father. He was married to another woman and considered Alvaro's mother his mistress. In 1996, when he turned fifty, Alvaro returned to Colombia and tracked him down in Honda, a village not far from where he grew up. His father owned a big house near a cemetery and had a little store—everybody who went to the cemetery stopped there for food and flowers. He assumed Alvaro wanted money.

I don't need your money, Alvaro told him. I'm not angry with you. I have no feelings toward you. I just want to know who you are.

They spoke for a short time. His father appeared indifferent that Alvaro, his only son, the result of a one-night fling, had appeared out of nowhere. It was like looking in a mirror, Alvaro reflected afterward. His father's disinterest, his lack of empathy, were characteristics Alvaro shared. A woman he had dated in New York told him, "You don't ask about my life or daughters. Your interest lasts only one night." He received her words as a revelation, and on his flight back to the States he thought of them again and decided that although he felt bad his father was the way he was, he did not have to be like him.

They never saw each other again. Blind, sick, and unable to walk, Alvaro's father died two years later.

When he was a boy, Alvaro watched Hollywood movies at a theater where his mother worked. On screen, actors smoked long cigarettes and ate in restaurants. He saw dashing detectives and strutting cowboys. That was the life he wanted. In 1967, when he was almost twenty-one, an aunt in Queens offered to fly him to New York. She didn't have to ask twice.

New York made an impression: The tall buildings, the busy streets, the stores with all the elegantly dressed people. He loved the seasons, especially winter. That something could fall from the sky and turn him white left him amazed and a believer in miracles. He thought pizza and canned foods with decorative labels the most wonderful of meals. He sorted through trash, collecting an odd assortment of junk: high school sports trophies, beat-up bowling balls, picture frames, and other garbage. *Get this out of my house*, his aunt scolded, but he continued adding to his collection. He had never had these things. Ownership represented the promise of America. With his aunt's help, he applied for citizenship and received his green card. He also registered with the Selective Service without fully understanding what that meant, but he felt he was on his way.

However, Alvaro soon faced difficulties. His aunt's American husband disliked him and kicked him out of the house two months after he arrived. Homeless and fearful of returning to Colombia a failure, he went to a church and prayed. God, he begged, you need to cut me a break. I'm screwed here. Any bone you can send my way, I'd appreciate. You're the guy who's supposed to help.

Two months later he was drafted into the Army. Having no skills, he joked, they put me in the infantry. Destination: Vietnam. It was not the divine intervention he had sought, but it got him off the street. His commanding officers trained him to hate the Vietnamese and kill them and he did. He won't elaborate, refuses to speak more about the war. Today, he doesn't see a connection between the person he was then and the man he is now. He was young, naïve, and stupid. He lacked compassion. He believes that with each cross he puts up today, he atones for his actions in Vietnam.

After his service, Alvaro returned to New York. He visited an Army buddy in New Mexico and fell in love with the desert, awed by its limitlessness, and promised to return and live there someday. Back in New York, he drove cabs, mopped the floors of a peep show, and worked as a photographer's assistant. He attended college and graduate school and earned three master's degrees: in anthropology, Latin American Studies, and Contemporary Hispanic Studies. In 1980, he took a job with the Department of Health and Human Services and stayed for almost twenty years before he got tired of the nine-to-five grind and decided to pursue an artistic career. He had always liked to draw. His savings, pension, and veterans benefits would support him. With art, he rationalized, he didn't need credentials.

In 1999, he moved to Placitas, New Mexico, an old hippie town north of Albuquerque, and bought a house. For two years he read books on philosophy and art criticism. He built boxes with cutout figures representative of the American West. He took large canvases and painted layers and layers of the same color paint in varying shades and made frames for them. *It's not bad*, he thought, *but it may not be good art*. Over the years, however, people bought his work and he felt their approval in the money they paid him, which in turn gave him the impetus to do more serious work that would encompass his ideas of being an outsider. After more than ten years in Placitas, Alvaro felt the need for a more urban environment. Albuquerque was close by, but he wanted a city with a better reputation for the arts. That led him to Tucson.

A hawk flies above the Jeep as Alvaro drives deeper into the desert, the sun higher and the air still cool although he feels it warming. Gusts rise off mountains sweeping the air ahead, fanning dust. Alvaro pulls off the road and parks near the spot where the remains of the nameless 2006 migrant were found. He had put up a cross for him last year. A migrant sleeping nearby awoke, startled to see him. Don't worry, Alvaro said, I'm here for a cross, nothing more.

Alvaro doesn't know what happened, but a short time later, someone destroyed the cross. Hunters have used his crosses for target practice. Other people break and remove them. He went to a swap meet one afternoon and saw one for sale. The cross he had placed here looked like it had been hit by a sledgehammer.

Stepping out of the Jeep, Alvaro stands stoop-shouldered and adjusts his cap. He wears jeans that pool around his ankles and a long sleeve shirt with triangular patterns that restrains his paunch. Gray hair falls to his neck and he removes his glasses and rubs his eyes.

Keep talk to a minimum, Alvaro says. We're going to a location where someone died.

He takes a blue cross from the back of the Jeep. Slivers of tin cans decorate the wood. A red dot on another piece of tin fills the center. Friends give him paint, off-white, beige—bland colors he brightens with whatever he has on hand in his shop.

The volunteers unload a shovel, bucket, bottled water, and a bag of concrete mix and follow Alvaro. The noise of their steps breaks against small stones and the scraping sound tears at the air like a ripped sheet.

Alvaro moves cautiously between jumping cholla cactus, whose stinging thorns collect like burrs and can easily penetrate clothing. Blankets, shoulder packs, worn sandals, plastic water jugs, and other supplies discarded by migrants litter the ground.

They may have camped here. They may have been picked up by family or the Border Patrol. Their abandoned possessions offer Alvaro no hint of their fate.

He searches the ground for bones. In 2017, a man driving home from a casino stopped to piss and saw a human skull. The skull belonged to forty-four-year-old Nancy Ganoza, from Peru, who had disappeared in the desert in 2009, cause of death unknown. A DNA sample found a match in New Jersey, where her two daughters and husband lived. Her family flew to Tucson and Alvaro built a cross and they joined him to raise it where her skull was found. Her husband propped a photograph against the cross below a red dot. She had black hair down to her shoulders and a winsome smile and she squinted as if she was facing the sun. Five candles surrounded the base of the cross and a white rosary with a crucifix hung loosely from it, and a circle of prickly pear cactus threw shadows beneath the twisted branches of velvet mesquite. Alvaro had planted dozens of crosses for people by then. Sometimes he knew their names, but he did not *know* them. Until now. The intimate presence of Nancy's family brought him to tears.

It's so sad, Alvaro thinks now. All of it. Each death, haunting. All of them tragic, some beyond tragic. Not too long ago, Alvaro built a cross for a young man who had died from hanging, a suicide, the medical examiner concluded. Alvaro could not conceive the agony and utter hopelessness that he must have experienced. Knowing it was too much to go on. Deciding with what strength he had left to take his own life rather than die of thirst, starvation, heatstroke, hypothermia, or madness.

The most disturbing moment for Alvaro, however, occurred last August when he found a body in the Roskruge Mountains, a remote area close to Tucson. Five miles from a paved highway and four miles from some houses but still in the middle of nowhere. He had just put up a cross and was following a stone path back to his Jeep when he disturbed two rattlesnakes, and his heart was racing from surprise and fear, the sound of their rattles still in his ears, when he saw a dead woman. For a moment, his reaction was similar to entering a room and encountering someone he had not expected.

A sharp odor rose from the corpse. The bones remained intact and her clothes lay around her, possibly torn off by animals. A T-shirt and blue jeans and a cell phone. She had a pair of yellow-and-pink sneakers that looked new. Very feminine and small. At first, Alvaro thought she was a child. He called 911. An autopsy revealed she had suffered from hypothermia and had been dead about two weeks. She had documents from Guatemala but no identification.

Days later, Alvaro marked the location with a cross. Was she a mother? he wondered. Did she leave children behind? What was she running from and to? In the following weeks he returned and looked for ID but found nothing. He lay on the ground and traced an outline of his body with flour. He stood and looked at the image like something from a crime scene. It was his way of sharing himself with her. Had his life been different, had his aunt not flown him to New York, he might have died as she had, or like the migrant he is about to acknowledge this morning, dead without a name.

Alvaro sets down the cross, takes the shovel, and digs a hole. He tosses dirt to one side, and when he stops to catch his breath, silence settles around him and he raises his head to listen to it. He asks Alicia to mix the concrete. He watches her shake it into the bucket, add water, and stir it with a stick.

That's enough, Alvaro says.

He inserts the cross into the hole and holds the top of it as Alicia distributes the concrete. Alvaro asks her if it's straight and she nods. He continues holding it as she and the other volunteers collect rocks and stack them in a small mound around the cross. Once it's secure, Alvaro steps back and ponders it within the vast solitude of the desert. Stalwart, like a sentry, unaware that soon it will be alone and appear quite small, dwarfed by the vastness of its surroundings.

Alicia removes a flute from her shoulder pack.

I'd like to play "Amazing Grace."

Play "Down in the Valley."

I don't know that one. I hope I can get through this without crying.

That's OK. Someone died here. Crying is what we do.

She begins playing and Alvaro bows his head. He has put up nine hundred crosses in six years but has no idea how many still stand. They last five, maybe ten years, eaten by termites, beaten by weather, turned to dust. Some nuns in a church in Cochise County heard about what he was doing and designed their own crosses. They did not place them where migrants died, but, as far as Alvaro saw it, where it was convenient. Their crosses have no relation to anything. The word got out that an old man was making crosses and the nuns wanted a piece of it.

He does not consider himself an activist. At home, he likes to read, go to restaurants, and play with his dog. He paints pictures with red dots in fragmented circles and lines to represent a splintered border and the ruptured lives of those who cross. He only wants the integrity of his project respected.

What's happening, he tells himself, is that instead of mellowing, he's becoming cantankerous in his old age. How does he tell nuns they're screwing up? They have a divine license to do what they do. They have God. How does he argue with God?

I'm an infidel, he reminds himself.

As Alicia plays, the plaintive notes drifting with the wind, Alvaro considers his own life. With each cross, he commemorates his journey as an immigrant and its inevitable end. His weekly desert sojourns have become a form of meditation in which he grieves his own losses— two failed marriages, the death of his mother, his time in Vietnam, his absent father. He is his father's son, but not his son. He does not conceal his emotions. He empathizes to the point of tears. He can't control what other people do with his art but only what he seeks to achieve with it: recognition of the dead, solace for himself.

The struggle of migrants, he knows, will outlive him. More will die today, tomorrow, and long after he has died. He'd like to paint three thousand red dots in a Tucson gallery but he doubts that will happen. Galleries don't appreciate art that won't sell. He will never build enough crosses.

That's all we know, right? It was a male? Alvaro asks Alicia when she finishes playing.

That's correct.

Does anyone want to say anything?

I hope he finds peace, Alicia says.

Alvaro lets her comment linger. The wind whistles and carries the sound of a semi, and the volunteers shift, twigs breaking beneath their feet. When the noise of the truck fades, Alvaro speaks.

In 2006, thirteen years ago more or less, a man came here looking for the American dream. He didn't find it, and all of his plans ended here. And those plans and his dream left a lot of suffering behind, perhaps with a family that was hoping for him to be the person who would send checks back home for them to survive. But this all ended here. We don't know his name, but he had a name, a family, and he had dreams and hopes. He had everything. That's why we do this, to give this person presence. To honor this person. But there will always be an empty space at the dinner table for this person, and that takes a long, long time to go away; in fact, it never will. He'll always be missing in some way.

At a loss to say anything more, Alvaro stares at the ground. He wonders how much longer he'll mark dead sites. His knees are shot. In the old days, he would start at seven, walk three hours to a site and three hours back, up and down mountains, sometimes not getting home before nightfall. These days, he seeks clusters, areas where several bodies have been found, so he can put up crosses without walking too far and adding mileage to the Jeep. It's old too.

He picks up the bucket and shovel. The two other sites are close by. He expects to finish before noon, an early day. Next Tuesday, he will return and carry more crosses into the desert and give the anonymous dead presence with a marker no one will see. Art without a viewer. He considers their shortened lives part of the American myth. Dying for a dream.

You Know Where I Am

Billie and Fabian sit at a round table in Billie's kitchen thinking out loud, considering his options. It's evening. Pitch black, with no stars. The damp air hints at rain. A dog barks.

"I don't know what I could do, but I'd do everything I possibly could," Billie says. "Joel would be so vocal. He's very to the point."

She speaks of her husband, Joel Tentori, as if he is still alive. She misses him and enjoys talking about him, but tears cloud her eyes. He died in 2013. He was born in Guadalajara, Mexico, and moved to Missouri in 1958 when he was 18. Two of his uncles worked in Kansas City, Missouri, at the time. He and Billie married in 1960 after they met at Nazarene Publishing House downtown where they both worked. A lifetime ago. She's seventy-six now.

"My husband came here for the opportunity," Billie says.

Joel told her about the first time he used a public restroom in Missouri. He entered one marked "colored only." When he came out, a man told him the bathroom was only for black people. The story surprised Billie when he told her. She had been born into an affluent Kansas City family. The social issues of the day never crossed her doorstep. The civil rights movement was something

she read about in the newspaper. Really, she says, that sort of thing
was not part of her life. Until now, year four of the Trump presidency. Everything feels so uncertain.

"I'd provide sanctuary for you and your family if immigration
officials attempted to deport you," Billie tells Fabian.

His mother cleans Billie's house but doesn't have papers and
neither neither do Fabian, his father and sister. Fabian is twenty-four and knows he should be concerned, but he has lived in
Missouri since he was eight and doesn't feel the threat of deportation. Not in a nervous, preoccupied, gut-fearing way. The idea
of it—that he could just get picked up and thrown out of a state
where he has lived almost his entire life—defies comprehension.
Look at him. Big guy. Thin mustache. Soft-spoken, easygoing. Just
taking things in. He can't conceive of deportation. Not like the
glass of water he holds. Something tangible. It's not like that at all.

"I'm not naive," he tells Billie. "We have a president now who
said things while he was campaigning and now he's actually doing
them."

Like the ban on refugees and people from some predominant-
ly Muslim countries. Who would have thought? Politicians don't
normally do what they say they'll do. He's already started detaining
undocumented people.

"It would be impossible to round up everyone," Billie says.

"Yes," Fabian agrees.

In 2012, Fabian applied to the Deferred Action for Childhood
Arrivals program, commonly known as DACA. The directive,
established in 2012 by executive action, provides work authori-

zation and a temporary reprieve from deportation for immigrants who entered the U.S. illegally as children before the age of sixteen. As Fabian waited to be covered by DACA, a police officer pulled him over for not fully stopping at a traffic light. He was just four blocks from his house on his way to pick up his sister from a party.

"Do you have a license?" the officer asked.

"No."

"Any ID?"

"Mexico ID."

The officer gave him two tickets. One for not stopping, the other for driving without proper identification. Four weeks after the officer stopped him, United States Citizenship and Immigration Services approved Fabian for DACA. He got his driver's license before his court date and a judge dismissed his case.

Fabian thinks about the officer who stopped him. He spelled his name incorrectly on the tickets and wrote the wrong age, too. An attorney told Fabian those two mistakes could have resulted in the case being thrown out, DACA or no DACA. Fabian doesn't know about all that. He's not a lawyer. At the time, he had no intention of taking chances but he wonders now whether the officer deliberately made those mistakes. Could he have been trying to help him?

"There are some good people in this world," Billie says.

She leans back from the table and brushes a strand of gray hair from her forehead. She met Fabian's mother in 2010. Billie was a nurse, a wife and the mother of three boys. She wanted to find someone to clean her house once a month. She contacted several people. One woman asked her how many bathrooms she had. Four, Billie told her. The woman said she wasn't interested. Another woman called, asked the same question and also turned down the job.

Then Fabian's mother stopped by for an interview. Billie was out but Joel was home. Fabian's mother looked all through the house before she made an offer. I'll do it one time, no charge, she told Joel. If you don't like it, that's fine. If you do, then I'll take the job.

Joel was taken by her straightforward approach and Billie hired her. Fabian's mother worked very hard. Self-employed, she soon began hiring women to help her and started her own house-cleaning business. One customer, she told Billie, accused one of her employees of stealing and she fired the woman, but it bothered her. She didn't believe the woman was a thief. Still doesn't, but she did what she felt she had to do.

Billie wonders about the fear Fabian's parents must live with. They have become part of her family. She and Joel spent part of every year in Mexico until he died. She carries Joel's green card. I love Mexico, he would tell her. It gave me my birth. But I love the United States because it gave me my life.

Fabian was born in Pueblo, Mexico. His mother cleaned houses there, too, and his father worked as an electrician. Fabian helped his mother make bread. He watched his younger sister after school. One day, his parents told him they were going to the United States for a long vacation in Kansas City. His father had a visa and moved first to arrange for a home. When it was time for the rest of the family to join him a year later, an American friend met them at the border. They were let in, no problem. When he was older, Fabian's mother told him they'd left Mexico to make a better life for themselves and to provide an education for Fabian and his sister.

Everything in Kansas City was so bright and well maintained, Fabian recalls. Street lights everywhere. All the long lines of traffic. It snowed four weeks after he arrived. He had really looked forward to snow and played in it all day. Snow no longer impresses him. But back then, it was very special.

As he got older, his mother told him not to discuss his status. If someone asks, just say you're working on it, she said. To become a citizen, she told him, you have to marry, join the military or go back to Mexico and apply. He didn't understand how he was different from his friends until he reached high school.

Because of his status, he could not get a driver's license. He was ineligible for college scholarships. After he graduated, he worked at motels whose managers didn't ask for a Social Security number or, if they did, accepted any old number he gave them. At that time he was eighteen and still living at home and he could get by on minimum wage. He got into a community college with a fake ID. He was doing well until the traffic cop stopped him.

When he applied for DACA, his mother was worried. If Fabian applies, she asked Billie, will the government have all of his information? Maybe then, immigration would come for her?

"I'd open my home," Billie told her. "I'd take you in. You know where I am."

The issue of immigration has split Billie's family. When President Barack Obama issued DACA, her nephew, a retired firefighter in his fifties, complained about his taxes going to illegals.

"I don't believe you're saying this about children," Billie said. "Children have no say about coming over here."

Her comment surprised him, and he said nothing more. They don't talk to each other now.

Fabian got married in 2016. He lives in a trailer park not far from Billie and drops by from time to time to help her around the house. Ford Motor Company's Kansas City assembly plant recently laid him off after eight months. He knew the position was temporary and had another job at a title loan company until that work dried up, too. He hopes to get an apprenticeship with a labor union.

A loophole in DACA, Fabian thinks, may allow him to avoid deportation should worse come to worst. Under DACA, an immigrant may leave the country with a temporary visa in the case of a family emergency and return legally. As Fabian understands it, immigration only cares about an immigrant's last known status. Under this scenario, Fabian thinks they couldn't deport him because technically he would no longer be undocumented. He'd have a temporary visa. If he has to fabricate a family crisis to meet the criteria, so be it. He has no idea if this would really work, but his American-born wife likes the plan. She has two children from a previous marriage. Fabian treats them as his own and doesn't want to be separated from his family. Every day, he gets online and checks the status of DACA.

"If it's canceled, I'm screwed," he says.

Billie considers his plan. She doesn't know the ins and outs of DACA. She hopes he's right. One of Billie's three sons lives in Colorado. His oldest boy's high school basketball team, the Spartans, played a private Christian high school team recently. A number of Mexican students are on the Spartans team. Parents of the opposing team held signs: "Make Our Team Great Again. Send the Spartans Over the Wall!"

Fabian never spoke about his status at the Ford plant but sometimes some knucklehead would mention immigration. Try living in their shoes, Fabian would say. Your family is struggling. You're scared of the cartels. You can wait years for a visa or you risk everything for an opportunity.

Some people heard him. Not all. More often, co-workers would get very vocal on Facebook. In person, he finds they back down. They get quiet. Doesn't mean they've changed their thinking, though.

Billie watches Fabian. He sips a glass of water, says nothing more. She tells him not to think about those people. Instead he should focus on his family. Do what needs to be done for himself and them. If ICE comes, she'll take him in, her house his underground railroad.

"You know where I am," she says.

Acknowledgments

My deep appreciation to Marc Estrin and Donna Bister at Fomite Press for taking on this book. Special thanks to the editors of *Global Sisters Report, Tampa Review* and *New Letters* where versions of some of these stories first appeared. Finally, my gratitude to Jesse Barker, Bruce Janseen, Susan Curtis, Roland Sharillo, and Sarah Madges for their patient and thoughtful critiques of the early drafts.

More essays from Fomite...
William Benton — *Eye Contact: Writing on Art*
Robert Sommer — *Losing Francis: Essays on the Wars at Home*
George Ovitt & Peter Nash — *Trotsky's Sink: Ninety-Eight Short Essays on Literature*

Writing a review on social media sites for readers will help the progress of independent publishing. To submit a review, go to the book page on any of the sites and follow the links for reviews. More reviews help books get more attention from readers and other reviewers.

For more information or to order any of our books, visit:
http://www.fomitepress.com/our-books.html

CPSIA information can be obtained
at www.ICGtesting.com
Printed in the USA
LVHW030353300421
686058LV00006B/565

9 781953 236180